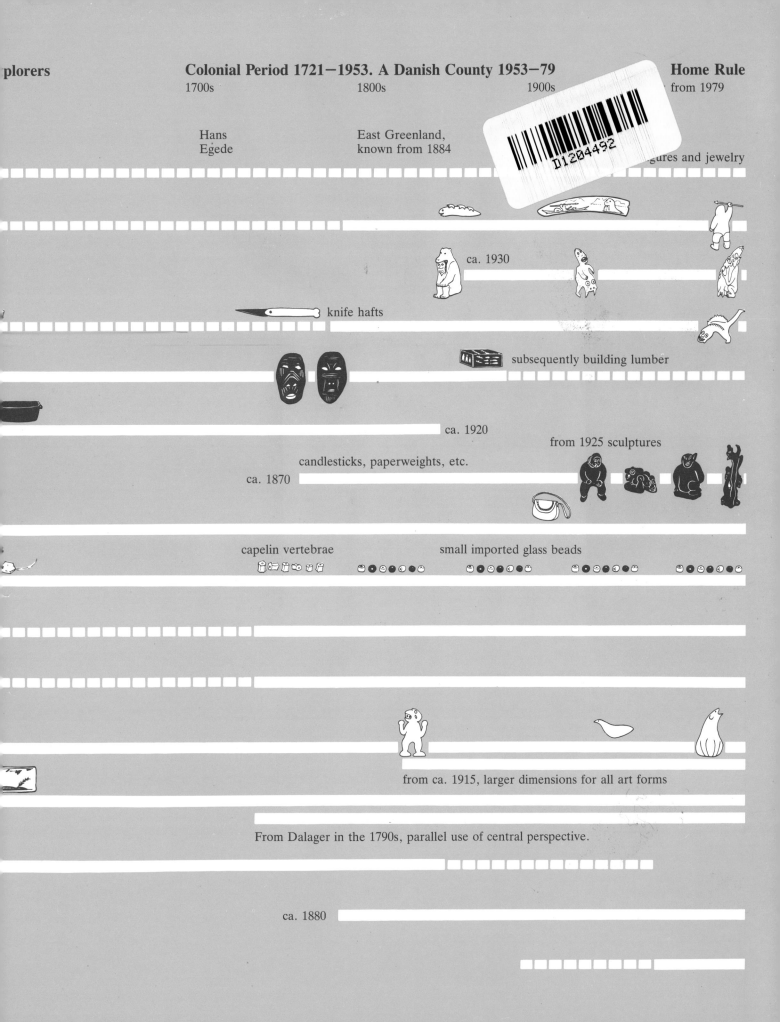

plorers

Colonial Period 1721–1953. A Danish County 1953–79

1700s   1800s   1900s

Home Rule

from 1979

Hans
Egede

East Greenland,
known from 1884

gures and jewelry

ca. 1930

knife hafts

subsequently building lumber

ca. 1920

from 1925 sculptures

candlesticks, paperweights, etc.

ca. 1870

capelin vertebrae   small imported glass beads

from ca. 1915, larger dimensions for all art forms

From Dalager in the 1790s, parallel use of central perspective.

ca. 1880

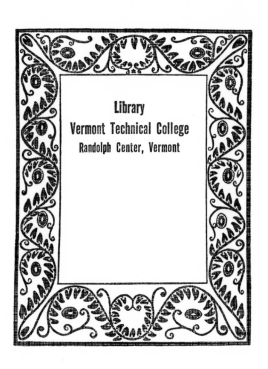

The Art of
Greenland

Publication of this book has been supported by

The Bikuben Foundation
The Foundation for the Welfare of Denmark
The Danish Government Committee for Cultural Exchange

The Art of Greenland

Sculpture
Crafts
Painting

By Bodil Kaalund

Translated by
Kenneth Tindall

University of California Press

Berkeley   Los Angeles   London

Translated from *Grønlands Kunst* published in Denmark
by Politikens Forlag A.S. 1979
Copyright © 1979 by Bodil Kaalund and Politikens Forlag A.S.

The University of California Press
Berkeley and Los Angeles, California
University of California Press, Ltd.
London, England
United States text adaptation copyright © 1983 by
The Regents of the University of California
All rights reserved

Library of Congress Cataloging in Publication Data

Kaalund, Bodil, 1930-
    The art of Greenland

    Translation of: Grønlands kunst
    Bibliography: p.
    Includes index.
    1. Eskimos – Greenland – Art. 2. Eskimos – Greenland. Industries.
3. Art – Greenland. I. Title.
E99.E7K12213 1983   704'.0397   82-45908
ISBN 0-520-04840-7

This edition has been produced for University of California Press
by Gyldendalske Boghandel, Nordisk Forlag A.S., Copenhagen

Printed in Denmark 1983 by Grafodan Offset, Værløse

Contents

A people of wanderers

Sculpture

Crafts

Painting

Preface

Let no one doubt that the new home government in Greenland is very much concerned with cultural life up here. For generations our people, using their imagination and talent, have formed our society and created the most ingenious forms of technical competence under difficult arctic conditions.

The art of Greenland is a part of our lives, and a part of our Eskimo souls. We have never lacked imagination. Like so many other forms of culture, Greenlandic art has been much characterized by the human conception of the struggle between good and evil, the negative and the positive forces in life, and, last but not least, by the knowledge that we must be able to survive under harsh and forbidding circumstances.

I would like to express the hope that this book will be a source of inspiration to our artists under Home Rule. The decisive cultural awakening still lies ahead of us, just as political awakening was the basis for the introduction of Home Rule and the new government.

Our warmest thanks to Bodil Kaalund for her contribution with this, the first comprehensive and coherent work about Greenlandic art.

Jonathan Motzfeldt
Premier
Greenland's Home Rule

Greenland is a land for visions and visionaries. Immensely remote and unknown to Americans, it seems centuries old still. Physically, Greenland is a monumental bowl filled with ice thousands of feet thick, perched at the top of the habitable world. English speakers have known little about the pioneers who for 5000 years have projected a thin stream of humanity around Greenland's shores. Who are they? How have they lived? What have they believed in? Where are they going? Answers to some of these questions can be found in Bodil Kaalund's account of Greenlandic art, produced by generations of Eskimos who have materialized their experiences and dreams in artistic images.

As Greenlandic culture has changed, so have the works produced by Greenlanders. Thus, the breadth of images, of subject matter, of styles and materials presented in this volume is staggering, for Kaalund has taken as her field of study the total range of Greenlandic material creations. Prehistoric Dorset Eskimo culture carvings loom out from antler, peopling the past with scarred and tattooed faces. Magic ivory polar bears appear as men, beasts, and weapons. Ivory and wooden dolls produced by Thule Eskimos stand silent and featureless. Within the historic period beautiful traditional skin clothing undergoes modification with the introduction of colorful cloth and intricate beadwork. Traditional myths and tales, as well as the Greenlandic experience with Europeans, find new and eloquent expression as images executed in pencil, ink, and paint. The works of 19th and 20th century Greenlandic artists at once reach back to traditional lifeways and forward, joining the international contemporary artistic traditions from which some works are indistinguishable. Here then is a kaleidoscopic view encompassing thousands of years and spanning vast cultural chasms.

Knowledge of the Greenlander's unique cultural and artistic traditions is almost non-existent in North America, the primary reason for this being the lack of comprehensive works dealing with Greenland written in the English language. Bodil Kaalund's book fills this void and is an excellent addition to the body of literature on Eskimo peoples of Greenland, Canada, Alaska, and Siberia. As a result of Bodil Kaalund's efforts Americans can now appreciate the diversity of experience, culture, and imagination of the Greenlandic people.

William W. Fitzhugh
Susan A. Kaplan

Smithsonian Institution
Washington, D.C.

Piecing together the past is a painstaking business. So much does not survive the passage of time. The student of culture must rely upon the enduring fragments. The so-called "soft parts" of culture disappear all too easily; some through the processes of decay, others pass into oblivion with the demise of those who carried them in their consciousness.

Fortunately, there is much that can be gleaned from cultural remnants of stone, bone, shell, ivory, antler, metal, and wood. And because of the remarkable persistence of traditions, the latter day products of crafts and the lore that surrounds them can be of great aid to the art historian. Careful analysis allows one to generalize about technology, styles, cultural foci, sorcery, religion, exploitive activity, and even social organisation.

Among the Eskimo life has always been perilous. But, as the following pages testify, it would be wrong to assume that the harshness of the environment and the limited resources of the arctic resulted in a poverty of culture. Instead, it is clear that the native inhabitants of Greenland, like their counterparts in other regions of the far north, possessed a richness of life and of artistic creativity that was quite remarkable. And contemporary practitioners are carrying on viable time-honored traditions. Of course there have been adaptations. And these, in and of themselves, are contributions to the whole. There is a clearly definable art that is Greenlandic.

It has surprised many to learn that the Eskimo had no word for art. They obviously had no need for it. As Kaalund notes, among the Eskimo there is no such thing as art for art's sake. Rather, for them, art is for the sake of people. And over the ages it has maintained a vital continuity; their art is eminently human. Perhaps this is the greatest tribute that can be paid to any artistic tradition. The pages that follow make this tribute clear.

Roland Force
The Museum of the
American Indian
New York

A People of Wanderers

The hunter follows the game

To understand the art of Greenland, we need to know something about its background. What were external conditions like? What were the original religious beliefs?

Eskimos, or Eskimo-like peoples, have lived in the arctic for about 5,000 years, but they have wandered. In a perpetual search for better places to settle, better hunting grounds, they journeyed around the Northern hemisphere from Siberia to Alaska, Canada and Greenland. Climate determined whether the game moved south or north, into the interior or out to the coasts – and man followed.

Immigration from Canadian regions moved around the northern end of Greenland down along the east coast. The first traces of man in Greenland are from around the year 2200 B.C. Arrowheads, adzes, and knives have been found from this period, designated Independence Culture I. Harpoons, as well as knives and adzes, have been found from what is called Independence II (ca. 700 B.C.).

Another immigration, the Sarqaq Culture (ca. 1600 B.C.), probably moved down the west coast, judging from finds made at the Sarqaq trading station there, and part way up the east coast. Finds from this period include arrows, knives, adzes, a lamp, a kind of dwelling, and other human traces. Here, too, we encounter the first testimony to artistic development, in the shape of a bone joint with scratched-in skeleton ornamentation and a little bone spatula with a carved face found at Itivnera on the Godthåb Fjord. The two predominant traits of Greenlandic art, which prevail to this day, are already evident: an interest in depicting the human form and a sense of ornamentation.

There are several testimonies to artistic development from the next immigrations, called Dorset I and II (ca. 100 B.C. and A.D. 700): a block of wood covered with carved faces (fig. 2), and small, compact, expressive bone figures of humans or bears.

Finally, from A.D. 900 to 1200, we have the last great immigration, called the Thule Culture. Like the others, it came from the west, across the narrow Smith Sound, and its descendents inhabit Greenland today. With it came the kayak, the *umiak* and the dog-sled. The artists of the Thule Culture have left us a number of wonderful small wooden figures. Lacking arms and feet and with only a rudimentary indication of a face, these figures show the body, the *torso,* as most important.

Simultaneously with the immigration of the Thule people came the European immigration from the south. The Norsemen, Norwegian-Icelandic vikings, arrived in the 900s and settled permanently in South and West Greenland for nearly 500 years, until they succumbed to hunger, cold, or feuding. In the following centuries, many European whalers, traders, and explorers called at the west coast of Greenland and brought with them new materials and usages. But they left again, in ships laden with skins, oil for the lamps of Europe, whalebone for crinolines, and narwhal tusks.

In 1721 people arrived who remained in the country. One of them was the minister Hans Egede, who looked for the vanished Norsemen and began missionary work among the Eskimos of the west coast of Green-

2. *Faces carved in a block of wood sent to the National Museum in Copenhagen in 1889 with the remark, "Found in an old grave at the colony of Upernavik." Dorset culture. 6″ high. National Museum, Copenhagen.*

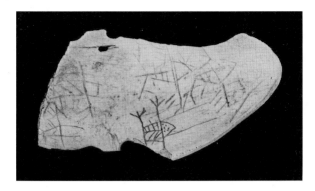

3 a. *Caribou bone with engraved drawings. Dorset culture. 2⁹/₁₆″ long. Shown full size. University Museum, Cambridge.*

3 b. *Bottom or lid of amulet box, carved as a face. Dorset culture. Caribou antler, 2⁷/₁₆″ high. Shown full size. University Museum, Cambridge.*

land. With him began the colonization that has continued to the present day, resulting in Greenlandic Home Rule within the Danish Commonwealth for a Greenlandic population of 40,000 and a resident Danish population of 10,000.

On the east coast Eskimo groups lived without contact with Europeans until 1884, and Angmagssalik was not colonized until 1894. There has therefore been a great difference in the development of the east and the west coasts, including the development of their art.

In this first chapter, I shall try to explain some of the ideas of the "old" Eskimo world – that is to say, the period before the introduction of Christianity and the new habits, usages and ideas. Here I use the term *Eskimo art* and compare art objects from Alaska, Canada, and Greenland to establish the uniformity of the culture and to show that certain cultural traits have a common root. Apart from this, the book deals exclusively with art found in Greenland or made by Greenlandic artists, and the term *Greenlandic art* is used subsequently.

From what kind of society did the art we admire today arise: expressive figures of people and animals, beautifully carved in bone, ivory or wood? Not from a close-knit, permanently settled society with written laws and statutes, but from a society of hunters who wandered over an immense area, from the Bering Straits to East Greenland, following the movements of the game, divided up into small groups, sometimes even single families. It is inconceivable that a uniform cultural tradition could arise and be maintained over so vast a land area through 5,000 years.

The artistic necessity

The conditions were harsh: merciless climate, ice-locked waters the year round, ten months of snow and cold. To survive here, to manufacture bone and stone tools and with them kill musk oxen, caribou, whales, walruses, and seals, seems worthy of our admiration. And that there was surplus enough, both spiritually and materially, to produce works of art is even more wonderful.

One asks immediately: but what is art? Is it art to decorate your clothes and your tools? To carve small figures as amulets for protection – is that conscious art? Admittedly the boundaries between art and artisanry are fluid, just as they are between individual works of art and magical figures whose appearance is prescribed. Nevertheless I will reply that, yes, it *is* art. And what is so impressive about Eskimo art is precisely that it originated in a hard and frugal life, often on the edge of subsistence – and that it was necessary to make tools with great skill and artistic ability and just as necessary to create pictorial expression for spiritual concepts. The fact that the small figures radiate vitality and the will to live is for me proof that art arises out of necessity. Art is not merely the frippery of a society of abundance. Art is the nucleus of our existence. By concerning ourselves with these works of art, we can approach an understanding of the inhabitants of the arctic regions, of their thoughts and existence.

Like the prehistoric cave painters, these hunting people were predominantly interested in the life-giving animals and their own relationship to them. The first figurative signs we know of are scratchings on pieces of bone – small stylized figures among which a few birds' feet are recognizable. From the same period we also see a face, which forms the bottom of an amulet box (fig. 3*b*). So already we sense that existence must have been hard – there was a need for amulets, a need to be on good terms with the higher powers. Hunger and cold were daily enemies, and even though there must have been periods with good catches and a favorable climate in some places, I think nevertheless that what the shaman Aua of

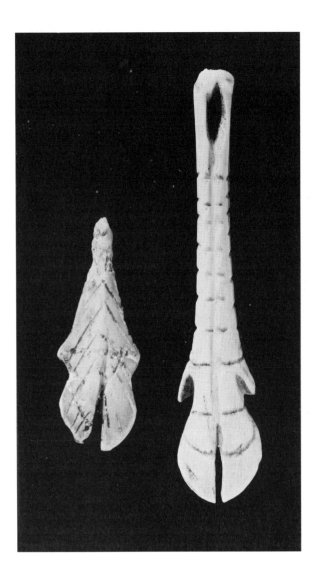

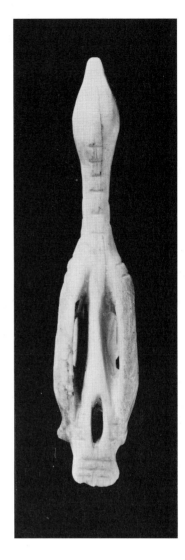

the Melville Peninsula told Knud Rasmussen in 1921 was often true for the old Eskimo tribes: existence was marked by fear and the religious beliefs implied a long series of complex taboos to be observed scrupulously. At Knud Rasmussen's attempt to find justification for these rules, Aua replied:

Not even you can give reasons when we ask you why life is the way it is. And that is as it must be. All of our customs come from life and go to life; we explain nothing, we believe nothing, but in what I have just shown you lie all of our answers.
We're afraid.
We're afraid of the earth's weather, which we have to fight in order to wrest a living from the land and the sea.
We're afraid of want and hunger in the cold igloos.
We're afraid of the sickness we experience daily all around us. Not of death, but of suffering.
We're afraid of dead people's and killed animals' souls.
We're afraid of the spirits of the earth and air.
Therefore have our fathers and their fathers armed themselves with all the old rules which are based on the experience and life wisdom of generations. We don't know how, we don't know why, but we follow them in order to be allowed to live without care. And so ignorant are we in spite of all our shamans that we fear everything we don't know. We fear what we see around us, and we fear what we know from the

6. Tupilak *figure with skeleton-motif female face, a male head on the back, and a bear's head on each hip. One of the bear's heads has a cross on the forehead (cf. fig. 15). Angmagssalik, ca. 1900. Driftwood, rubbed with lampblack and oil. 6⅛" long. National Museum, Copenhagen.*

tales and myths of our forefathers. Therefore we have our customs, and therefore we observe our taboos.

Aua's younger brother continued on the same topic and said:

Life's greatest danger lies in the fact that human food consists entirely of souls. All of the creatures we have to kill and eat, and the ones we have to slaughter and destroy in order to make clothing for ourselves have souls just like us, souls which don't perish with the body and which therefore must be appeased or else they will avenge themselves on us because we have stolen their bodies.

In order to comprehend art closely connected to magic, we must – as mentioned earlier – know something about the associated religious beliefs. The entire surrounding world was alive: each stone, piece of wood, turbulence of the water – every single thing – was alive, had its *inua*, its owner. Not only things but also concepts such as food, sleep, and laughter possessed one.

The Eskimos thus had an extensive belief in souls. People and animals – as evidenced by the foregoing quotation – possessed souls. The great mask feasts of the Alaskan Eskimos were held to appease the souls of the game animals, and this respectful, loving, cultic attitude toward animals is reflected in the little Dorset period amulets of bears, walruses, birds, caribou hooves, and seals (figs. 4 and 5).

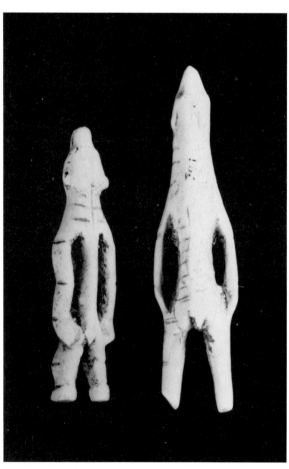

8. *Bears with skeleton motif, probably amulet figures. Dorset culture. Igdloolik, Canada. Walrus ivory, 1⅝″ and 2⅛″ long. University Museum, Cambridge.*

But people and animals did not have only one soul, they had many – one for each joint of the body (fig. 6). These souls were not equally important or equally great. It was said that there were three great souls: one in the throat and the other two in the groin. The place between the eyes, at the root of the nose, was also a very important point – "there where the intelligence lives." The body was only a temporary dwelling, whereas the name lived on. A person was divided into a name, a body, and a soul. An East Greenlander explained it thus to Knud Rasmussen:

A body is perishable and putrifies like all other flesh, and therefore the soul cannot be bound to it. A human being has many souls distributed over the entire body; each joint has its soul and each soul lives in a human likeness, a tiny little human being the size of a thumb. These souls gather all the person's life force, which emanates from the mouth. When a human being dies, it therefore stops breathing. The human being's souls are made like small humans, because each single part of the body which they maintain is like an independent piece of a human being.

When a person wants to do another human being ill, he therefore always endeavors to steal one of its souls, because then that part of the body which has been robbed of its soul must get sick. It is considered one of a shaman's most important tasks to get stolen souls back to their human beings.

Besides these concrete personified conceptualizations, people also believed in a special power, a universal magic force called *sila*. The word variously means the universe, intellect, and weather, the force residing in all things, which is not personified, is neither good nor evil, but determines everything and is in all things. Finally, there were the mythological figures, and it was exceedingly important to be on good terms with them: the Sea's Mother, who ruled over the animals of the sea; the Ruler of the Winds; and the Moon Man, who determined the tides and the course of the year. To these and many other supernatural beings were connected numerous legends still alive among the Eskimo peoples, of which we will meet many interpretations in this book.

To return to the belief in souls, when we look at a caribou antler from the Dorset period (fig. 7) or a block of wood covered with closely set faces turning in all directions, are we seeing a human being with all of its tiny souls gathered into one, an entire human being? So it would appear – in any case, it is a strongly sculptural message; compact and closed in form, the objects radiate an intense feeling of the human.

With the sculpturally closed form is found the engraved figure: symmetrically ornamented bears, walrus heads, caribou hooves, birds, and seals. Perhaps some of the markings indicate that here resided an important soul, perhaps the intention is to show the animal's skeleton – so familiar from flensing – or perhaps there was a special cult centered on these animals, and their images were borne as amulets or jewelry. The stylizing of bear figures, in particular, could indicate the latter (fig. 8).

This ornamentation, usually called "skeleton motif", is still used in present-day East Greenland art, though probably more for the sake of decorative effect and because of tradition. "It is the way we are accustomed to." "That's how the old ones did it." "That's the way my father did it." "I don't know, but that's how we've always done it." Those are the replies I got to questions as to why these particular carvings are used.

But surely it is this very respect for tradition, for the rules and injunctions of the ancestors, that has held Eskimo art and culture together – despite every influence. It is conceivable, too, that skeleton ornamentation derived from a now-forgotten death cult. Carvings such as death masks and ornamented skeletons from the Ipiutak period in northwestern Alaska also point in this direction.

15

Cult and magic

I earlier mentioned the existence of a bear cult. This is not strange, considering that the polar bear is large and dangerous and, at the same time, an extremely desirable animal, to which many legends and beliefs are attached. It was thought that the bear possessed human intelligence and that one had to beware of it because it could understand what people said (figs. 10-12).

A bear could be killed only if it wanted to be. It wanted to trade with human beings, to receive a gift in return for its meat and skin. After skinning, the head was kept in the house for a few days and hung with gifts such as *kamik* sole skin, which the bear was especially fond of and needed, too, for no animal walks as much as the bear and wears out its soles so often.

In Signe Rink's memoirs there is a description of how a bear was caught at a settlement in South Greenland near Cape Farewell in 1882-83. The narrator, called "I.H.", tells what happened after the bear was killed:

> When the head had been carried inside, I went inside too because I knew that certain tricks would be performed with it. First it was placed on the edge of the lamp platform with its face turned to the southeast, whereupon its eyes and nostrils were plugged with lamp waste and the like, and the top of the head was decorated with all kinds of trifles such as boot soles, knives, glass beads, saw chips, and other things.
>
> The direction (southeast) points to the way from which bears are accustomed to come; that is with the great ice around the south point of the land. The moss in its nostrils is supposed to keep the bear you want to catch from scenting the approach of humans, and the grease in its mouth is supposed to please it, as it is fond of all kinds of burnt fat. They decorate the top of its head because they think that the bear has been sent on an errand to them for these things by their ancestors, and, as they reckon that the bear's soul won't arrive home again before five days have gone by, they never eat the head of their bear before this time has elapsed, as the bear's soul might die on the way (and the trifles for the family be lost).

The polar bear was a messenger between people and their dead ancestors. There was also a giant polar bear that lived in the sea, "the Sea's Bear," and it was so huge that when it inhaled "such whirlpools were caused that icebergs and whole *umiak*s rush into its nostrils." Here, perhaps, is another connection with the dead, one of whose realms was located in the depths of the sea.

It is certain that wearing amulets was a common practice and that they were worn next to the skin, placed in the kayak, under the bed, or sewed into the amulet harness or the anorak. Women also wore amulets inside their topknots.

There exist accounts of the use of amulets from both West and East Greenland. The first comes from the English explorer John Davis, who in the years 1585-87, in his attempt to discover the Northwest Passage, sailed up the west coast of Greenland all the way to Upernavik. Davis was the first European since the Norsemen to make contact with the Greenland Eskimos, and his observations were published in London in 1589 in an account of the voyage. Of the Eskimos, Davis writes in his journal: "They are idolaters, and have images great store, which they were about them, and in theyr boats, which we suppose they worship."

Hans Egede, too, writes in his *The Old Greenland's New Perlustration* (1741) that the use of amulets was common. They were, however, "nothing more than a little piece of an old tree, stones or bones, birds'

10. The hunter has lost his harpoon and the bear is pulling him and his kayak down. Drawn in 1933 by Kârale Andreassen, Angmagssalik. Pencil on writing pad paper, watermarked "Holland." Collected by the Dutch ethnologist and Nobel Prize winner Nico Tinbergen. Museum voor het Onderwijs, The Hague.

11 a. Polar bear, Alaska. Dorset culture. Walrus ivory, with hole for use as pendant, 4¾″ long. University Museum, Cambridge.

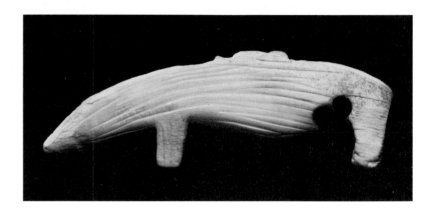

11 b. Polar bear, Canada. Dorset culture. Found in 1875 at Hayes Sound. Longitudinal furrows. Walrus ivory, 3⅝″ long. British Museum.

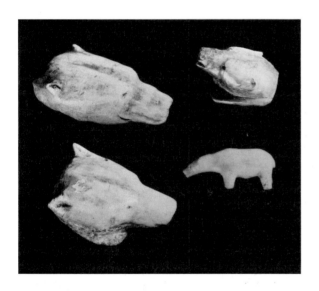

11 c. Three bears' heads, and a miniature bear. Amulet figures, found at Igdloolik, Canada. Dorset culture, ca. A. D. 1000. Walrus ivory, the largest head 1⅜″ long. Shown full size. University Museum, Cambridge.

beaks or claws, or whatever each's phantasie chooses." In particular, Egede mentions that barren women believed they would become fertile if they got as an amulet a piece of a European's shoe sole. "For as they regard our nation as a fecund people and being of a strong nature and very capable, they think that the power they possess goes with their clothing and that it will be of like service to them."

From the same century, the merchant Lars Dalager writes of amulets, in his book *Greenlandic Relations* (1752), that the Greenlanders for their life and health wear so many of them that it would be too exhausting to go into detail, but he touches on the subject:

Some use something like a cartridge belt, hanging diagonally from the shoulder down to the other side, together with a belt around the waist. Others use belts around their arms above the elbow, but around the neck hangs the finest and most important, seeing that the best medicine is inlaid and sewn onto those, which can consist of hair, feathers, pumice, fish scales, and birds' eyes.

Dalager notes, however, that it was not always out of superstition that these trimmings were worn. "For some use bands around the neck with claws on them for decoration only. Some also use bindings around their arms and hands in order to feel how they lose and gain in fatness."

Even though Dalager may be correct in noting that not all use of decorations should be attributed to their supernatural value, magical uses were nonetheless made of those amulets that were not visible, and the belief in their worth in bringing good fortune has flourished all the way up to our own day. Thus the Swedish painter Ossian Elgström relates from his journey along the west coast in 1915 that a sealer asked to be given back a carved piece of bone from his kayak, which he had just sold, as his hunting luck had "disappeared".

On the east coast, the use of amulets was very common. Captain

Gustav Holm, who in 1884 met an isolated tribe at Angmagssalik, related that "many have sitting in the skin harness a male and a female figure which are carved from wood taken from the house entryway." The female figure was worn on the chest, the male on the back, while smaller pieces of wood were placed under the arms. A pregnant woman should carve two little dolls from the wooden handle of a skin-scraper that had belonged to someone who had died and place them as amulets in her underfur, one at each armpit, so that the childbirth would be easy.

All sorts of odds and ends could be used as amulets: pieces of iron, hair, splinters of bone, or bits of clothing that had belonged to particular persons, but also blubber sludge, blood residues, fingernails – especially from the ring finger (the finger the midwife held when she named the child). Many amulets were carved in the form of humans or animals and thus became small works of art with magical content.

Birds, or parts of them, also possessed potent qualities as amulets. Thus it was said that if a man were killed by sorcery, his son could protect himself by making an amulet from a raven. The raven was to be skinned in such a way that the skin retained the claws, head, and beak, and afterwards it was to be hung up in the house or tent directly over the place where the man usually sat. As soon as the soul robber appeared, the raven would start to scream, so that only the robber and not the people in the house could hear it. Feeling himself discovered in his designs, the soul robber immediately fled in terror. In order to protect a child, say, from soul robbery, you could place the raven's head and feet under the bed directly beneath the child's place, and over the child a raven figure, and should the avenger come, either the one or the other would discover him and protect the child.

An amulet of a raven's head with claws (fig. 13) also gave many catches during hunting, because the raven has the quality of always turning up where game is killed. A person who had committed murder, and was therefore exposed to revenge, could confuse the avenger by placing a piece of twig from a raven's nest – often carried in the shape of a little doll – in his amulet bag, because ravens are shrewd birds who place the dwarf willow twigs they use to build their nests with in such a way that the nest is both hard to see and difficult to get to.

Gustav Holm noted that a boy who spat blood and whose entire family was consumptive had a wound peg sewn into the chest of his anorak as an amulet. The stoppers of wood or bone were inserted in the wound of the harpooned animal so that the blood wouldn't run out. Often they were furnished with a beautifully carved face, presumably representing the soul of the wound peg or that of the animal. Or was it the hunter's? It might also be the hunter's mark of ownership, and it could possibly have

12. A supernatural bear collected by the umiak *expedition to East Greenland, 1884-85. Gustav Holm's remark: "A so-called* Angakoq *bear on wheels, recognized by its thick neck and skinny body." Also recognizable as supernatural by the skeleton motif. Used as a toy. Driftwood and bone, 8¼" long, 3½" high. National Museum, Copenhagen.*

13. Amulet made from a raven's head and talons, fastened together with a skin thong. Collected in Angmagssalik in 1902 by W. Thalbitzer. 9″ long. National Museum, Copenhagen.

the same purpose as in northern Alaska: the face was supposed to call the hunter if the seal drifted away. The throat peg (fig. 14) was decorated in a similar manner. It was placed in the windpipe of the killed seal after the lungs had been inflated so that the animal floated on the surface and was easy to transport.

Some of these small faces – with their ornamentation and distended mouths – are reminiscent of masks. Masks represent some intermediate point between portraitlike anthropomorphic art and magical art in which definite symbolic values are used for a definite purpose. From the Dorset period, there is a little mask with transverse lines and two diagonal grooves that cross at the root of the nose and between the eyes – there where "the intelligence lives" (fig. 15). From present-day Greenland, we still see masks with transverse lines and a marking at the root of the nose, and although these masks are made for sale and have lost their magical significance, it is nevertheless thought-provoking that Eskimo artists – either consciously or unconsciously – still make use of the age-old ornamentation.

Over the entire Eskimo area, the face has been decorated and "the loose face," the mask, has been utilized. At the Bering Strait the "wild men didn't wear masks but black paint on their faces." For the Siberian Eskimos, lines drawn around the eyes assured good luck in hunting, and in Alaska masks were used at the great feasts for the game animals. In Greenland, masks are alleged to represent the shaman's helping spirits or the spirits of his ancestors. Masks were personal objects and were often

*14. Throat peg, with carved
face. East Greenland.
Collected in the 1930s.
Driftwood, 8⅝" long.
Rijksmuseum voor
Volkenkunde, Leiden.*

*15. Mask, with skeleton motif, carved from a caribou shoulder blade,
2½" high. Dorset culture. University Museum, Cambridge.*

16. Female and male figures. Thule culture. East Greenland, ca. 1900. Collected by Kristian Rosing. Driftwood, 2¹³/₁₆" and 2⁹/₁₆" high. National Museum of Greenland, Godthåb-Nuuk.

17. Seated woman. Thule culture. Collected by C. Ryder's expedition to Angmagssalik in 1892. Driftwood, 2⁷/₁₆" high, 6⁷/₈" long. National Museum, Copenhagen.

18. Male figure with facial features, intended to represent a European. Thule culture. Collected by Gustav Holm's umiak expedition to East Greenland 1884-85. Driftwood, 2" high. National Museum, Copenhagen.

19. Pregnant woman. Thule culture. Found in arctic Canada. Walrus ivory, 1¹/₄" high. University Museum, Cambridge.

20. *Male figure collected on the east coast by Dr. Therkel Mathiassen 1931-32. Driftwood, with inlaid bone eyes and black pigment. National Museum, Copenhagen.*

placed in the grave with their owners. Their first use was as dance masks in cult ceremonies, and later they were used as frightening masks.

In a house ruin at Angmagssalik a little hand-held mask with one side male and the other female was found. This balance of nature is often seen depicted in Eskimo art. In the Thule period, the man-woman theme is the most important and the most appealing to artists. As dolls (fig. 16), as amulets, either carved in wood or bone or appliquéd onto fur, we see the human couple, now and then in the company of seals, kayaks, *umiak*s, and tents – the entire little world of the settlement.

Such everyday realism (figs. 17-18) flourished side by side with cultic beliefs, which led to far more stylized, abstract art.

A trace of fertility cult might perhaps be attributed to the small "family figures," such as the little pregnant woman in figure 19 and the androgynous figures we meet with right down to our own day. The cultivation of fertility seems reasonable in small, often languishing societies, and sexuality plays a very great part in their literary and pictorial art. The figure with the black phallus may thus very well be a fertility figure, but considering its frightening and caricatured expression, it might also be a lampoon (fig. 20). Black was regarded as a "dangerous" color. Thus it was said of the terrifying spirit Ajummaaq that it had a body something like a human's, but with only three fingers and three toes (fig. 98). Its head was like a dog's, and its arms and legs were black. Everything it touched with these black limbs putrified and died.

From more recent times, we also see terrifying figures with the phallus placed on the chest (fig. 22). Johan Petersen, first manager of the trading station established in Angmagssalik in 1894, ten years after Gustav Holm's *umiak* expedition, relates:

Our neighbours, who had returned from a visit in Sermilik, said that a young girl in Sermilik had been very sick. During her illness, she had confessed that in order to harm her family – she wanted to kill her father and stepmother, or rather her two stepmothers and her brothers and sisters – she had fashioned herself a *tupilak*. For some time she had been collecting the various parts – snarls of hair, fingernails, and bits of

21. *The terrifying spirit Amo, collected on the east coast in the 1930s by Nico Tinbergen. Driftwood with black pigment, 7⅞" long. Museum voor het Onderwijs, The Hague.*

22. *Androgynous figure carved by Adam Pîvât, Kungmiut, in the 1960s. Sperm-whale ivory, arms riveted on. 4¹¹/₁₆" high. Private Collection.*

27. *Portrait of the shaman Mitsivarniannga's* tupilak, *drawn by his son, Kârale Andreassen, in Angmagssalik in the 1920s. Pencil on paper, 4¼"×4½". Royal Engravings Collection, Copenhagen.*

clothing that had belonged to the intended victims – to make the *tupilak*, which was moreover tricked out with a male sexual organ on its chest. The girl had been assisted in working on the *tupilak* by one of the older women of the settlement, who wanted revenge on her divorced husband.

*Tupilak*s were sorcery monsters. They were fashioned by individuals skilled in sorcery to inflict death and disaster on their enemies. Containing parts of various animals and preferably also parts of a child's corpse, the *tupilak* was made according to definite rules. Charm songs were sung over it, whereupon it was left in a stream or in the sea to find its own way to its victim. If the intended victim possessed greater competence in magic, the *tupilak* emmisary returned and killed its maker. It was therefore an exceedingly dangerous process to set in motion (figs. 23-26).

There are no "authentic" *tupilak*s extant, but there are many accounts of them and many pictorial replicas. It would appear that the Greenlandic artist gets a great deal of release for his imagination and sense of the surreal in making these dread-inspiring figures.

Around the year 1920, the shaman Mitsivarniannga, whose son the catechist Kârale Andreassen drew his father's *tupilak* (fig. 27), told how it was made. Mitsivarniannga had lost his little brother and had to perform penance of various kinds. One day he was visited by an old shaman, who asked him if he didn't want to avenge himself on the person who was to blame for his brother's death. Mitsivarniannga said he did, and this is how it was done. The corpse of the child was dug up, and a dead and putrifying snow bunting, a living snipe, and a tendon from a seal caught by old Peqqissarpik, who had caused the child's death, were obtained.

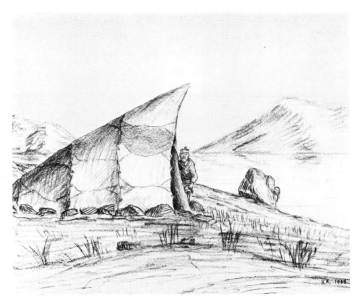

23-26. *Four drawings by Kârale Andreassen, made in 1933 for Nico Tinbergen, depicting the creation of a* tupilak *and the destruction of its maker. Figure 23 shows an old woman in the process of assembling a* tupilak, *with parts of a skeleton among the ingredients. Figure 24 shows her waiting at their tent for a young married couple whose happiness she is jealous of to come home. Figure 25 shows the live* tupilak. *The young couple have stronger powers of sorcery, however, and the* tupilak *therefore returns to the old woman and kills her (fig. 26). All drawn with pencil on 11³/4″×8¹/4″ writing pad paper. Museum voor het Onderwijs, The Hague.*

The shaman then created, according to the special rules, a thing with the child's head and body, the snipe's legs, the snow bunting's wings, and the seal's tendon across its back in order to give strength to the wings. After the shaman had recited the magic words, the *tupilak* came alive and flew away to get revenge on the old soul robber who had caused the child's death.

Naturally many misfortunes were said to have been brought about by *tupilak*s. There are, for example, numerous accounts of hunters who from their kayaks harpoon what they believe to be a seal but turns out to be a *tupilak*, which pulls the kayak man down with it into the deep. As late as the 1970s, East Greenland sealers spoke of this, and as an illustration carved a figure of the monster (fig. 28).

These composite beings are also known from other Eskimo regions. Thus one of the most common masks in Alaska represents the spirit of the half-human-half-animal, and on Nunivak Island the half-human-half-animal was sometimes depicted with a human face and an animal's body.

I have mentioned the shaman several times. One of the Alaskan Eskimo designations for a shaman is *tunvalik,* or "demon-intermediary." But toward the end of the 1800s, the common northern designation *angatuq,* in Greenlandic *angakkoq,* meaning "one who knows many arts," was used over most of western Alaska and Canada. According to Kaj Birket-Smith, the Chugach shaman was called *kalalik,* or "one who possesses spirits." Hence the shaman is the person who effects contact with the spirits, who had helping spirits for the purpose, and who is skilled at many arts.

His operations were especially important when there was poor hunting or bad weather, for then he could undertake journeys to the bottom of the sea to clean and comb the hair of the Sea's Mother. As thanks for his help, she would then send the sea animals up to the surface again. Or he could fly to the moon to appease the angry Moon Man, who punished humans when they did not observe their taboos. Both journeys were, of course, fraught with danger and difficult to carry out, just as the entire apprenticeship of an *angakkoq* was hard to undergo.

The shamanistic ritual was performed in the dark, and to the inciting accompaniment of the drum were heard the piping, growling, whistling voices of the spirits. Often the shaman was a good ventriloquist, but he could also disguise his voice by holding a stick lengthwise between his teeth. I am convinced that a state of ecstasy occurred in the condition of fear and excitement created by the ritual. I remember how great an

29. *Shaman figure collected by Dr. Therkel Mathiassen in 1931-32 in Angmagssalik. Driftwood, rubbed with lampblack and oil, gut, and depilated sealskin, 7¼" high. National Museum, Copenhagen.*

impression it made on me when Odin Maratse (from a family of shamans) late one evening at the Sermiligaq outpost in East Greenland got an old drum with a plastic head out from under the couch, and performed an eerily effective shamanistic seance with the rhythmic beat of the drum accompanied by the piping, squeaking "spirit" noises.

I was on the east coast with an exhibition of masks from the collections of the National Museum in Copenhagen, an exhibition that resulted in a flood of new masks, of which some appear to be portraits and others traditional masks adhering to the legacy of formalized ornamentation. (Now and then this ornamentation reminds one of tattoos, which among the Eskimos were also used both as decoration and for their magical powers). A favorite way of turning one's own face into a mask was to tie a string over the nose so that it was deformed. This comprised part of a specific personage, namely "the beggar," also called Uaajeerteq. This figure is represented by a man who dresses up like a pregnant woman (again an instance of androgyny), blackens his face, puts a stick crosswise in his mouth, and binds a thong across his nose (fig. 30). Thus deformed,

31. Mitaartut *mask collected in Jakobshavn in the 1950s by George Nelleman. Undepilated and depilated dog skin, buttonhole stitching around the eyes. 11″ long. Forhistorisk Museum, Moesgård, Århus.*

he goes around begging gifts to the accompaniment of the drum. At the same time, he spreads fright and panic among the sitting circle of spectators by laying into them with his drumstick.

Some of the elements of Uaajeerteq are found again in the so-called *mitaartut* mummers. *Mitaartut* is the plural of *mitaartoq,* used of "a disguised, unrecognizable, somber-looking figure." These costumed figures perform each evening from New Year's Eve until Epiphany. Often they pose as the Magi, at times in costumes strongly reminiscent of Uaajeerteq, with blackened cinched-up faces, padded stomachs, and sticks that are used energetically. And, finally, the *mitaartut* also use masks made of skin (fig. 31), paper, or, as recorded in a single case, rye-bread dough with glass Christmas-tree baubles inserted as eyes – but never made of wood (on masks in general, see pp. 54).

Other characteristics of *mitaartut* are that men perform in women's clothing and women in men's clothing, and that the sex is delineated in an unmistakable manner. The *mitaartut* are mute, and if one can't guess who they are, one must give them gifts. Perhaps in olden times *mitaartut* were poor people who in this way obtained something for their household; in any case the *mitaartut*'s clothing is on the whole wretched and tattered, and their appearance is repulsive. The entire custom suggests a blend of pagan and Christian usages in which a cult figure with obvious sexual content is amalgamated with the story of the three wise men.

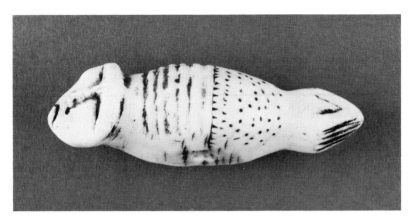

32. Seal figure with dot ornamentation. East Greenland or Thule, age uncertain. Made from a polar bear tooth without the form being altered appreciably. 1¼" long. National Museum, Copenhagen.

35. Handle for tow line, with carved face, line and dot ornamentation. Alaska, ca. 1890. Walrus ivory rubbed with lampblack, 2½" long. British Museum.

33. Bird with dot ornamentation. Arctic Canada, ca. 1890. Walrus ivory, 1⅛" long. British Museum.

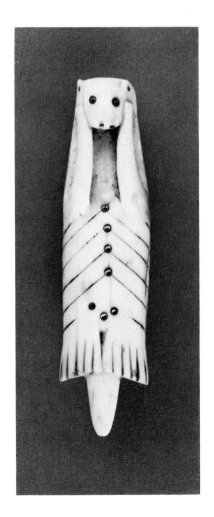

On *mitaartut* masks, we see no skeleton ornamentation, but there is explicit delineation of eyes, nose, and mouth.

Eyes, nose, mouth, and ears are symbolized in Eskimo art by seven dots – the seven openings of the human or animal head. On some occasions, there are long lines of dots, or the entire figure is strewn with dots, drilled into the bone or ivory and then rubbed with lampblack, a striking graphic effect. – The dot and the line, the oval, the circle, the triangle these are the simple, nearly elemental, geometric forms with which the Eskimo artist creates his world of ornament (figs. 32-35).

34. Sea otter with line and dot ornamentation. Alaska, ca. 1890. Walrus ivory with inlaid metal, 2⅝" long. British Museum.

36. *Eyeshade collected by the* umiak *expedition to East Greenland, 1884-85. Was used as a cap "especially for protection against ice-glare" (Gustav Holm). Driftwood with riveted bits of bone, 8⅝″ long. National Museum, Copenhagen.*

It can be difficult for us to interpret these signs properly: when do they possess evident symbolic value, and when are they created for the sake of aesthetic enjoyment? Sometimes there is no question about it – for example, when we regard the eyeshade from East Greenland shown in figure 36. The pattern on the top represents a face, with concentric circles as eyes. It is difficult to say anything definite about the pattern on the sides of the eyeshade, but the ornament might be derived from the oval, whose basic motif is a seal's body.

The most necessary and commonplace of game animals, the seal, provided meat for food, oil for heating and light, skin for clothing and the covering for kayaks and *umiak*s, fur for insulating the winter dwelling, skin for the summer tent, gut for shirts and windows. The indispensable seal is an oft-repeated motif, most beautifully as bone reliefs riveted on wooden chests, water buckets, and hunting implements, such as the throwing stick in figure 37. The great helping spirit Toornaarsuk had the body of a seal, and the stylization of Toornaarsuk and of the seal's hindquarters came to form a standard ornamentation that decorates many articles of everyday use.

37. Throwing stick carved in Angmagssalik in 1936-37 as a gift for the sculptor and polar explorer Eigil Knuth. Driftwood with riveted bone figures representing seal, narwhal, people, bear, and dog. The figure at bottom left represents a dancer. The two lowermost figures in the right hand row have the sign of Toornaarsuk – the stylized seal's hindquarters – as their heads. 19¼" long. Greenlanders' House, Copenhagen.

There was altogether an intimate connection between implement culture and the cultic world. The given material and the function of the implement to a large degree determined its shape and size, but nonetheless it was believed that the animal preferred to be caught with beautifully carved implements. Furthermore, one enjoyed good catches if one was on good terms with the Sea's Mother. If one hadn't abided by the taboos, she became angry and held on to the animals. Then, too, there was the Moon Man, who could punish with inundations and eclipses of the moon.

The very close connection between the occupations of the Eskimo and the spiritual world, as well as their perfect adaptation to nature, the climate, and the animals, is what arouses our admiration for this people. Nothing can be removed from the whole; everything has its place and meaning.

The individual artist in the ordinary sense was virtually nonexistent. The man who was good at making arrows and harpoons was also good at carving figures, and the woman who was able to sew good, impermeable skin clothing and impermeable kayak coverings knew how to turn her needle to fine embroidery. To this day, precise technical craftsmanship is highly esteemed among the Eskimos. In light of this, it is almost dangerous to experiment with artistic devices: the balance is disturbed, things will go wrong if you don't follow the rules of your ancestors.

Common cultural traits

Style changed slowly, and surely it is this fidelity to tradition that is the basis for the many common traits among the Eskimo peoples and for the close stylistic connection between the Sarqaq, Dorset, Thule, and Inussuk cultures and present-day artistic expression in Alaska, Canada, and Greenland.

And there are many common characteristics: in language, myths and legends, religious beliefs, songs, dances, hunting techniques, and building practices. This is mentioned only to point out that it is not only in the area of art that similarities exist. I would like to show some examples of relatedness in art apart from a self-evident uniformity in materials and dimensions determined beforehand by the same climate, nature, and game animals.

A common stylistic trait is the ability to produce a distinctive graphic effect, either by means of incised drawings on bone or ivory or by using appliqué with light fur on dark, dark on light, or juxtaposing them on a neutral background. The same appliqué effect is achieved by riveting figures, where not only the colors but also the materials contrast. Here the effect is both that of a relief and of a play of materials.

In the area of sculpture, there is great mutual cohesion with regard to the frontal principle (figs. 38-40). It is especially from earlier times that, from the whole Eskimo area, we see only figures facing straight ahead, weight squarely on both feet, eyes front. Everywhere in the Thule period, we meet the same interest in the body, the torso. The frontal is associated with the symmetrical. There is the same symmetry and graphic effect in the skeleton-ornamented bear figures from the Dorset period and in figures from modern-day Greenland.

As far as masks are concerned, there is greater variation, as Alaskan masks occupy a special position. Yet we see masks with inlaid eyes from both Greenland and Alaska, and the marking of the wings of the nose – so common in Greenlandic masks – is seen in Alaska as well. Skin masks from Labrador and from the west coast of Greenland are identical in having "pointed," or ogival, eyes, noses, and mouths, and in the way smooth and furry skin are juxtaposed.

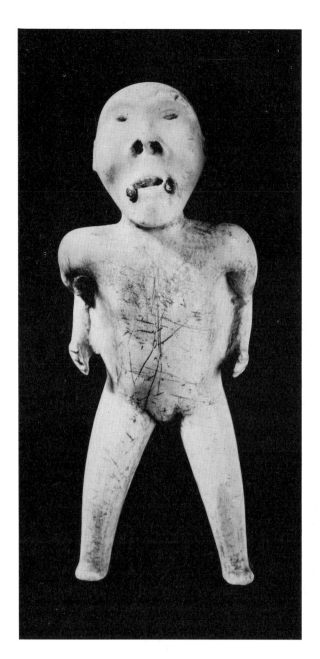

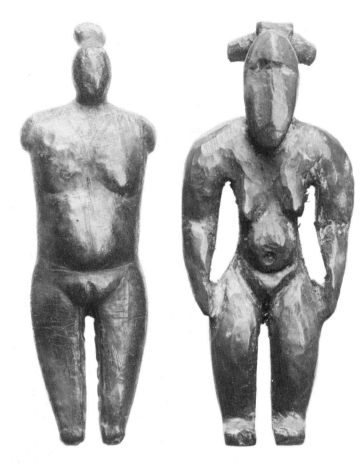

40. Two female figures, collected in Thule in 1939. The figure on the right, on account of its style and patina, is considered to be from the Dorset culture; the one on the left, because of its truncated arms, from the Thule culture. Walrus molar ivory, 3³/₁₆″ high. National Museum, Copenhagen.

38. Male figure, Alaska, collected in the 1800s. Walrus ivory with metal labrets at the corners of the mouth, representing the lip jewelry worn by the Alaskan Eskimos well into our own century. 5¹/₈″ high. University Museum, Cambridge.

39. Two figures, both representing a man carrying a child on his shoulders, presumably father and son. On the left hand figure, the father has rotated his face completely toward the child. Igdloolik, Canada. Dorset culture. Walrus ivory, 1⁷/₈″ and 2″. University Museum, Cambridge.

41. *Detail from the bow of a bow drill, showing dancing figures with Indian-like feathered dress. West Canadian Eskimos. Acquired in 1847. Walrus ivory with engravings rubbed with lampblack. Entire bow about 11¾" long. National Museum, Helsinki.*

42. *Detail from reverse of fig. 41. Scene representing whale hunting from an* umiak. *The men, who only row the* umiak *in hunting situations, are paddling the boat forward, whereas women row facing aft.*

43. *Various situations from hunting and daily life. From the Tjukter Eskimos of East Cape, collected by Knud Rasmussen on the fifth Thule expedition in 1924. Large walrus tusk cut and polished at either end, engraved drawings rubbed with lampblack. 3⁵⁄₁₆" long, 2" high, ¹¹⁄₁₆" thick. National Museum, Copenhagen.*

44. *Animal figures, including bear hunting seal. Tjukter Eskimos (Bering Straits), 1921. Walrus ivory with blacked engravings, 11³⁄₈" long. Finnish National Museum, Helsinki.*

45. *Women at a tent, men coming home with the catch, seal. East Greenland, 1950s. Whole walrus tusk with part of jaw, engraved drawings. 13³⁄₄" long. Private collection.*

In painting and drawing, the similarity lies mainly in the lack of central perspective – I disregard similarities in choice of motif, as this is generally in keeping with the common conditions of life. For example, when a hunting scene is engraved in ivory or bone, the figures are seen from the side progressing as though on a line everywhere in the Eskimo area. Usually they describe a series of actions. Starting from one side or the other, the frieze tells of a hunting situation, say, or a journey (figs. 41-45).

I regard this manner of making a sequential series of scenes as typical of Eskimo artists. We see it in engravings from northern Siberia, from Alaska, Canada, and Greenland, and we find the same pictorial concept in Gormansen's watercolors (the first known paintings from Greenland) and in Jakob Danielsen's urge to continue his motif through a series of pictures.

Perspective was not used, and again this is surely associated with the Eskimo sense of ornamentation. The ornaments never fill out the whole surface, but run on as bands, lines, or "friezes" (fig. 46). For example, if

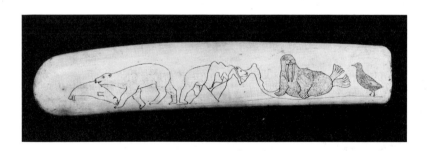

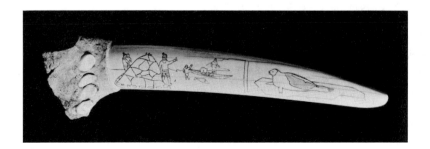

46. *Gut strip with appliquéd figures of eight couples and an* umiak *in depilated sealskin. 16¹/₈" long, 4" high. East Greenland. Collected during the* umiak *expedition, 1884-85. National Museum, Copenhagen.*

riveted figures were used (fig. 47), they were usually placed side by side, forming a frieze.

Do we not suddenly sense a profound relationship between these pictorial friezes and ornamental borders and the long word-sentences formed in Greenlandic by adding suffixes to roots? And doesn't the effect of songs and magical incantations, too, lie in repetition and the refrain that recurs again and again like a pattern?

Earth colors and plant colors were used in addition to blood and lampblack. Black could also be made by mixing graphite, crushed charcoal, or gunpowder with fermented urine, blood, or water. These limited materials inevitably resulted in a restrained color scale, probably the reason why the black-white effect has been cultivated with such virtuosity. When color finally came to the Eskimos in the form of the beads and cotton cloth that the strangers brought as trading goods, pure, clear colors were the ones preferred. They were strong and unmixed, as we see them in the Greenlandic national costume, for example, and in the choice of colors for painting frame houses.

Beads were already popular, either carved out of bone or ivory or made from the vertebrae of the capelin fish, but the bartered manufactured beads were highly prized – it was a sign of affluence and prestige when a skillful sealer's wife had many beads. Besides, one of the good things about beads was that there was a hole through them. Evil could not, therefore, remain in a bead, but must needs fall through the hole.

As already mentioned, many similarities derive from common conditions of life and common materials. It is obvious that a sealing and hunting people who followed the game in their journeyings – now and then breaking up and families setting out in search of new hunting grounds with all their goods and chattels – could not create masonry or monumental works of art. Their effects had to go with them, and not take up too much space. Besides, one had to be sparing with precious materials. Killed animals and gathered driftwood were exploited to the utmost. The small format is thus almost a necessity of nature for all Eskimos. The motif is likewise to a large extent in keeping with the shape of the material. Naturally, you did not carve away a lot of excess from a large piece of ivory or wood, but rather found precisely the little chip that embodied the doll or the harpoon point you wanted to make. The materials were the same: stone, bone, ivory, wood, and skin.

The implements were also related. Finds by archaeologists of homogeneous arrows, chips, scrapers, axes, and knives are the evidence by which the dissemination of the various cultures has been established. What is also obvious is that the form of a figure is largely determined by the tool.

But most important, when speaking of artistic coherence, is that the Eskimo conceptual world is firmly cemented through myths and legends transmitted orally from generation to generation and from tribe to tribe –

47. *Tool chest, East Greenland, purchased in the 1890s by Angmagssalik's first colony manager, Johan Petersen. Driftwood, covered with riveted bone figures, fifteen figures on the lid alone, carved bone bead handle. 9³/₄" long, 4¹/₈" wide, 5" high. National Museum, Copenhagen.*

the same belief in *sila* (or mana), in *inua,* and in souls, the same fundamental belief in the close connection between humans and animals. Numerous animal legends indicate that originally there was not such a great difference and that animals frequently turned into humans and vice versa.

The belief in spirits, the use of amulets and magic words also manifest a coherent people, though the names may be a little different. For instance, the name for the Sea Woman among the Eskimos of Baffin Island is Sedna ("She down in the Sea"), while the Polar Eskimos call her Nerrivik ("the Food Place"), the West Greenlanders say Arnaqquagssaaq ("the Old Woman"), and the East Greenlanders Immap Ukuua ("the Sea's Mother"). But her function is the same. She is the ruler of the sea animals and is also associated with the realm of the dead under the sea.

There are divergencies and slightly different conceptions, just as there are within a family, but the conspicuously collective heritage is unmistakable. Asiatic Eskimos, Bering Sea Eskimos, Pacific Eskimos, Colville Eskimos, Point Barrow Eskimos, Mackenzie Eskimos, Copper Eskimos, Netsilik Eskimos, Caribou Eskimos, Iglulik Eskimos, Labrador Eskimos, Baffinlanders, Polar Eskimos, Angmagssalik Eskimos, and West

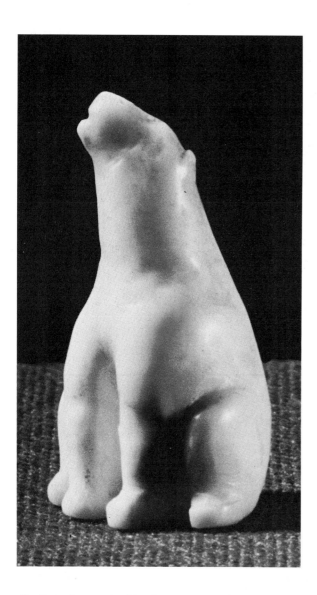

48. *Polar bear carved by Qaaqqutsiap of Etah (Thule) ca. 1958-60. Walrus ivory, 1" high. Private collection.*

Greenlanders all incorporate the most important Eskimo dialect groups of recent times.

In all this immense area, people understand one another, both mentally and, for the most part, linguistically. How reasonable, then, to conclude that their art is related and to speak of an Eskimo culture – the Eskimo culture as the root of the Greenlandic people.

In this chapter I have sought to trace the faint outlines of the culture that has been the wellspring of life for the Eskimo artist, and whose ideas are still an important source of inspiration. Although the Eskimo cultural picture is waning in today's Greenland and the function of art has changed radically, we can – outside influences notwithstanding – trace many cultural traits that have remained alive through several thousand years.

But Greenlandic art history follows a different pattern from the one we immediately comprehend. We of the European cultural tradition are accustomed to regarding the development of art as a continuous history of style, progressing, for example, from romanesque to gothic, from renaissance to baroque, and so on. This is not the case with Greenlandic art. The ideas, craftsmanship, and materials of the past are still alive in certain areas; you can hold in your hand a tiny modern figure (figs. 48-49) that could just as well have been made during the Dorset period (see fig. 11c).

Naturally European influence has powerfully transformed art. Entire disciplines such as drawing and painting first arose after the cultural confrontation. The Danes have been permanent residents on the west coast of Greenland since 1721, and many European ships traded with the Greenlanders in the period following the 1500s. It was only in 1884 that contact was established on the east coast, however, which is why the development of East and West Greenland has been quite different.

Despite contact with other cultures and missionary activity, many customs, cultural patterns, and artistic traits remained unchanged – or only a little changed – for many years. It was the period after the Second World War that first brought about fundamental changes in society, and for the

49. *Bird. Thule, ca. 1950. Carved from a polar bear tooth, black dots for eyes, 1³/₁₆" high. Private collection.*

50. Legendary being known as Quperlussuaq (the Worm), with four bears on its back. The figure previously had a bear's head in its mouth. Carved in 1956-57 by Qaaqqutsiap of Etah (Thule). Walrus ivory, 4½" long. Private collection.

past twenty years the building up of an industrial society along European lines has taken place very rapidly.

When I mention "old" figures and "old" cultural traits, I may therefore be referring to figures from the 1930s. Many people believe that the most typical sculptures found in Greenland today – figures carved in sperm-whale ivory and soapstone – are expressions of an old cultural tradition, and that that is the way figures have always been carved.

But they haven't. Sperm-whale ivory figures were at the very earliest carved in Kangaamiut in the latter part of the 1920s, and so far I have not been able to trace a soapstone figure from before that time. Between the Dorset and Thule cultures – when the small bone and wood figures were carved – and the 1900s there is a vast interval. Painting – which, being European inspired, is the youngest art form – enjoyed a flowering in the 1850s. On the other hand, we know of no sculpture from that period. In the area of the everyday arts, the line is more continuous until the Second World War, when the Americans brought much that was new to the country.

The table on the front end paper of this book illustrates the course of cultural development in materials, subjects and styles in broad outline. For me, the most important thing in this introductory chapter has been to show that the spiritual impetus behind artistic endeavor has not been forgotten in Greenland (see, for example, figure 50, carved in the 1950s), the Greenland I love, whose art and artists – both named and anonymous – will be described in the remaining pages.

Sculpture

The significance of the material and the function of sculpture

51. Figure group of father, mother, and child. Bought in Ole's Department Store, Godthåb, 1976. Signed "S L Nûk" on bottom. Dark soapstone, 5⅛" high. Private collection.

Anyone who has held a Greenlandic figure in his hand, turned and weighed it, felt the shape of it between his fingers, knows that the material, form, and expression of the sculpture are resolved into a higher unity. This is true both of figures from the Dorset and Thule periods and of those of the present day. How does this unity arise?

I think it has to do with the way in which we most intensely experience sculpture. We perceive color, line, and light with our sight, tones with our hearing, and form primarily with our *feeling*. All of us have picked up a stone from the beach, say, and held it in our fingers, perhaps carried it in a pocket for a long time for reassurance and pleasure. We also prefer to *feel* sculpture in order to come to the proper experience and understanding of its essence. We need to feel the coolness or warmth of the material, the rough or smooth character of the surface; to follow the contours.

Most Greenlandic sculptures by far are small. They were intended to hold in the hand or wear on the person, as amulets, dolls, or as parts of implements or articles of everyday use. Dorset and Thule figures are exceptionally small. From bits of bone, ivory, or wood only a couple of inches long, human and animal effigies have been carved that contain – their size, or minuteness notwithstanding – an assured sculptural power that one might be tempted to call monumental (see figs. 40 and 113).

52. Woman with child in amaut, *acquired in 1936 in Angmagssalik by the painter Aage Gitz-Johansen. Artist unknown. Upper arm bone of seal, with attached base and arms of ivory, 3" high. Private collection.*

This capacity for powerful expression in small volumes has remained unchanged from the early amulet and doll figures to the "Thule charm necklaces" of our own day and Simon Kristoffersen's tiny figure groups in silver.

But homogeneous expression goes hand in hand with respect for the given form – and with knowledge of the material and tools, or technical skill. The form and character of a material determine in advance a great deal about the making and appearance of any work of art, but with the Greenlandic artist there is a particularly great respect for the form as provided by nature, perhaps unconsciously inspired by the ancient belief that all things are alive, that each stone and piece of wood has its *inua,* its owner.

It is as though the artist were trying to find out what is "living" in the piece of wood, tooth, or bone. For example, the upper arm bone of a seal resembles a woman carrying an infant in her back pouch – it just has to be perceived, and then liberated as a figure (fig. 52). The form inspires creation of a particular figure. That is why we see so many figures around five to six and one-half inches high and in a closed, compact cone, carved from the popular sperm-whale ivory. Again, if you have a walrus tusk or a caribou bone, in other words material of greater length, it inspires a longer narrative, a frieze of pictures either carved in relief or engraved as drawings.

A walrus's lower jaw becomes a figure with bowed legs (fig. 53), or a piece of the jaw including the worn teeth becomes an assembly of faces. From a dog's or a polar bear's tooth there emerges a compact little effigy.

39

53. Terrifying spirits. Thule, 1970s. Carved from the lower jaws of walrus. Some of the teeth in the jaw are visible in the figure on the left. Ca. 5½" high, 6" wide. Collection of the Queen and Prince Consort of Denmark.

54 a. Tupilak *figure carved by Lunde Kúko, Kûngmiut, in 1973. Seal earbone, 2½" long. Private collection.*

54 b. The same figure from behind, where the shape of the bone is seen clearly.

But from a whole caribou antler there appears so large and convoluted a ground figure that the artist elects to engrave some long picture sequences. The convoluted ear bone of a seal appears random and confused when seen from one side, but if you turn it around there materializes – almost by itself – the nicest little *tupilak* figure (figs. 54*a* and *b*).

This applies to ivory and bone figures in particular. When it comes to wood, it is probably the universal – and necessary – sparingness with materials that determines the small size. Driftwood, brought by currents all the way from the pine forests of Siberia to the coasts of Greenland, was utilized for many purposes. It was a necessity for the frameworks of kayaks and *umiak*s, to reinforce dwellings, for the dog-sled, and for household utensils. Whatever was left was used for making sculpture. If you had wood enough, you could afford to carve a large doll or a mask.

Wood became hard from being in the water and probably offered the same resistance to the knife as ivory or bone. The grain was beautifully exploited by the artists, and it is a pity that this material is no longer used. The boles lie unclaimed along the coasts.

The softer soapstone, on the other hand, was not used for making figures. At any rate, none prior to 1900 have been found in Greenland. Soapstone was used for lamps and boiling pots, and no decorated examples have been found. Any soapstone figures have either been destroyed in the course of time, or it simply was not a material worthy of being used for purposes of art.

Some of the earliest soapstone figures I have come across had functional value as carved and ornamented tobacco boxes, candlesticks, inkstands, or ashtrays made for Danes stationed in Greenland. Where soapstone figures have no actual functional value, the oldest of them at least assume the form of useful objects, such as the group of figures carved by Peter Rosing of Kangaamiut (1934), in which the basic form of the sculpture is that of the blubber lamp (fig. 55).

Gradually a particular size of soapstone figure became commonplace – a gift-shop size? – suitable for standing on the mantlepiece or the bookcase like a porcelain figurine, something between bric-a-brac and sculpture, depending on the artistic quality. Only in more official connections – as gifts for the royal family, memorial stones, or representative figures in public buildings – did the artist work in larger volumes.

Other than that, sculpture in stone takes compact forms, in which the figures seem to grow out from the interior of the stone. There is one

55. *Frightened by a settlement fellow wearing a bear skin, a man who is building a kayak falls over backward and crushes the boat. Peter Rosing of Kangaamiut, 1934. Dark soapstone, 15" long, 8¾" wide. Private collection. Several Kangaamiut artists have worked with the theme of the man wearing a bear skin (see fig. 62a). It can either represent the Moon Man, who visited the earth in the shape of a polar bear, or be a depiction of a hunter training his dogs to attack bear.*

exception: since the 1950s a special style has arisen among a group of artists from the Kangaamiut outpost, in which the basic form is dissolved and perforated so that the figure stands as an armature, and both the stone elements and the space between them are equally important for the total perception of form.

Recently soapstone has become nearly the most widely used material of all. Many artists have their own quarries, often located in inaccessible places. The stone can have many nuances within the gray. There are greenish and reddish tints, and often attractive designs in the stone that are utilized by the artist, and the light gray stone can be made dark by absorbing fat. The usual method is to heat the figure and then rub it with candle wax.

Other kinds of stone are only very seldom used by Greenlandic artists. In recent years, I have seen only a single figure in marble, one in cryolite, and none in granite, which otherwise appears in many beautiful colors. There are also no stonecutters in Greenland but many stone carvers. This is associated with the fact that the knife has been the tool of preference, together with the scraper, awl, drill and file. With these tools, one carved, abraded, and polished works of art until they stood forth in precise, taut forms. To be sure, the adze – the *ulimat* – has been used for thousands of years, but only for rough cutting, the preparatory process.

Just as Greenlandic sculptors have not used hammer and chisel except in very rare cases, it is very seldom – and only in the most recent times – that artists have worked with clay, even though this material is found in a number of places. Ceramics, which appears early in nearly all cultures, is not practiced by the Eskimo. One does not shape figures, but rather breaks in from without and *liberates* the form.

What is it, then, that one liberates from the tooth, the piece of wood, or the stone? It is beings, *living* beings – animals and humans and their relationship to one another. In spite of the changing function of sculpture, this basic element has lasted throughout the ages.

Originally, the small figures were amulets, and cult was associated with them: ancestor cults, death cults, and the cult of bears and other animals, as is natural in a hunting people. The figures were worn on the person, were quite diminutive, and were often stylized and ornamented.

In contrast, dolls and toys were naturalistic. Here the function was to give children an introduction to everyday life, to show them a miniature version of the real world in order to give them an understanding of, and a readiness for, the daily life of adults.

And then the strange people came to the west coast of Greenland with new needs and desires. Dolls and toys were still carved, together with household utensils and decorative objects, such as candlesticks and the like, while the cultic figures, including masks, were forbidden by the missionary.

Then on the east coast, at the same time as the arrival of the merchant and the minister, the man of science turned up. He was interested in those very figures that had to do with cult; he admired the old culture, asked questions about it, and bought up everything that had belonged to it (thus fortunately preserving a considerable part of the Eskimo cultural heritage for posterity). It became profitable for the Greenlandic artist to take account of the old faith. As the function of art went from the cultic to the commercial, the size of the figures became that suitable for souvenirs and knick-knacks – but always within the given form of the material.

Most recently, a new need has arisen: that of official prestige sculptures, such as memorials to Greenlandic personages. With us, such memorial stones are now and then placed in cemeteries in connection with graves, but not in Greenland, where graves are decorated with a simple wooden cross and the intransient bloom of plastic flowers. Freestanding large sculpture has hitherto been known, however, in the form of anthropomorphic stone cairns.

When speaking of large outdoor sculpture, it is important to remember that nature has provided a wealth of forms. Here I am thinking not only of the shapes of the mountains, but also of the prodigiously varied and beautiful world created by glaciation. Water, wind, and ice have ground and shaped some sculptural elements that must both have been outdoor sculpture enough and have inspired minds to create perfect, closed figures – as though scoured by ice and polished by wind and weather. By far the greatest proportion of Greenland's artists are sculptors, especially the men. But then it was the men who, as hunters and fishermen, were in close daily contact with nature and from ancient times had the adze, the drill, and the knife as their tools.

Even in our own day, many of these sculptors are anonymous. Carving figures is a matter of course, and nearly everybody can do it. If, for some reason, you don't have any other work, you can make a little money selling figures to tourists, resident Danes, the local furniture store, or the Royal Greenland Trading Company's home crafts department.

I picture to myself the multitude of these folk artists who from the time of the Dorset and Thule cultures to our own day have casually picked up a piece of wood, bone, or stone and conjured forth a distinguished little sculpture, who unconsciously – and with no other ambition than to be good craftsmen – can render a situation, a movement, or a human type vividly and precisely.

It is odd that, while sculpture is the oldest and most deep-rooted art form in Greenland, it is not until our own century that we encounter named artists in this discipline. Painting, the youngest of the arts in Greenland, has had named artists since 1840, while not until the 1900s do the names of sculptors occur.

Apart from the shaman Mitsivarniannga, who at the beginning of the century made *tupilak* models in Angmagssalik, the first named sculptors we know of are people from Sukkertoppen and Kangaamuit. They are Gerth Lyberth, from around 1915; and, in the twenties and thirties, Johannes Kreutzmann, Esra Berthelsen, and Peter Rosing. From Upernavik there was Otto Thomassen, and, in the latter part of the forties, Hans Lynge started sculpting in Copenhagen and Godthåb. Among the important names of the last twenty years are those of Aron Kleist, Knud Petrussen and Simon Kristoffersen.

All the dynamic artists gave rise to schools and came to put their mark on the districts where they lived (and still live) as others around them were influenced by their style, took it up, and furthered it. Function and tradition are now no longer all-determining for style. The individualistic sculptor in Greenland came into being with these people, and it is therefore natural to accord them a special chapter.

Outstanding sculptors

While Greenlandic art displays great commitment to tradition and distinct continuity in the choice of motifs and materials, there are among the mass of carvers individual breakaways – people who, while having their roots in tradition, have nevertheless had the courage and drive to go new ways, either by bursting out of the established format, by using new material devices and expanding the sphere of available motifs, or simply by convincing through sheer talent.

One of them was the trading post manager in K'errortussoq and Napassoq (Holsteinsborg and Sukkertoppen districts), Gerth Lyberth. Besides attending to his job as manager of the trading post, Lyberth was a productive pictorial artist. Possibly inspired by the painter Harald Moltke, and in any case encouraged by Knud Rasmussen, he drew illustrations for the latter's *Myths and Legends*, while being inspired, as seldom seen among Greenlandic artists, by the stories of the Bible. He also carved large statues.

All this reflected the upheavals taking place in Lyberth's lifetime (1868-1929). In 1915 the Swedish artist Ossian Elgström visited the west coast of Greenland. While at Napassoq, he wrote that Lyberth was working on portrait busts in larger than life size, carved from driftwood and painted in strong colors, and in addition on a large relief depicting the catching of a shark on the ice and teeming with figures, all of it painted, about twenty inches high.

Elgström relates, too, that for American museums Lyberth had made models of Greenlandic dwellings with all their furnishings down to the smallest detail. Today one of these models is in the possession of the Royal Greenland Trading Company – a complete and detailed miniature of Lyberth's own house, with his own paintings on the walls, the harmonium, wall clock, and everything else belonging to a Danish-Greenlandic home of the time. It both reflects cultural upheaval and gives a good impression of Lyberth's dexterity.

The busts, on the other hand, show Gerth Lyberth the artist. The wood sculptures are unusually large, around twenty-eight inches high. Outspokenly carved, vividly painted, and with inlaid glass in the eyes and skin attached to the carved collar, they represent a realism that tells forcefully and simply about the people who were the artist's neighbors. He repeatedly sculpts the human couple – "A Hunter and his Wife," as he calls them (fig. 56).

The hunting was good in those districts at that time, and the portraits show us confident, independent people, somewhat humorously depicted to be sure, but with a predominantly proud and self-assured mien. The first pair of busts (now vanished) were sculpted for the new museum in Godthåb, another pair are in the Knud Rasmussen Museum in Hundested, north of Copenhagen, and the rest are privately owned. The sculptures have no other purpose than as portraits – a new concept. Their size and the way the shoulders are contoured could indicate that Lyberth had seen European busts or photographs of them and copied something of their outer form, but the artistic expression is entirely original.

At nearly the same time, there lived another artist in the Sukkertoppen district. This was the great hunter and sculptor Johannes Kreutzmann of Kangaamiut (1862-1940), and the two men must have known each other. At any rate, there are points of resemblance in their technique, and although they did not live in the same township, they could have met in Sukkertoppen. While Lyberth played on many strings – writing poetry, painting, drawing, and sculpting – Kreutzmann displayed his artistic abilities in one field – the familiar art of wood carving.

It is odd that Kreutzmann, who was a very successful kayak man and hunter, and was therefore envied and respected among his fellows of the

57. *Golgotha scene acquired in Sukkertoppen before 1930. Signature lacking, but said to have been executed by Johannes Kreutzmann. Driftwood with inlaid mica and soapstone. Inscribed above with "INRI" and below with "Golkata." Total height 9¹/₁₆″. National Museum of Greenland, Godthåb-Nuuk.*

settlement, never carved any of the animals he must have known so well. He depicted people, now and then in work situations.

It all started when Kreutzmann carved figures as dolls for his small children, but as they aroused the admiration of others, the impulse was provided for an extensive series of sculptures, all carved in wood and painted with oil colors, most of them around seventeen inches high, but a few up to thirty-two inches.

It was especially in his later years that Kreutzmann worked with these figures, both because the times were better and because he had attained greater artistic clarification. He expressed it to the artist Hans Lynge in these words: "With age it is as though the past stands out more clearly in one's thoughts. The many unusual people I had been fond of and admired came alive for me, so I started trying to make their figures in wood."

And what we see before us is a whole portrait gallery, a bringing to life of a Greenlandic community from the turn of the century. We see women with infants in their back pouches, women scraping skins, in everyday garb and in festive costume. Men with packs on their shoulders on their way to or from the summer hunting grounds, the sealer in his kayak jacket, and a man wearing a tie over his anorak (fig. 58).

We see an entire mini-world, captured with a sure eye for small details: the flat-footed boy with his broken-down *kamik*s, the old woman's patches, the fat-bellied man whose anorak is too short, or women bend-

58. Settlement fellows carved by Johannes Kreutzmann at the beginning of the 1900s. Painted driftwood. Full height of figures about 15¾". Presented to Thisted Museum by the engineer M. I. Nyboe, who, because of his efforts on behalf of Thule and his practical help to Peter Freuchen and Knud Rasmussen, had a region of Greenland named for him: Nyboe's Land.

59. Boy carrying home fish carved by Peter Rosing, Kangaamiut, in the 1930s. Walrus ivory, 4⅞" high. Private collection.

60. Hunter with club carved by Peter Rosing, Kangaamiut, in the 1930s. Acquired (as were figs. 62b and c) by Captain Johan Bendsen, who was in Greenland in 1936 as geodesist. Walrus ivory, 4⅛" high. National Museum of Greenland, Godthåb-Nuuk.

ing over with the skin peeping through the gap in their clothes at the waist.

These human situations contribute to the creation of an observant, cheerful realism, which together with the beautifully carved form and splendid use of colors makes the figures far more than dolls. Both as a document of the times and as independent creations, they represent superb folk art.

Here were two artists who each went his own way and who worked with innovations in size and with painted sculpture – that is, in a combination of the devices of form and color. But it was also here in the Sukkertoppen district that the basis was laid for the traditional small sculpture of West Greenland. The oldest were tiny figures carved in bone, ivory, or untreated wood, but gradually these very diminutive figures gave way to a size more suitable for holding in the hand, with a height of around four inches to four and three-quarter inches.

Sperm-whale ivory was the favorite material for this type of figure, first carved at the Kangaamiut outpost, where the motifs and artistic traits considered typically West Greenlandic were thus born.

The pioneers in this development were Peter Vallentin Rosing (1871-1938) and Esra Berthelsen (1889-1954). Rosing was a hunter and sculptor and worked in walrus or narwhal ivory with tremendous accuracy and wealth of detail. Berthelsen commanded a more outspoken line, and there is a forceful, vivid expressiveness to his figures, which were also carried out in ivory. After them came many who worked within the same tradition. A distinguished representative of this art, Ole Kreutzmann (b. 1898), is still living in Kangaamiut.

A tradition was established, but naturally there were individual characteristics among the artists. Peter Rosing made human figures – hunters in furs and with hunting implements (fig. 60); a man and wife on their way to church, a boy carrying home fish (fig. 59) – in a natural, precisely proportioned style, the subjects always with beautiful, slightly smiling faces.

Esra Berthelsen, on the other hand, exhibits an entirely different register and style. With him, the heads of the figures are oversized, their expression coarse, the noses broader, and the whole effect somewhat more grotesque. Besides the same themes of everyday realism – such as "Woman Smoking a Pipe" and "Father, Mother and Child" (fig. 61) – Berthelsen also worked with legendary figures and illustrated ancient Eskimo concepts whose meaning is not clear to us today, and which therefore engender a variety of interpretations (figs. 62a, b, and c).

45

62 a. *Man wearing bear skin, and with a bear's head on a stick, carved by Esra Berthelsen in Kangaamiut in the 1930s. Sperm-whale ivory, 4⅛" high. Private collection.*

62 b. *An unknown legendary figure, carved by Rasmus Berthelsen in Kangaamiut in the 1930s. Sperm-whale ivory 3¾" high. National Museum of Greenland, Godthåb-Nuuk.*

62 c. *Woman smoking pipe, carved by Rasmus Berthelsen in Kangaamiut in the 1930s. Sperm-whale ivory, 3" high. National Museum of Greenland, Godthåb-Nuuk.*

61. *Man, and woman with child on her back, carved by Rasmus Berthelsen in Kangaamiut, ca. 1940. Sperm-whale ivory, 5" high. Private collection.*

The same world of dual motif is characteristic of Ole Kreutzmann and his brother Karl. In them, we meet the hunter with his implements, a man with his hands in his pockets, and a man riding on an imaginary being (fig. 63). And early in their production (in the 1930s and 40s), both artists worked with diminutive ivory figures where, unlike in the East Greenland *tupilak* figures, the composite parts can be discerned – human faces, seal bodies, dog's legs, wings. Here the figure has merely been turned and twisted and made into a little caricature of a being (see fig. 137).

Here we see a mental image of the grotesque, the forerunner of the style that grew up around Knud Petrussen (in the 1950s) and Aron Berthelsen, again from Kangaamiut. Now it was soapstone that became the preferred material, and in contrast to the fixed tradition of creating sculpture in a tightly closed form showing great respect for the matrix, we see a dissolution of the form, a perforated and hollowed-out matrix. The experience, or rather shock that it was for Petrussen to see a horse, provided the thrust for a carving in which the horse's head with its huge grin is recognizable (fig. 64) but where the motif is otherwise deformed and broken down and rises again in morbid growths with unerring effect – that of the ghastly. As sculpture, these surrealistic works are enormously refined and make beautiful use of the space between the elements of the figure.

Thus we have seen in a single locality – Kangaamiut in West Greenland – an extraordinary artistic manifestation, with strong individuals augmenting and renewing both the naturalistic tradition and the fantastic, the spirit world. Still, all the figures have one thing in common; all stand

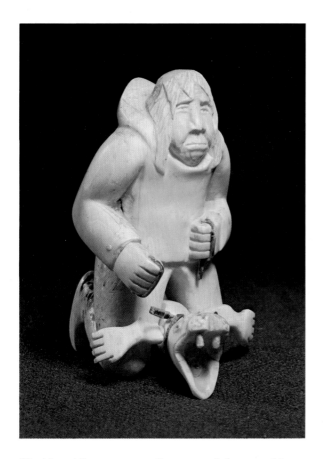

63. *Man riding – or strangling – a* tupilak, *carved by Ole Kreutzmann in Kangaamiut, ca. 1930. Walrus ivory. A narrow thong originally ran from the hands down around the creature's throat. 4⁵/₁₆″×2³/₄″. National Museum, Copenhagen.*

64. *Fantastic being of a* tupilak-*like character, carved by Knud Petrussen in Kangaamiut. Acquired in 1964 by Birte Christensen, who founded the Association for Greenlandic Folk Art. Soapstone, 9″×5¹/₂″×6⁵/₁₆″. Private collection.*

upright and deal with human beings or distortions of human beings.

But there were other places along the coast of West Greenland where an artistic tradition arose around a single talent. It was natural that the first *tupilak* figures came into being in Upernavik, where the old faith and the use of amulets and magic formulas have lasted into our own century. The trading station had been established rather late there, and for a long time the mission met with great unwillingness to convert. At the same time, the isolated location far in the north, with a colder climate and longer periods of darkness, provided good conditions for the nurturing of superstition and flights of fancy. As late as 1946-52, the artist Hans Lynge collected invaluable material from the Upernavik district about the heathen faith people still remembered.

This fidelity to the old Eskimo culture is apparent in certain stylistic traits too. The artists of Upernavik are the only ones in Greenland to use concentric circles for eyes (fig. 65), which seems to indicate a connection with Alaskan cultures, and hence deeper Eskimo origin. This may be explained by the fact that (besides the abovementioned circumstances) Upernavik lies close to the immigration route from Canada and at the same time is so far away from the ice-free towns that Danish-European visits have not occurred as frequently here.

It was Otto Thomassen (1895-1971) who in the 1930s began carving delicate little ivory figures either of "A Man" or "A Hunter," or depicting a world of ideas that, while not forgotten on the west coast, had been suppressed there, and included cults surrounding certain animals and the misfortune-bringing *tupilak*s. The situation whereby the composite

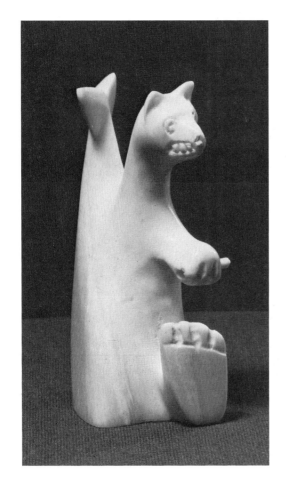 

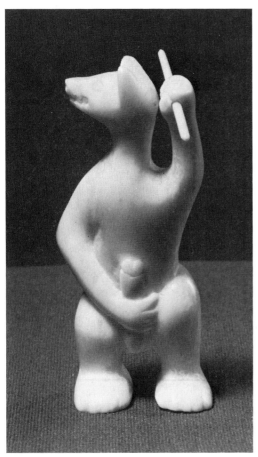 

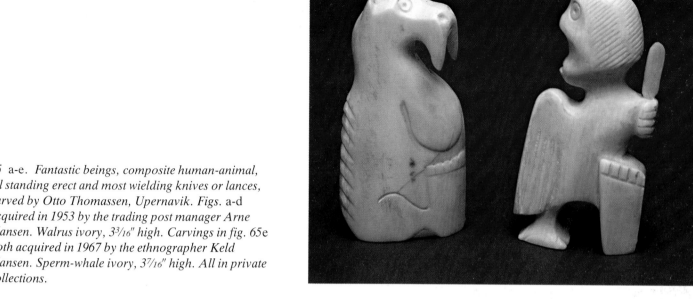

65 a-e. Fantastic beings, composite human-animal, all standing erect and most wielding knives or lances, carved by Otto Thomassen, Upernavik. Figs. a-d acquired in 1953 by the trading post manager Arne Hansen. Walrus ivory, 3³/₁₆" high. Carvings in fig. 65e both acquired in 1967 by the ethnographer Keld Hansen. Sperm-whale ivory, 3⁷/₁₆" high. All in private collections.

being, the *tupilak,* receives life and potency from the man's vivifying seed has been depicted by Thomassen a number of times, and the male sexual organ often appears on his *tupilak* figures in other respects. In order to power the figure? Or could it be an unconscious expression of a now-forgotten fertility cult? We also see in Thomassen some kind of bird cult – a man with a bird growing out of his body, or with a bird in his hand or on his head. *Tupilak*s with birds' heads also appear. But we ought to consider that the artist lived beside the largest sea-bird rookery in Greenland, Agparssuit. Birds were a part of his daily surroundings.

It may be surprising that the fantastic world of forms in wind- and water-eroded rocks and icebergs is not directly evident in Greenlandic sculpture in a naturalistic sense. Indirectly, however, these impressions from nature mean a great deal. Thomassen's carving, in particular, brings to mind half-thawed, hollowed-out ice floes. Certain of his sculptures are just such round, polished forms, with delicately worked recesses for ears, mouth, eyes. As a rule, the ears on Thomassen's figures are holes like a seal's ears – a naturalistic detail on an otherwise fabulous creature with a human face, a bear's paw with raised lance, and extended wings (figs. 65*a – e*).

This expressive art, which virtually arises like a necessity of nature out of the form of the ivory and gives utterance to both the seen, the naturalistic, and the mysterious old pagan world, has been carried on by Thomassen's three sons, Kaspar (1935-74), Kornelius (b. 1936), and Rasmus (b. 1937). Accomplished craftsmanship and artistic imagination characterize their work.

In Greenland an artistic tradition is often carried on in the family. This does not only apply to pictorial art. In olden times, songs and poems and magic charms were passed on as gifts and could then no longer be used by their author. If one had a son, it was natural that he took over one's artistic heritage. If not, it was entrusted to the most worthy heir. This custom may account for the fact that sons or brothers or settlement fellows regard it as proper and an honor to continue working in a particular style.

In the Kristoffersen family of Godthåb, we see a clear example of such a tradition. The father, Kristoffer Kristoffersen, began sculpting in soapstone toward the end of the 1950s. His sons Simon (b. 1933) and Karl

66. *Man's head carved by Karl Kristoffersen, Godthåb-Nuuk, in 1972. This artist works mostly with simple figures: a strong man, a figure lifting a weight, or, as here, simply a head. Whale vertebra, 9⁷⁄₁₆″×9⁷⁄₈″×5¹⁄₂″. Private collection.*

(b. 1943) and daughters Sara (b. 1937) and K'iture quickly followed suit, as did their mother, Dorte (1906-77). All were talented, though it was Simon who was given the greatest chance of developing his talent by being trained at the Royal Academy of Art in Copenhagen. He has worked in clay, wood, plaster of Paris, marble, and silver, and has been given commissions. Back home, the brothers sculpted distinguished monumental figures in whale bone (fig. 67), a material of very exciting effect much used in Canada, but which in Greenland has been utilized only by Simon and Karl Kristoffersen. Simon Kristoffersen is the only Greenlandic artist who has received an official commission in Denmark: standing in the garden of the National Hospital in Copenhagen is a large bronze version of one of his favorite motifs – the Lord of Strength wrapping his tail around the legendary hero Kagssagssuk.

Other than that, soapstone was, and remains, the material preferred by the Kristoffersens, to such a degree that the family have their own quarry in Godthåb Fjord, a soapstone vein with wonderful golden-green nuances in the gray.

Everybody in the family carves soft, compact, somewhat lumpy sculptures, often groups of two or three figures in a situation either of play or struggle or relating to an old legend. The legend of the orphan Kagssagssuk, who grows up to be strong and becomes the big man of the settlement – the underdog who wins in the end – is a popular motif. The Sea's Mother and situations with mother and child and with married couples are portrayed with great warmth and tenderness by Dorte Kristoffersen, and it is Sara who probably has the greatest feeling for imaginary and fabulous beings. Otherwise the family is to all intents and purposes an artists' commune, working together in close understanding of one another. Their work (figs. 67, 109, 110, and 111) can be compared with that of the living Canadian artists who express themselves with such sureness in the medium of soapstone.

67. *Men struggling during seal ball game (a contest whose object is a stuffed sealskin). One of Simon Kristoffersen's early figure groups from 1959. Godthåb-Nuuk. Light soapstone, 5"×7⅞"×5½". Private collection.*

68. *Man carrying a burden on his shoulders, carved by Aron Kleist, Julianehåb, in 1969. Dark soapstone, 14⁷/₁₆" high. Private collection.*

But there are other renewers of tradition. In Julianehåb, in South Greenland, Aron Kleist (b. 1923) and his daughter Cecilie (b. 1949) carve figures of legend, drum dances, and *tupilak*s in a highly personal and refined style. In a couple of cases, Aron has sculpted unusually large soapstone figures twelve inches to sixteen inches in height, with a motile rhythm in the line despite being of monumental massiveness. In other respects, father and daughter prefer using sperm-whale, narwhal, walrus, and even elephant ivory.

Producing a texturally varied surface, a semi bas-relief is cut in the ivory, so that shapes arise in a closely entwined movement within the basic form (fig. 69). Aron, who was a successful hunter, adheres to the patterns of someone who is good at making his implements and also skilled at making figures – the craftsmanship is perfect. Even though the thematic world is well-known, the expression is new and reveals original talent.

In this discussion of forceful, individualistic artists, we have stayed within our own century for the simple reason that we do not know of any named sculptors of earlier date, or even of art objects as a concept divorced from implement culture and magic. These people have become very significant as renewers of the old culture in the context of the present, and their development constitutes part of the backbone of Greenlandic national consciousness.

An artist who is fully conscious of this role and who is preeminent in the Greenlandic art world is Hans Lynge (b. 1906), who is active as an author and dramatist, painter, printmaker, and – what concerns us here – sculptor. This versatility makes itself felt in his choice of materials as well. Lynge, who studied at the Royal Academy of Art in Copenhagen and who also has a good knowledge of European art from several study tours, has worked in clay, wood, and stone, and has had various pieces cast in bronze. His special motif is woman and the mother, but the figures and deeds of Eskimo legend are also a source of inspiration for him, and in nearly all of his works there is a narrative point (see, e.g., fig. 70). The mode of expression may be inspired by European art, but the content and the thought behind it is Greenlandic. Lynge is qualified to carry out the official sculpture of Greenland, such as memorials and

70. *"Gold Has Been Discovered in Greenland."*
Fabulous animal, sculpted by Hans Lynge in 1968.
Greenland marble with lumps of fool's gold (iron
pyrites) in the animal's raised palm, hence the title of
the work. 4³/₄" × 5¹⁵/₁₆" × 4³/₄". Property of the artist.

69. *Fantastic creature with fish, carved by Aron*
Kleist in Julianehåb in the latter part of the 1960s.
Sperm-whale ivory with pupils of inlaid black
material, 6¹/₈" high. Private collection.

portrait busts of such well-known Greenlanders as Arqaluk (Lars Møller), Augo Lynge, Henrik Lund, Jonathan Petersen (fig. 71), and Frederik Nielsen, with vivid textural treatment and with a sense of the personalities of his subjects. But it is when he combines the portrait with a narrative relief (fig. 72) that we experience what is so typical of him and of Greenlandic culture in general – the ability to tell a story. From out of the bone, stone, or wood sides of the relief grow a wealth of details, a myriad of figures in series of episodes that all but presume a close acquaintanceship with the subject of the portrait. The closeness of the figures to one another, their togetherness, is also characteristic of Lynge's sculptures, and corresponds to a quality in the Greenlandic character and way of life.

Portrait making – the art of rendering personal facial characteristics – was practiced in anonymous Greenlandic art, but not for the purpose of depicting a particular person. What was wanted was to portray types with definite qualities of character – the happy, the evil, and the oafish, but especially the ghastly and the ludicrous. This entire spectrum of facial expressions we see in the art of *masks*.

71. *Portrait bust of the poet and organist Jonathan Petersen, comprising the upper part of a monument executed by Hans Lynge in 1977-78, paid for by subscription and erected on the Church Square beside Godthåb's old church. Modeled in clay and subsequently cast in bronze. Somewhat larger than life size. City of Godthåb-Nuuk.*

72. *From the same sculpture as figure 71. One of the three bronze reliefs in the stone base of the monument. Executed by Hans Lynge in 1977-78. Modeled in clay and subsequently cast in bronze. 24³⁄₈″×20¹⁄₂″. The relief depicts an episode in Jonathan Petersen's life when his artistically gifted son Pavia (painter, poet, and catechist) was on his deathbed in Sukkertoppen. In the middle of the relief is the waiting coffin, and behind it the dying man, surrounded by deceased relations, whom he would soon be united with in heaven. In the right foreground, the scene is no longer in Sukkertoppen but in Godthåb. In front of the organ in Godthåb Church – the organ Jonathan Petersen played for so many years – Jonathan is seen holding a microphone, sending a greeting to his son via the newly started radio.*

The mask – portrait or cult accessory?

In a magic formula recited by Eskimos in the fall on moving from the tents into their winter dwellings are the words: "The skin of my face have I covered and I am wearing a mask ..." When you were in contact with the higher powers, it was necessary to hide behind a mask, to change identity, to make yourself unrecognizable to the spirits.

Masks were mainly of skin or wood, and the size varied from around two and three-quarter inches up to sixteen inches in height – depending on function. Skin masks were either flat face masks, hood masks, or hand masks, and were made of depilated sealskin or shark skin and had skin strips in a contrasting color sewed around the eyes, nose, and mouth (fig. 73). Such masks may have been used in healing (or preventive) rituals, as amulets were sewed under the edgings so that sickness and soul-robbers could not penetrate the openings of the face – the organs of sense. When the amulet mask was sewed in the form of a hood, the head was entirely protected (fig. 74). From West Greenland come appliquéd *mitaartut* masks made of skin, and from East Greenland we see skin masks with white strips sewn in skeleton motif (fig. 75).

74. *Hood mask from West Greenland. Age and location unknown. Sealskin with the fur inside, sewn-on nose. Depilated sealskin edging around mouth and eyes. Eyebrows, eyelashes, and moustache of dog skin. 13"×9⁷/₁₆". National Museum of Greenland, Godthåb-Nuuk.*

73. *Flat face mask purchased in Angmagssalik in 1911 by colony manager Johan Petersen. Shark skin with white depilated skin sewn around the eyes, nose, and mouth 14³/₁₆"×10⁷/₁₆". National Museum, Copenhagen.*

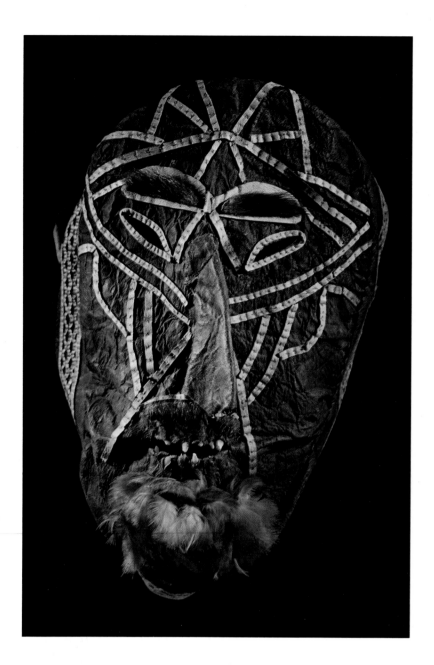

75. *Face mask collected in the Angmagssalik district in 1934-35 by Robert Gessain, a member of Paul Emile Victor's expedition to East Greenland with the ship* Pourquoi Pas? *Depilated dark sealskin ornamented with sewn-on white skin strips. Around the entire edge there is attached an embroidered border, some of which is visible on the right side of the mask. Inlaid seal teeth in the mouth, dog skin eyebrows, and feather beard. About 10¼″ high. Musée de l'Homme, Paris.*

By far the majority of masks were made of wood, including the few very large masks, numerous face masks, hand masks, house masks, and mask copies. Most are either carved with a skeleton motif, or skin strips are applied to the wood with the same linear effect. Feathers, sealskin, and musk ox skin were also attached to wooden masks, and teeth – either genuine or carved – were often set in the mouth, especially in more recent times. Colors other than black are seldom seen on wooden masks, and riveted bone figures never. Nor were there animal masks. The mask was always a human or spirit likeness.

One of the simplest methods of altering the face was to rub it with lampblack, tie a thong over the cheeks and nose (fig. 30) so that a snub nose was formed, and place a stick crosswise in the mouth so that the cheeks were distended and the voice distorted. Then neither the features nor the voice would be recognized.

This method is still used by *mitaartut* mummers (see page 28), and for them it is a matter of being unrecognizable to one another and to their settlement fellows. When the shaman, on the other hand, made his face and voice unrecognizable, it was not for the benefit of his fellow tribesmen. They knew who he was. It was for the sake of the powers, the spirits, for it would be unfortunate were they to recognize and avenge themselves on the man who invoked and challenged them.

We know little with certainty about the cult use of masks. Were they a prescribed accessory at fertility rituals or burial ceremonies? Did they represent departed ancestors? Were they used at memorial feasts or in connection with a death cult? Are there relatively so few masks in archaeological finds because they were personal effects and were buried or burned at the death of their bearers? Or were they so sacred that after being used in ritual they had to be destroyed?

On the basis of our knowledge of the use of masks in East Greenland in the brief period from 1884-85 (when Gustav Holm established communication between Angmagssalik and Denmark) to the ascendency of Christianity around 1930, the functions of masks can be roughly divided into the following categories:

(1) Dance masks intended for rites of various kinds, such as the drum dances preceding the lights-out spouse-swapping game or performed before song contests. These face masks frequently represent the Ua-ajeerteq figure (see page 27), which exhibits traces of a fertility cult (fig. 76). Other dance masks project the dancer's mime, either ludicrous or strongly terrifying (fig. 77).

(2) Theatrical masks used for entertainment. For instance, there was the "shaman game", in which an actual shamanistic seance was imitated and the person who played the shaman wore masks representing his helping spirits. Hand masks were used in the same manner – from behind the crackling gut curtain first one face and then another was shown in illustration of narratives and songs (fig. 78).

(3) House masks representing "the house's spirit." Smaller in size, these were placed on the east wall of the dwelling and acted as protection, as strangers lost their power on seeing them (fig. 79).

76. Face mask representing a man (moustache) dressed up as a woman (topknot). With a thong over the wings of the nose, vestiges of black pigment, and a transverse stick inside the mouth, the mask is typical of the Uaajeerteq figure. Age unknown. Gift from an old man to the author Kirsten Bang, private tutor in the household of Pastor Otto Rosing in Angmagssalik in the 1930s. Driftwood with glued-on strips of depilated sealskin; eyebrows, eyelashes, and beard of dog skin. About 11^{13}/₁₆" high. Private collection.

77. Face mask, strongly carved with transverse furrows, representing a face with bound nose and a stick in mouth. Collected by the botanist Christian Kruuse, who was in Angmagssalik in 1901-02. A man by the name of Akernilik gave the mask to Kruuse, saying that it was "very old." Driftwood, rubbed with lampblack, 10"×5¼". National Museum, Copenhagen.

(4) Masks carved by children and young people, presumably as part of a kind of training for the grownups' world. These masks are solid and were not intended to be held before the face. They must be regarded as small facsimiles of masks – or hand masks used in the games of the children.

But we still lack any clear evaluation of the place of masks in religious or daily life, and the material available for study is not large. In museums in Paris, Vienna, The Hague, Leyden, Godthåb, and Copenhagen, and in private collections, there exist in all around 200 masks, and none of them can be dated from before the end of the 1800s. (This refers to masks from pre-Christian times or from the period of transition – more recent souvenir masks are far more numerous). During the introduction of Christianity, zealous missionaries and ministers ordered masks and drums in particular to be burned. Regrettably, many masks were lost in this way. Nevertheless, the prohibition in itself is evidence that masks were cult implements.

One of the cultic functions we know something about is shamanism for the purpose of obtaining better hunting. The shaman had his necessary personal helping spirits, and according to one interpretation, the masks represent these spirits. As the latter generally had a terrifying appearance, the predominating expression of the masks would seem to corroborate this.

As mentioned earlier, we know that one of the purposes of masks in pre-Christian times was as an accessory in cultic dances, and this accords well with their animated, sinuous ornamentation and the frequently distorted mouths and noses (figs. 80 and 81). They were definitely not intended for static exaltation as idols or death masks. They were part of a dramatic, physical mode of expression, created for movement. With their ornamentation and countenances, they enhanced the effect of the dance.

Later, when the old beliefs had waned and lost their power, the masks were used to frighten the children when they became noisy in the big

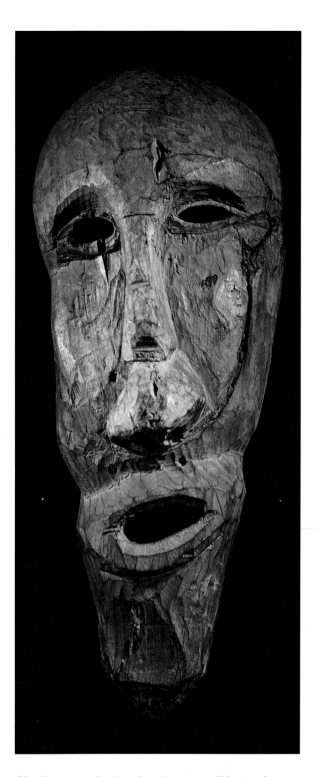

78. Small hand mask with base, collected in the Angmagssalik district in 1934-35 by Robert Gessain. Executed in driftwood by children or young people. Total height around 7½". Musée de l'Homme, Paris.

79. House mask, placed on the east wall facing the sunrise. Collected in the Angmagssalik district in 1934-35 by Robert Gessain. Roughly carved from light driftwood. The nose has a transverse indentation also seen on other masks, such as the one from West Greenland in figure 83. About 9" high. Musée de l'Homme, Paris.

81. Face mask with two noses, collected in the Angmagssalik district in 1934-35 by Robert Gessain. Driftwood rubbed with lampblack, 13"×7⅛", 4⁵/₁₆" deep. Musée de l'Homme, Paris.

80. Face mask collected in the Angmagssalik district in 1934-35 by Robert Gessain. Carved by Silas Silassen (b. 1895). Driftwood rubbed with lampblack. Attached sealskin beard and eyebrows, inlaid bone teeth. 10¼"×4⁵/₁₆", 3½" deep. Musée de l'Homme, Paris.

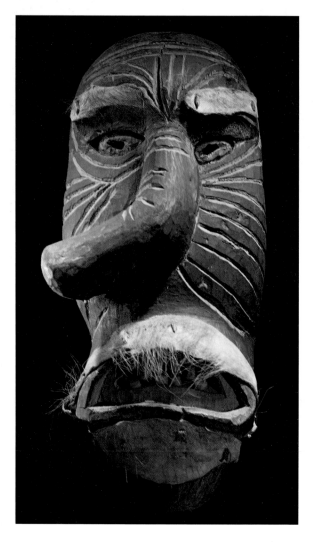

common houses. Still later, during the past few decades, the mask has been reduced to the status of a souvenir object.

The mask and the drum functioned together in various situations, one being the shamanistic ritual. The contorted, ghastly mask, together with the inciting monotony of the drum and the subdued lighting that was part of the whole setting, contributed to the onset of ecstasy, with accompanying relief from apprehension afterwards.

And as we see in Knud Rasmussen's film *Palo's Wedding* (1933), the dancers with grotesque masks on their faces helped to whip up feeling prior to the song contest. The contest itself, which was, in fact, litigation – a deadly serious joust in which the two contending parties sang their pleas (for homicide, theft, and other misdeeds) and the winner was the one who got laughter on his side – has, to all appearances, been a source of inspiration to mask makers. Most Greenlandic masks are correspondingly exaggerated and acrimonious. The drum and the ugly mug were also part of the equipment of "She Who Devours Intestines" (see page 72), the grotesque old woman whom the shaman had to get past on his perilous journey to the Moon Man. With the figure "Uaajeerteq," the

82. *Unusually large mask from West Greenland, collected by the painter Aage Gitz-Johansen during his stay in Sukkertoppen in the 1930s. The mask belonged to Gustav Olsen of Kangaamiut, who stated that it had been in his family for several generations. He knew nothing of its use. Driftwood, vestiges of black pigment, 16½" high. National Museum, Copenhagen.*

face was blackened, the nose cinched up with a thong, and the drum a part of the trappings. In this situation, the drumstick was used to lay into the audience. Pretty young girls were especially liable to these attentions.

We find an obvious cultic remnant in the *mitaartut,* who also wear masks – a definite type of mask into the bargain, always of skin, paper, cloth, or, in a few cases, of rye-bread dough, but never ornamented and never made of wood like all other masks. Don't we sense here a connection with the inland Eskimos of Canada, where for obvious reasons driftwood doesn't occur and skin masks were therefore used? And couldn't it be that the fertility cult perceived behind the *mitaartut* originally came from those regions?

The few wooden masks found on the west coast of Greenland have their own special appearance. They are very large and rather solid, colored but without ornamentation, and present a cheerful, baroque expression (figs. 82 and 83) in contrast to East Greenland masks. The latter are by far the most numerous, which is why it is only in East Greenland that a true mask cult can be referred to.

What do East Greenlandic masks look like, and what can be read from

83. Face mask from the west coast, mentioned as being nearly finished in 1915 in Ossian Elgström's book Moderna Eskimåer *and designated a dance mask. Driftwood, vestiges of paint around the mouth, 10¼" high. Now in a private collection in Vienna.*

84 a and b. Front and reverse of small hand mask. Hole in top (to insert a topknot?), handle below. Collected in the Angmagssalik district in 1911 by colony manager Johan Petersen, who reports that the mask was found during the excavation of an old dwelling on the Angmagssalik Fjord. Driftwood, 4³/8"×2⁵/16". National Museum, Copenhagen.

their expressional characteristics? The oldest Greenlandic mask we know is a small hand mask found in the ruins of a dwelling at Angmagssalik (fig. 84). It is only four inches high, carved from wood, with a face on either side and a hole in the top – presumably for a removable topknot, so that one face could represent a man and the other, with the topknot inserted, a woman. The mask is deeply furrowed, with transverse lines across the saddle of the nose and the forehead, around the eyes, and either emanating from or surrounding the mouth. We see the same lines again and again, though with variations. Do they represent a tattooed face? Or does the ornamentation have some cultic significance, both as tattoos and as carvings on a mask?

From the Central Eskimos, we know the meaning of certain tattoos on women. Important events in a woman's life were marked: her first menstruation, marriage, the birth of her first child, the birth of the first boy, the first seal caught by her eldest son (the latter indicated by vertical stripes on the chin, as in figure 85) – all events having to do with reproduction, the perpetuation of the family, the hunt, and survival. Such tattoos were used all the way into the 1900s, providing highly concrete information about the woman in question. One could, so to speak, read her life history in her face. In evaluating the profound connection tattooing had with the perpetuation of life, it should be remembered that the Moon Man became angry and withheld game animals if the women were poorly tattooed – for the moon held sway over menstruation and childbirth.

But the ornamentation could also be the expression of a death cult, recognizable in an artistic sense in the use of skeleton motif, which was employed from the time of the Dorset culture up to our own (fig. 86).

Finally, the lines can indicate important centers, such as the place between the eyes, where the intellect lives, or organs of sense – eyes, nose, mouth – can be emphasized. The ears were omitted on the old

85. Face mask representing a woman collected in the Angmagssalik district by colony manager Johan Petersen. Driftwood, ornamented with carved furrows. Around the topknot there is a strip of depilated sealskin, from which there hang strings beaded with capelin vertebrae and a bead of blue glass. 11⁷/₁₆" high. National Museum, Copenhagen.

86. Face mask acquired in 1941-42 in East Greenland by telegraph manager Leo Christiansen from an unknown artist from Cape Dan. Driftwood, 10⁵/₈" high. Private collection.

87. Large face mask, representing a cinched-up face with a stick in its mouth. Collected on the east coast in the 1930s by British ethnologists. Driftwood, 13³/₈" high. University Museum, Cambridge.

masks. Only in our own time do they make their appearance, though without much importance. The mouth is open on practically all Greenlandic masks, even on the little hand mask in figure 84. Likewise, eye sockets were carved even though the masks were solid and they could not be looked through.

Perhaps we are making too much of these ornaments. Couldn't the mask in figure 85 simply be a portrait of a wrinkled old woman? I don't think so. The decided portrait masks we know of are all smooth-faced. Although they sometimes have characteristic grooves, these parallel incisions, which partly emphasize certain forms (fig. 87) and partly run contrary to and therefore dissolve the form, may either have a cultic meaning or be an artistic abstraction.

All artists know what it is to work with a form, to make it more forceful and resilient and then break it down in order to find the balance between the object's inner force and the external pressures. But nothing about the structure of Greenlandic society gives any indication that there was use for experimentation. Patterns and styles evolved quite slowly and with great respect for tradition. When relatively small groups of people live in isolation, one sees, as a rule, a very static conception of art. The injunctions of ancestors, including artistic directives, must not be violated, the hard-won balance must not be disturbed.

When, at length, communication with other cultures was established and the whole pattern of life changed as it did in Greenland, there was reason to be apprehensive that cultural distinctiveness might disappear entirely. But as it turns out, Greenlandic artists have displayed unusual fidelity to traditional styles, sizes, ornamentation, and basic concepts. It is my opinion that the incised ornamentation – the so-called skeleton motif – on most of the masks manifests a now-forgotten cultic phenomenon, which gradually became a tradition and appealed to the artists' sense of decorative effect.

88 a and b. *Two hand masks. a: Front of female mask. b: Reverse of male mask. Carved by Efraim Singertât, Angmagssalik, 1973. Imported lumber painted with black enamel paint, with inlaid eyes and walrus ivory teeth. a: 10¹/₄″×5³/₄″, 2³/₈″ deep. b: 7¹/₂″×5³/₄″, 2¹/₄″ deep. Private collection.*

89 a, b, *and* c. *Three face masks acquired in Angmagssalik in 1935-36 by Aage Gitz-Johansen. a: carved by Pavia (year unknown), 11³/₄″ high, 2³/₄″ deep. b: Carved by Pavia's son Georg (1901-62), who at his baptism took the last name Poulsen, 10¹³/₁₆″ high, 3³/₁₆″ deep. c: Carved by Pavia's youngest son, Nuka (b. 1912), also called Utuak Poulsen, 11¹³/₁₆″ high, 2³/₄″ deep. All in brown wood: a and b masks polished, c with rough surface. Private collection.*

In Gustav Holm's 1884-85 collection, we find a pair of closely ornamented masks of somber countenance, with strongly protuberant mouths; and from around the same point in time there are several masks that obviously belong together in pairs, man and wife. With one of the couples, one face is covered almost entirely by transverse compressed lines, while on the other face the lines seem to point to eyes, nostrils, and mouth. The female masks are recognizable by their topknots. It is conceivable that they were used by men who were supposed to be impersonating women. All of the mouths are open, distorted outwards (see fig. 77), and rectangular in shape, never round.

Where the little hand mask in figure 84 represents both man and woman – and while as a parallel many figures possess the characteristics of both sexes – it subsequently became more and more common, and in our own day nearly obligatory, to carve a mask couple. When I was in East Greenland in 1973 with an exhibition of masks, one of the old experienced mask makers wanted to carve a mask couple for me "the way they're really supposed to be". At first I was disappointed with the otherwise lovely masks – carved in wood, painted black, and with inlaid eyes and teeth – because they were so small, smaller than life size, and therefore in my opinion useless except to hang on the wall as souvenirs. But it was when I turned them around and saw how painstakingly room had been made for fingers to slip into the nostrils that I realized I had judged too quickly. The masks were hand masks, and were intended to be used in the manner of hand puppets in a play about a man and a woman (figs. 88a and b).

During this century, Dutch, French, English, and Danish ethnologists have collected the last masks remaining in East Greenland, which was the last area to be Christianized. It was only in 1921 that all East Greenlanders were baptized. The masks and drums were probably in use for a few years more, though in secret, and slowly the mask went over to being a trade object and a home crafts product.

In these masks from the thirties up to our own day, it is possible to discern an effort to attain an ever wilder and more grotesque appearance (figs. 89a, b, and c). It is as though the further away masks get from their

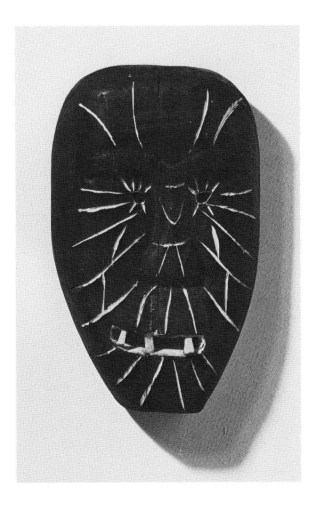

90 a, b, *and* c. a *and* b: *Souvenir masks, representing a man and a woman, carved by Jakob Amátangneq (1900-73), Angmagssalik. Imported lumber rubbed with 2728lampblack, inlaid bone teeth, about 11¾″ high. Private collection.* c: *Souvenir mask representing a weeping man, carved by Jonas Bâjaqe in Kungmiut, 1973. Imported lumber, black acrylic paint, 10⅝″×6¾″, 3⅛″ deep. Tukaq Theater, Fjaltring.*

function, the more outlandish their style becomes. It seems like a kind of convulsion of the culture.

Each mask maker has his own style within the given boundaries (figs. 90a, b, and c) of natural size, black ground color, inlaid teeth, and incised lines in the wood that show up light against the black ground. The teeth may be real animals' teeth or bone and wood teeth carved for the purpose. In present-day masks, there is often a tongue behind the teeth. Inlaid eyes of bone or ivory are occasionally seen. On masks from Scoresbysund, one finds the practice of attaching fur to the wood, and sometimes beards of musk ox hair and eyebrows indicated with skin or feathers. Generally, however, the effect is accomplished using wood alone, with the aid of the black ground.

Despite the traditional forms of the masks, one discerns, under the stylistic straightjacket, a recognizable human face (such as the weeping face in figure 90c), a portrait. It is as if some of the mask carvers had used themselves as models, so that behind the standard ornamentation a self-portrait is seen. Regular portraits are known too – lightly caricatured likenesses of numerous Danish and other European ethnologists. Most probably these individuals made inquiries about masks and perhaps offered to buy some; since they were so interested, masks were made of them.

In South Greenland, where the population includes East Greenlanders, a special type of mask is made: flat wooden masks intended to be hung on the wall, with black painted hair and eyebrows but no ornamentation. The masks are clearly portraits of family members and neighbors and are now and then rather broad caricatures. One artist from South Greenland, however, avails himself of ornamentation in his crazily exaggerated, nearly surrealistic suggestions of the human face.

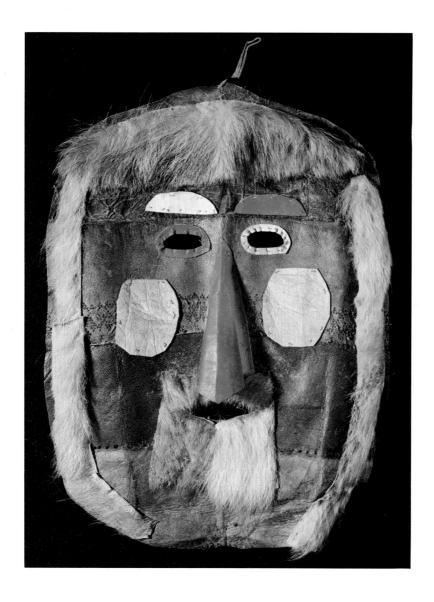

91 a. Mitaartut *mask collected in Jakobshavn in the 1950s by the ethnologist George Nellemann. Sewn by an old woman "the way it was done before." Depilated sealskin with sewn-on nose, edgings, and appliqués of dyed depilated sealskin and dog skin. 11" high. Private collection.*

Mitaartut masks follow another pattern. They do not represent persons or spirits, but are simply intended to make their wearer unrecognizable. Usually they are made of skin, with a decorative effect in the contrast between smooth and furred parts. Artistically, they represent a form compounded of sculpture, handicraft, and painting, as patches of colored skin are often sewed on – either that or a kind of object art, as in the case of the mask with eyes consisting of the paper jackets from flashlight batteries, or the rye-dough masks with Christmas-tree bauble eyes. *Mitaartut* masks can have all kinds of expressions – anger, joy, oafishness – whereas traditional wooden masks practically all represent apprehension and terror.

By now it must be obvious that the question as to whether the mask is a portrait or a cultic accessory can't be answered unequivocally. That mask art has cultic roots seems beyond doubt, and the very system of line ornamentation – three or four lines across the forehead, three or four lines at the root of the nose, and so forth – suggests a special significance, a fixed tradition having to do with cult. But that the artists have looked "realistically" at themselves and others close to them when rendering physiognomy also seems apparent.

Even masks intended to represent helping spirits could be realistically conceived, as these beings were accepted as having a definite appearance and manifestation. Nobody doubted that they looked the way they were described by the shaman. They were realities.

91 b. Mitaartut *mask collected in Jakobshavn in the 1950s by George Nellemann. Depilated skin appliquéd with dyed depilated skin and furred dog skin, 11⁷/₁₆" high. Forhistorisk Museum, Moesgaard, Århus.*

92 a *and* b. *Front and reverse of hand mask with removable topknot. Carved in Tiniteqilaaq by Harald Boassen. Polyester foam and paint. Topknot held in place with a nail. Topknot 2³/₈" high, mask 7⁷/₈" × 5³/₈" × 1¹/₂". Private collection.*

On the whole, the artistic worth of mask art seems to me to be great, especially in the more contained expressions of the baroque and the terrifying – that is, the older mask art in particular and the *mitaartut* masks. In the past, the black coloring was made from lampblack and oil, and gave greater warmth and depth to the wood than the acrylic paint of today, which conceals and shuts off the effect of the wood. And the driftwood used in the past had a noble character, containing a play within itself unmatched by imported building lumber.

Still, artistic quality is not dependent on the use of the old materials. There is a very expressive and beautiful mask from 1973 made of the very un-noble material polyester foam, from the packing for a transistor radio, carved and painted on both sides. The polyester mask has a removable topknot, enabling it to represent either a man or a woman – precisely the same configuration as the oldest known Greenlandic mask (fig. 84). Inasmuch as the latter is hidden away in the basement of the National Museum in Copenhagen and unknown to the ordinary populace of Greenland, there is no possibility of the polyester mask being a copy.

This polyester mask and other present-day masks are evidence that the old concepts are still alive and the depictions of humans and spirits are still being rendered with artistic force by Greenlandic mask makers.

It was mentioned that the missionaries had no appreciation of the artistic and cultural value of the masks, but saw them only as a threat to Christianity and, in their eagerness to make conversions, had them destroyed. Furthermore, the ministers most likely shared the opinion of most Europeans that the masks were ghastly and ugly.

Even in our own century, the usual view of art was so dominated by central perspective and other ideas of the renaissance that the art of primitive peoples long appeared clumsy and rude. At best, their works were regarded as curiosities, and it is typical of this attitude that art from Africa and the islands of the Pacific and Indian and Eskimo art was placed in ethnographic museums and not in art museums.

It was European pictorial artists who discovered what a wealth of forms, colors, and lines primitive art offered – and most important, how charged with expression and life these sculptures and masks were (fig. 93). Even though cult and magic were often the basis for the precepts within which "primitive" artists felt obliged to create their works, they expressed themselves with a freedom and sense of abstraction that came to have the effect of a liberation on European artists.

As a result of the voyages of discovery, nineteenth-century artists began looking for inspiration in other cultures than the Greco-Roman. They began by turning their attention to the art of the East, starting in France with Delacroix's interest in the oriental and continuing with the impressionists' preoccupation with Japanese art. It is well known that their acquaintanceship with Japanese woodcuts had a decisive influence on artists like van Gogh and Toulouse-Lautrec. With his paintings and books from Tahiti, Paul Gauguin, at the end of the 1800s, opened the eyes both of fellow artists and the public to the hitherto unsuspected merits of the art and culture of Oceania.

It wasn't until around 1906 that African art became appreciated and found its way into museums, via artists like Matisse, Vlaminck, Derain and Picasso. In 1907 Picasso painted his famous "Les Desmoiselles d'Avignon," in which the women's faces are obviously inspired by West African mask art, a painting that is a clear break with classical pictorial concepts and that came to represent the breakthrough of abstract art.

Through the works of these artists – particularly Matisse and Picasso – interest spread in the art of primitive peoples, in "primeval" art. People began investigating the sources of culture in a search for unspoiled, spontaneous expression. This effort to uncover the deeper layers of con-

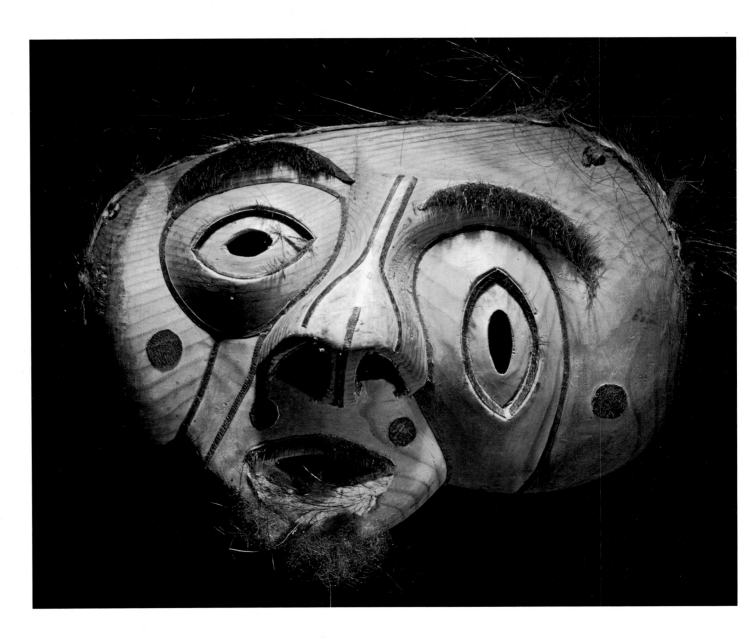

sciousness was also connected with the interest at the time in psycho-analysis and the theories of Freud.

Artists like Paul Klee and Joan Miró carried on this development, and it is revealing that in New York in 1943, when the Museum of the American Indian was in dire financial straits and put objects from its collections, including Eskimo masks, on sale, they were immediately bought by artists – among them André Breton, Max Ernst, Roberto Matta, Yves Tanguy, Kurt Seligmann, and Enrico Donati – leading surrealist painters and writers who had escaped from the war in Europe and continued their work in the United States.

In Denmark, it was artists who worked spontaneously and sought the greatest possible emotional expression who visited the National Museum and saw the Kjersmeier collection, or went to the Musée de l'Homme in Paris for inspiration, including Asger Jorn, Ejler Bille, Carl Henning Pedersen, Robert Jacobsen, and Knud Nielsen.

Most deeply influenced by mask art, however, was Egill Jacobsen, whose works from the 1930s were simply mask pictures. Jacobsen says that for him the mask is the medium that expresses the movements of the mind, and that it itself becomes pictorial language. "Often there is an underlying experience that can't immediately be read. Masks don't always relay the impression of faces or people, but can express powerful perceptions of nature, experiences of wind and weather, the universe and the oneness of people with it – a sensation of the cosmic that expresses all the states of the mind in intense colors in the form of a mask." These remarks impart a sense of how closely related artists from different cultures can be.

The Greenlandic sculptor Aron Kleist (see fig. 69), many of whose productions are spirit figures – twisted and convoluted forms with mythic content, reflecting violent states of mind – surely expresses a cosmic trend of mind, too, when he says: "My qualifications for being an artist are my background as a hunter. When I am out in nature, I observe precisely the wildlife and the changes of the weather – all these relationships are the background for everything I make."

The old Greenlanders believed in *sila* – a force flowing through everything. How revealing that *sila* simultaneously means weather, the universe, and intellect. We can understand why the mask, which as a symbol was capable of expressing all these things, was an inspiration and a liberation for other cultures, and for ourselves.

Tupilak figures and figures with mythical background

Masks are not the only things that represent the world of spirits or reveal murky remnants of former ages' cults and magic. Greenlandic sculptural art is rich in portrayals of concepts and figures from ancient Eskimo mythology – the Sea's Mother, the Lord of the Winds, the Moon Man, and the hag Naligateq, whom the shaman had to get past on his way to the moon. Commonest of all are the composite misfortune beings called *tupilek* (plural of *tupilak*).

The belief in *tupilek* was great. Life was full of danger, and the fear of sickness, famine, and especially of sorcery has persisted into our era of affluence – fear of unknown forces, of the evil always lying in wait.

In dealing with *tupilak* figures, we will be concerning ourselves mainly with works by East Greenland artists. Apart from the fact that the old concepts are still remembered in East Greenland, exceptionally many and talented artists are found there. This is probably the reason why so many people automatically associate Greenlandic sculpture with *tupilak* figures.

As mentioned before (see page 24), a *tupilak* was a misfortune-bringing creature fashioned in utmost secrecy by someone skilled in sorcery from parts of various animals and humans. It was made alive by the singing of a charm song and grew large by sucking from the sexual organ of its maker. Then it was put in the sea to swim to its victim and do away with him. Possibly the victim himself was skilled in sorcery and so strong that the *tupilak* instead turned around and killed its maker.

The fear of being the object of these avenging beings was undoubtedly great, and the fear itself, possibly in combination with hunger and exhaustion – and perhaps a guilty conscience – can well have brought about the death.

No one has ever found a genuine *tupilak,* but when the Danes came to East Greenland and heard so much about *tupilek* and wanted to know what they looked like, people began carving models in order to illustrate the concept. It soon proved that the more bizarre and alarming the figure appeared, the more fascinating it was to the European purchasers. Gradually, it became a business to make corporeal the magical beings that figured so largely in the old world of ideas. Meanwhile, the same thing happened as with mask art: the style became wilder and more

93. *Assymetrical face mask carved by George Poulsen, Kulusuk, acquired in 1934-35 by Robert Gessain. Light driftwood with attached skin strips and paint, 7½″×10⅝″. Musée de l'Homme, Paris.*

94. Tupilak *effigy carved by the shaman Mitsivarniannga in Angmagssalik in 1905 for the ethnologist William Thalbitzer, depicting a* tupilak *that harassed the family. Driftwood, wound about with a thong, eyes and teeth from a child's corpse, 11¹³/₁₆″ high. Museum of Trade and Shipping, Elsinore.*

mannered the further away people got from believing in the supernatural power of the *tupilak.*

The first figures were carved in 1905 by the shaman Mitsivarniannga for the Danish ethnologist William Thalbitzer, and were "*tupilak* portraits" of the shaman and his family's altogether concrete misfortune-beings. Mitsivarniannga's models all have one consistent ingredient: parts of a child's corpse. We have a figure wound tightly in a strip of skin, with inlaid eyes, and teeth from a real child (fig. 94); a wooden figure that is a combination of bird and human; and, finally, a combination of dog and human, swaddled in skin, with two floatation bladders attached to its back.

The latter theme is known in our own day as well: the hunter thinks he has caught a seal, but it turns out to be a *tupilak* (figs. 28 and 95). Either the monster pulls the hunter with it down into the deep, or the hunter succeeds in killing the *tupilak.*

As *tupilek* sneaking up on their victims either swam in the water, flew through the air, or crept along the ground, they are nearly always seen in a couchant position – at any rate as far as the older *tupilak* figures are concerned (figs. 96a – d). As a rule, the *tupilak* is furnished with a human face and an animal's body and legs, and only if the body is anthropomorphic does the figure stand erect.

Numerous modern erect figures called *tupilek* on account of their bizarre appearance – or perhaps on account of having the characteristic skeleton parts or the indication of ribs of the *tupilak* – possibly represent a mythical figure instead. It can be difficult to differentiate clearly between concepts.

The *tupilek* were bringers of misfortune, but they could be vanquished – for example, with the aid of a shaman's helping spirits. These could be very miscellaneous, and are described by the shamans themselves as being strange, but highly concrete, beings. They were the shaman's personal assistants, and he obtained sway over them through ecstatic or trance states. There were both great and small helping spirits, but there were also the more powerful terrifying spirits and spirits of the dead (figs. 97a and b).

Some figures assumed to be *tupilek* may represent these spirits, and the skeleton motif that decorates *tupilak* figures presumably may also belong to spirits of the dead. Spirits appeared having definite animal shapes, such as the black guillemot, for example, or the ice diver, the prawn, or the sandhopper. Often they would reveal themselves in human

95. *Harpooned* tupilak, *skeleton decorated, with both male and female characteristics. Collected in Angmagssalik in the 1930s by the Dutch ethnologist H. P. T. van Lohuizen. Driftwood with black paint, inlaid bone teeth, thong from float bladder to body of* tupilak, *4⅛″ high. Museum voor het Onderwijs, The Hague.*

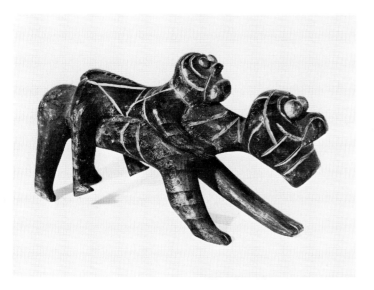

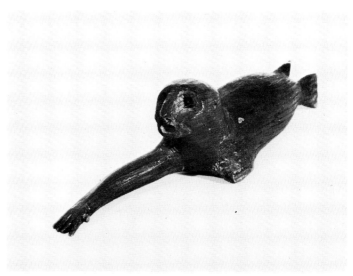

96 a-d. Tupilak *figures, all from East Greenland, collected in the 1930s by van Lohuizen. Driftwood, some with black paint, from* 4¹⁵/₁₆″ *to* 7⁷/₈″ *long. Museum voor het Onderwijs, The Hague.*

form, but naturally with the characteristics of the animal in question.

Certain of the spirits are described as having a particular appearance, such as the terrifying spirit Amô. Its body is small and shrivelled and with small, shrunken legs, whereas the head is large and nearly bald and the eyes strongly luminous (fig. 21). The arms are very long, and it has three fingers on each hand and three toes on each foot. The dangerous terrifying spirit Ajummaaq, too, has three fingers and three toes. They are black all the way to elbow and knee, and it is said that everything these black extremities touch putrifies and dies. Ajummaaq has the head of a dog (fig. 98).

Whatever the composite figures represent, they express the same thing in an artistically convincing way: fear of evil in the shape of creeping monsters with gaping mouths, protuberant eyes, and grasping black limbs. The skeleton beating the drum is a memento mori: life can quickly end.

It is in the genre of ghastly beings that Greenlandic artists – anonymous as well as named – give by far the greatest play to their talents. In a land where one is constantly reminded that the forces of nature are strongest, and where people have had to constantly battle against dark-

97 b. *Spirit named "Takusasiaq", deeply incised with skeleton ornamentation. Collected in the Angmagssalik district in 1931-32 by the archaeologist Therkel Mathiassen. Driftwood, inlaid bone eyes and teeth, 4³/₄″×6¹/₈″. National Museum, Copenhagen.*

97 a. *Dwarf spirit with pointed head, carved by Adam Pîvât in Kungmiut in the 1960s. Sperm-whale ivory, about 2³/₄″ high. Knud Rasmussen High School, Holsteinsborg.*

ness, hunger, and cold, fear is inevitably deeply ingrained. The means of combatting it is humor, another typical trait of Greenlandic art. Often the ghastly and the humorous are joined together; the most deformed and twisted figures can have an assuaging touch of the comical about them.

Recounting the old spiritual concepts in pictorial form developed – at any rate on the east coast – into a considerable industry. At first certain hunters carved figures in idle moments or in their old age, but soon it turned out to be a profitable business, so that now many families in outposts like Kungmiut and Kulusuk work at an extensive production of *tupilak* souvenirs.

There are many repetitions in this category of art works. Even though the objects are made by hand, they acquire something of the assembly line. As one expects of a people with so pronounced an artistic sensibility, however, there are original and distinguished works of art among them (fig. 99). The audacious pictorial vision of the East Greenland talent pool has, moreover, been significant for West Greenland artists, who have been given encouragement to let their visions unfold. "*Tupilak*s" are now being carved everywhere in Greenland. Even in Godthåb, the most modern city in Greenland, artists are found who carve fabulous composite creatures. The murky background of cult and magic grants artistic freedom and lets imagination and the talent for combining be the deciding factors (figs. 100 and 101). The cultivation of these often rather surrealistic figures is not made less worthwhile by the interest and urge of the outside world to buy.

Of all the many figures from Eskimo mythology – such as the Great Worm, the Beast with the Iron Tail, the Gobajaks (fat-bellied women with iron claws), the Ice Cap Dwellers (an amalgamation of dog and human), the Giants, and many others – a few especially have appealed to the imagination of artists.

Remarkably, the wrathful Moon Man (unless some of the masks represent him) is not among them – he who otherwise played such an impor-

99. *Fantastic creature carved in East Greenland in the 1960s by Gaba Poulsen. Blue-green soapstone with inlaid bone teeth, 7¹/₈″×3¹⁵/₁₆″×3¹/₈″. Private collection.*

98. *The terrifying spirit Ajummaaq, carved by Adam Pîvât, Kungmiut, in the 1960s. Imported lumber and black paint, articulated shoulder joints, 5¹⁵/₁₆″ high. Knud Rasmussen High School, Holsteinsborg.*

100. *Fantastic creature, carved in Godthåb in 1973 by Takisunguaq Petersen. Light soapstone, 6″×7¹/₂″×5¹/₈″. Signed "TAKI 73" on bottom. Private collection.*

101. Sculpture with fragments of hands, feet, faces, carved by Rasmus Thomassen in Godthåb, ca. 1973. Light soapstone. 5¹⁵/₁₆" high, bottom 2"×2". Private collection.

tant role in taking away the souls of those who failed to observe taboos such as performing penances for the deceased. For the same offences, he could hold back the tides or keep the seals from having young, thus influencing fertility.

If the Moon Man became angry, the shaman had to undertake a journey to the moon to find out the reasons for his anger and try to appease him. On his way to the moon, the shaman passed the woman Naligateq, who is often depicted as a hideous old hag with a dog skin, a father-lasher, or the like dangling between her legs. By making faces to the accompaniment of the drum song, she tries to get the shaman to laugh, and if she succeeds she rips his intestines out and devours them.

Naligateq (meaning "the big-crotched one") appears both in a naturalistic (fig. 102) and in a more stylized version (fig. 103). In the course of time, her face, too, became heavily decorated with skeleton motif. On another figure, she has the same ugly face and the dog's head hanging between her legs, while the head of a walrus protrudes from her belly (fig. 104). We also know a figure in which "the animal" has a dog's ears and a walrus's jaw, and here the topknot has become a bird's head. Finally, in one version (fig. 105) only the grotesque face and the walrus head remain. Here the walrus has become a phallic symbol, an obvious pictorial element throughout – the subject is, after all, a journey to the lord of fertility, the moon.

The Moon Man had a woman living with him. From the front, she seemed like an ordinary woman, but when she turned her back, the shaman saw to his horror that she was a skeleton (figs. 106a and b).

As mentioned, no definite depictions of the Moon Man himself have been found. It is conceivable, however, that the soapstone carving shown in figure 107, with its round, severe visage and downturned mouth, represented the moon – just as Alaskan masks with the corners of the mouth turned down are moon masks. Similarly, the figure of a rampant polar bear with raised lance and a human face under the bear skin may be an effigy of the wrathful Moon Man – the legends relate that the moon came to the earth in the shape of a polar bear (fig. 55).

The Uaajeerteq figure (see fig. 76), which obviously derives from a fertility rite, has also appealed to the imaginations of artists. With its distorted, masked face, the figure appears as a representative of both sexes – with topknot and pregnant belly, but at the same time equipped with a phallus (fig. 22). Uaajeerteq is also seen with female sexual characteristics alone; whatever the circumstances, she seems to be a stern sex goddess (fig. 108).

The Lady of the Winds, Asiaq, is another mythological being portrayed. As everything about her was topsy-turvy, she is seen with her mouth a vertical slit and her nose and eyes askew.

A much beloved mythological figure, the Sea's Mother is especially fascinating to West Greenland artists. She was an old woman who, as previously noted, was associated with the realm of the dead in the sea. (The other was in the sky, connected with the moon – it is still said that when the northern lights appear, it is the dead playing football with walrus skulls). The realm of the dead down in the sea was a fat and good place to be, because that was where the sea mammals stayed. In times of poor hunting, it was said that the bad deeds of humans attached themselves like lice to the hair of the Sea Woman, and the shaman therefore had to journey to the bottom of the sea and comb her hair so that the animals would rise to the surface and allow themselves to be caught. The artist of figure 109 told me that the sculpture represented the Sea's Mother consoling a child whose mother had just died: the mother was all right down in her realm, for there was plenty of food.

There are certain legends especially cultivated on the west coast. One of them is the tale of the orphan Kagssagssuk who was so poorly treated

102. *Naligateq, carved in the late 1960s by Cecilie Kleist in Julianehåb. Sperm-whale ivory, about 5⅛″ high. Bone drum and drumstick loosely attached. Private collection.*

103. *Naligateq, carved in East Greenland in the 1940s. Artist unknown. Seal bone, inlaid black eyes, ivory drum, 3⁹⁄₁₆″ high. Private collection.*

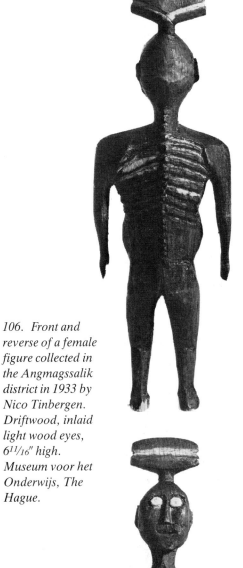

106. *Front and reverse of a female figure collected in the Angmagssalik district in 1933 by Nico Tinbergen. Driftwood, inlaid light wood eyes, 6¹¹⁄₁₆″ high. Museum voor het Onderwijs, The Hague.*

104. *Naligateq with an axe in her hand, carved in East Greenland in the 1950s, signed "J. K." on bottom. Sperm-whale ivory, inlaid black eyes, 5½″×1⅜″×2⁹⁄₁₆″. Private collection.*

105. *Naligateq, carved by unknown East Greenlandic artist in the 1970s. Sperm-whale ivory, inlaid black eyes, 6½″×1⅛″× 1⁹⁄₁₆″. Private collection.*

107. *Male figure acquired in Godthåb in the late 1950s by telegraph manager Leo Christiansen. Artist unknown. Soapstone, 4⅜″ high. Private collection.*

108. *Dread-inspiring female figure collected in Angmagssalik in 1931-32 by the archaeologist Therkel Mathiassen. Driftwood, bone eyes and teeth, 4⅞″ high. National Museum, Copenhagen.*

by his fellows in the settlement, with the exception of an old woman who was kind to him and lent him her *kamik*s. The Kagssagssuk figure is recognizable by these outsized *kamik*s and by his very large nostrils. It was a favorite sport, when the boy came crawling in through the house entrance passage, for his fellows to stick their fingers in his nostrils and haul him inside by them.

By following the advice of his foster mother to go to the Lord of Strength, however, Kagssagssuk, after training hard, became so strong that first he carried a whole tree trunk from the shore up to the house and later killed three polar bears with his bare hands. Afterwards, he avenged himself on his tormenters and killed everybody in the settlement. The only ones to be spared were the old foster mother and an old married couple.

This legend of the runt who fights his way to the top is very popular and is often depicted – especially his trials of strength; so, too, is the Lord of Strength himself, who takes the shape of a kind of dog or fox with a long tail (fig. 110) and flings the tail around his victim and hurls him far away.

Now and then, we see a figure with one ear larger and more erect than the other (fig. 111), representing a *qivittoq* – an individual who for some reason or another has made it impossible for himself to live as a member of society and who therefore goes into the mountains to live as a hermit. For these outcasts to have a chance of survival, their senses had to be extremely highly developed. Their hearing, for example, needed to be extraordinarily keen, so that they could hear the distant approach of people. Therefore the ear grew. Many *qivittoq* stories were in circulation, and there was great fear, especially among the children, of meeting one of these solitary wanderers.

What conclusions may be drawn from this enumeration of figures and concepts from Eskimo mythology? Does an emotional relationship with these things still exist? Do people believe in them?

I definitely think Greenlanders have a deep sense of their history and cultural origins. In the same sense that European artists "believe" in the Annunciation, Golgotha, and the Resurrection, Greenlandic artists "believe" in *tupilek*, spirits, and the Sea's Mother. They have become classic themes with a long tradition to draw on, a form of religious art one doesn't associate with faith proper, but with deep familiarity, and with which simple emotions and basic concepts can be expressed – fear, joy, the mystery of the continuity of life, death. (The Christian church has an unusually lively and whole-hearted following in Greenland, but only in very few cases have Christian concepts and figures found expression in sculpture).

In some cases, it is not a question of carving imaginary beings, but of making realistic effigies. Such and such a spirit, such and such a *tupilak* really looked exactly that way, the artists say.

109. *The Sea's Mother, carved by Dorte Kristoffersen, Godthåb-Nuuk. Signed "DK 1972" on bottom. Dark Soapstone, 6½"×3⁹/₁₆"×8½". Private collection.*

110. *The Lord of Strength, carved by Simon Kristoffersen, Godthåb-Nuuk, in 1972. Light soapstone, 6¾"×5½"×4¾". Purchased by the State Art Foundation and subsequently placed at the Knud Rasmussen High School, Holsteinsborg.*

111. *Figure carved by Sara Kristoffersen, Godthåb-Nuuk, 1974. Dark soapstone. 5½"×5¼"×3⅛". On account of its erect ear, the figure possibly represents a mountain wanderer, or qivittoq, as these hermits had to have exceptionally keen hearing in order to survive. It was also said that qivittoqs learned the language of the animals. Private collection.*

112. *Tupilak figure composed of parts of dog, bird, whale, and pig (?). Acquired in Egedesminde in 1966. Artist unknown. Dark soapstone, 3¹⁵/₁₆" high. Private collection.*

113. *Figures with characteristic Thule culture traits: truncated legs, no arms, and, in some cases, no facial features; flat facial surface. Collected in the Angmagssalik district in 1891 by C. H. Ryder's expedition up the east coast to Scoresbysund. All of driftwood, the tallest 3½" high. National Museum, Copenhagen.*

Everyday realism and everyday poetry

Simple concepts: A man. A woman. A mother with her child. A hunter bringing home a seal. Flensing the seal. These facets of everyday life have been described by Greenlandic artists through all periods with humor, poetry, and realism.

The Eskimo of the Dorset period with his high collar and the Norseman with his liripipe hood were both readily depicted by a simple nuance of dress. A doll that is only a lump of wood with a head, and probably intended to be dressed often, in return gets a particularly expressive face, while others have their entire sculptural expression in the body, with the head not much more than a necessary point of balance – especially when the figure is female and the little topknot practically determines the entire harmony of the sculpture. For a time, hands and feet are immaterial for the artists. From the Thule culture up to our own day, we see superb renderings of humans in the form of small wooden dolls without arms or feet.

The oldest of these human couples displays a stylized, simplified mode of expression – they are types, made according to fixed tradition. Nonetheless, the sculptures possess many details: one is wearing *naatsit* (tiny panties, nearly like our bikini shorts, intended to be worn indoors in the dwelling, where the oil lamps provided abundant warmth); another is flat-chested; a third has her topknot practically sitting on her neck; a fourth is wearing the new hair style for men, the saucepan cut; and so forth (fig. 113).

114. Man and woman. He with unequivocal determination, blackened on thighs and face; she pregnant, blackened in groin, sinew thread wound around thigh. East Greenland. Artist unknown. Acquired in 1924 by colony manager A. T. Hedegaard. Driftwood, 5½" and 4¾" high. National Museum, Copenhagen.

This sense of small realistic detail, which derives from the powers of observation, reveals itself more and more clearly. As in other cultures (such as the Greek), the severe, archaic frontal style – which regardless of the sculptures' physical size usually has something monumental about it – is supplanted by a more dynamic, more realistic and detailed conception of art. An example is the couple in figure 114, where one of the realistic features is the sinew thread wound around the woman's thigh. At first I thought that the leg was broken and that the binding was there to hold it together. But not so. The sinew thread represents a bandage. In those days, it was very common for a husband to cut the woman's thigh with his knife in order to show his dissatisfaction with her. The thigh, which was visible between the *kamik* and the trousers, is considered by Eskimos to be a very attractive place on a woman, and was moreover a visible place on which to demonstrate his displeasure. Now and then such a cut was used to signify that one wanted a divorce.

Later, that is to say in our own time, the realistic style was replaced by a far more varied and differentiated concept of art. Style now belongs to the individual artist. Some still carry on the old tradition, others blend something of the *tupilak* style into ordinary figures, but each follows his own bent and invents his individual style.

Children are seldom depicted alone, or even in a family group of father, mother and child. Rather the mother is shown with her child in an *amaut* (an anorak with a roomy back to carry the child in). But the theme is not seen nearly as often as in Canadian Eskimo art (fig. 115).

We nearly always see human figures represented full length, though in some cases in half length or as busts – especially large and beautifully

116. Bust of woman, carved by sheep-farmer Hans Jacob Frederiksen, Qingua, near Narssarsuaq, around 1969. Local mulberry wood, 8¼" high. Private collection.
115. Mother with child in amaut. Frederikshåb, 1960s. Artist unknown. Dark soapstone. Entire figure about 8⅝" high. Private collection.

117. Bust of woman, carved by Jacob Amátangneq in Angmagssalik, 1935-36. Acquired by Aage Gitz-Johansen. Very heavy soapstone with pyrites, 3⅞"×2¾". Private collection.

118. *Polar bear and walrus, carved by catechist Qipissorssurratsiaq Alataq (1913-72), Thule. Acquired by ethnologist Rolf Gilberg in 1969. Light, polished soapstone, with inlaid bone. Polar bear 5⅞″ long, walrus 5⅛″ long, both 2⅜″ high. Private collection.*

119. *Ptarmigan, collected in the Angmagssalik district in 1884-85 by Gustav Holm. Driftwood with inlaid walrus ivory, 2⁷/₁₆″ high. National Museum, Copenhagen.*

executed portrait busts in wood like the ones from South Greenland, where birches and junipers grow large enough for their roots to be used as material (fig. 116).

Busts in bone and soapstone are known too, as is a single instance of a head resting directly on the surface without neck or plinth – a marvellously simple and expressive little stone sculpture that brings to mind Egyptian art (fig. 117).

Entirely in line with the wood-block and carbou-antler sculpture of the Dorset period (see figs. 2-7), contemporary artists carve blocks consisting of nothing but figures (see fig. 51) or faces. While having nothing to do with the belief in souls, these modern counterparts have much to do with the close human fellowship so typical of Greenlandic behavioral norms. The groups simply represent people who are together.

In these often beautifully composed lumps of humanity lies the embryo – in my opinion – of good Greenlandic monumental sculpture. The human being is the grand theme, and depictions of humans together with animals in everyday situations is also very popular.

First something about the animals. The statuesque is what characterizes some of these sculptures. The shapes of the arctic animals often invite treatment as a tight, closed lump. The neat oval of the seal, the walrus's head sticking up out of the water like a stone, and the polar bear with its pigeon-toed gait and small head, with the ears close to the skull (fig. 118), comprise closed forms – almost like a part of the terrain, a lump of ice, a rock. The whale, too, can be experienced as a great black wave breaking, or as a submarine, when it slides up over the sea's surface and down into the deep again. If you have seen wildlife in the Greenland habitat, it is almost as though a part of the mountains, the ice, or the sea has come alive. It is easy to understand how the old belief that everything has a soul could arise; you might feel it yourself. The plump little mountain hare with its stubby ears looks like a lump of snow (see fig. 133), and the ptarmigan changes its plumage with the seasons so that it blends in completely with the colors of the terrain and becomes part of it.

A distinguished little representation of the ptarmigan is to be found in the Danish National Museum in Copenhagen (fig. 119). It is not properly naturalistic, as white bone drops have been inlaid on the round, taut form. Strangely enough, they don't explode the form but emphasize it.

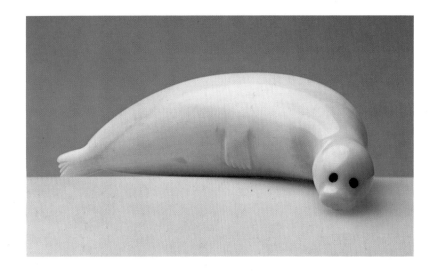

121. *Seal lying on the edge of the ice, on its way down into the water, carved by Rasmus Massanti, Tiniteqilaaq, in 1973 for the Dutch anthropologist Gert Nooter. Sperm-whale ivory, 4⁵/₁₆″ long. Private collection.*

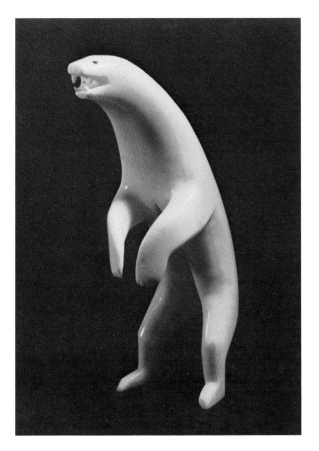

120. *Rampant polar bear. Angmagssalik, ca. 1969. Artist unknown. Sperm-whale ivory, 4¹/₈″ high. Private collection.*

122 a. *Figure group with dog-sled, driver, and six dogs. Artist unknown. Acquired by trading-post manager Egon Mørk Rasmussen in Thule in the 1940s. Walrus ivory. Length of sled, 4⁵/₁₆″. Dogs, about 1⁵/₈″ long. Sled driver, 1³/₄″ high. Private collection.*

Take away the dots and the bird looses its power and aura, and becomes an inelastic lump.

Otherwise most animal sculptures (apart from the Dorset period's skeleton-ornamented animal amulets, which were associated with cult and are therefore not included in this context) always have something of the seen and experienced about them – the bear standing on its hind legs and growling, ready to attack (fig. 120); the seal sporting on the ice in the spring sun, or scenting danger and already with its head over the edge of the ice in order to glide down into its breathing hole if necessary (fig. 121).

The small ways and peculiarities of sled dogs have been delicately recorded, particularly by a number of artists from the Thule region (fig. 122a). When traveling by dog-sled, the human being is very dependent on the strength and endurance of his dogs. In dangerous situations men have avoided freezing to death by warming themselves with them, or kept from starving by eating some of them. Considering how vital a role sled dogs play in the long winter periods and in large areas of Greenland, there exist remarkably few sculptures of dogs. For Greenlanders the dog is a utilitarian animal and not nearly as interesting to portray as large and dangerous animals such as the polar bear and the walrus.

Here we approach the subject of figurative depictions of animals in interplay with humans. Besides dog-sled groups, the abovementioned Thule artists have also given us a series of details from life on a dog-sled journey: the primus stove being lighted, dogs being prevented from devouring human excrement (fig. 122b), as well as implements such as the rifle, coffee mugs, and so on, are carved from bone in minute size and detail.

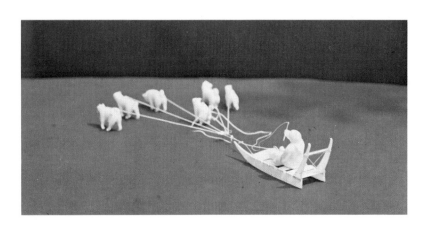

123. Hunting scene carved by production foreman
Peter Egede, Godthåb-Nuuk, ca. 1950. Walrus ivory,
about 8⅝″ long. Private collection.

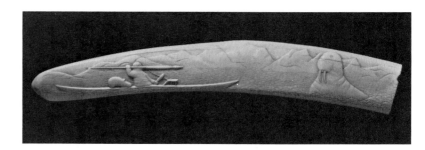

122 b. *Scene from sled trip. Same as 122a. Man*
squatting, 1⅜″ high. Standing man, 1¹³/₁₆″ high. Private
collection.

The hunting situation itself, naturally enough, is a beloved theme. Depictions of the struggle between the hunter and the hunted are often represented by several figures that – arranged in a sequential series – relate the action and the outcome of the contest. Or the situation is shown at its most dramatic moment – just before the well-aimed thrust, as in the walrus tusk relief in figure 123, the hunter in his kayak with harpoon raised and aimed at the walrus. Hunter and animal are looking at each other in this fine composition, the two parallel lines of the kayak and harpoon at right angles to the walrus's two tusks, and the equality of the battle is sensed.

"The Man with the Raised Lance" (fig. 124) is a solitary figure, but situations such as "Man Dragging Home a Seal," and "Flensing the Seal" are the popular motifs, carried out in bone and ivory, and especially in soapstone. In Frederikshåb, in particular, there is a huge output of these "everyday figures," nearly all carved with folds in the clothing like those of Anton Thorsen (figs. 125a and b) and Elias Eigilsen. Many followed the lead of these two artists, so that now such figurines are practically being mass-produced.

In "Flensing the Seal," it is the woman who is portrayed. The man catches the seal and drags it home, but the work of flensing is – or was – the woman's job. We find figures of the woman with a child in her back pouch, carrying a bucket and an *ulo* (the woman's knife with its semilunar blade), on her way to flense a seal. In others, she stands over the animal with her legs apart and her rump in the air – the typical work posture of the Greenlandic woman – or sits doing the scraping with her legs apart in front of her, again with a 90° angle at the pelvis, a tiring posture for us, but natural for Greenlanders.

We see the industrious and busy Greenlandic woman again in the statuette "Woman Carrying Coal" (figs. 126a and b). In those days, when homes were heated with coal and firewood, it was the job of the grown girls and the women to carry the sacks up from the harbor to the houses. In the figure, the sack is represented by a rough stone, which is a good contrast texturally with the woman's soft, smoothly polished back.

But there are innumerable such scenes, both of daily work and of Sunday's occupations. Besides those already mentioned, there exist countless portrayals of minor situations – to name a few, "Boy Carrying Home Fish" (fig. 59), "Woman Smoking a Pipe" (fig. 62c), "Man Carrying a Heavy Load," "Distributing Flensing Tidbits," "Man and Wife on Their Way to Church," and "The Catechist Reads from the Bible" (fig. 134). Daily life was seen from both a realistic and a humorous point of view, and portrayed with tenderness.

124. *Hunter with raised lance carved on the west*
coast in the 1930s. Artist unknown. Walrus ivory, 3⅛″
high. National Museum of Greenland, Godthåb-
Nuuk.

125 a *and* b. *Flensing and butchering seal, carved by Anton Thorsen in Frederikshåb in the 1970s. Soapstone; the woman's* ulo, *bone. 5^{15}/$_{16}$" and 6^{5}/$_{16}$" high. Collection of the Queen and Prince Consort of Denmark.*

126 a *and* b. *Front and reverse of a woman carrying coal, carved by an unknown artist from Frederikshåb in the 1960s. Dark polished soapstone, about 7^{1}/$_{16}$" high. Private collection.*

127. Death spirit carved by an East Greenlandic
artist in the 1970s. Walrus ivory with inlaid black
eyes, 4¾″ long. Collection of the Queen and Prince
Consort of Denmark.

127. Death spirit carved by an East Greenlandic
artist in the 1970s. Walrus ivory with inlaid black
eyes, 4¾″ long. Collection of the Queen and Prince
Consort of Denmark.

128. Dread-inspiring creature, wearing bearskin (the
Moon Man?), carved by Aron Qavigak (b. 1934), in
Thule, in 1969. Acquired by Rolf Gilberg. Sperm-
whale ivory, 4¾″ high. Private collection.

Style characteristics and local traits

Whether it manifests itself in the imaginative or the observing style,
sculpture enjoys a secure position as the oldest, most deeply rooted and
familiar art form in Greenland, the one in which people – with sureness
and naturalness, and regardless of changes in material and function –
have given concrete form to their feelings and their skill.

Certain characteristics of style can be traced through several thousand
years, and local traits exist as well. Greenlandic sculpture of today is a
peculiar combination of age-old traditions and inherited themes and
craftsmanship. It has adapted itself to the needs of the present and to a
certain extent adjusted itself to the taste of its buyers. To put it another
way; we encounter here a richly faceted folk art in which old concepts
remain alive without people allowing themselves to be bound by or stag-
nate because of them.

The old stylistic traits are most pronounced on the east coast. Here the
skeleton motif of the Dorset culture continues to be used (fig. 127), and
here the themes are still associated with the old faith. In a figure with
inlaid black eyes, we see a very old trait, but one nonetheless typical of
East Greenland art at the present time – although it also appears in South
Greenland, where people from the east coast have settled, and is used by
the occasional Thule artist. The Thule region was the port of entry for
the Eskimo immigrations and is thus close to the cultural source.

In some ways, things have changed. In the old days, black dots were
obtained by rubbing soot into a depression, or with inlaid baleen. Nowadays you heat a black plastic comb to just below melting point, press a
piece of comb tooth into a pre-drilled hole, and smooth over.

Size is another traditional characteristic. Only in Thule is sculpting still
being done in the same diminutive format as in the Dorset period. Yet
sculpture everywhere in Greenland is still remarkably small, as a rule
from four to eight inches in height.

As mentioned earlier, a specific style often arises around forceful artists,
with a family or an entire settlement imitating the dominant individual
and thus building up a tradition.

Looking at the map of Greenland and starting in the north at Thule,
we find, as mentioned, a tradition of very small figures, of Thule charm
necklaces and dog-sled teams, and of figures carved from the lower jaw
of the walrus (see figs. 53 and 122a). Figures with pointed oval eyes set
vertically and sometimes with black pupils are also typical of the Thule

130. *Fantastic creature carved by Ferdinand Broberg, Godhavn, in 1976. Soapstone, 7¹¹/₁₆" long. National Library of Greenland, Godthåb-Nuuk.*

129. *Woman smoking pipe, and man with a knife in his hand, carved by Kasper Thomassen in the 1960s. Walrus ivory, about 3³/₈" high. Knud Rasmussen High School, Holsteinsborg.*

area, as are lines radiating from the eyes (fig. 128). Only bone and ivory figures are found.

Upernavik is the scene of a tradition that has grown up around the Thomassen family, producing ivory figures with broad, slightly pigeon-toed feet, long triangular noses, and, frequently, concentric rings around the eyes (fig. 129).

In Godhavn at the present time, a style is beginning to coalesce around two first-rate artists, Ferdinand Broberg (b. 1914) and Knud Kristiansen (1932-78). The work of both takes sculpturally strong forms in bone and soapstone, using a lot of space between the parts of the sculpture, without breaking up the lump as much as is seen in Kangaamiut. Broberg (who, incidentally, has also taught at the Art School of Greenland in Godthåb-Nuuk) is an exceedingly skillful technician, who stresses the perfection of craftsmanship in the execution of his work. Kristiansen, who as a member of the National Council spoke out for improving the situation of Greenlandic artists, was interested primarily in depicting the experience lying behind the impulse to the work of art. He was an expressionist who transformed his dreams and visions in stone, often in relief.

In Jakobshavn, Johan Halsøe (b. 1911) works in soapstone and occasionally in caribou antler; and in Egedesminde we find one of the few wood carvers on the west coast, Hans Alaufesen (b. 1922), who has executed distinctive portrait busts in wood, but whose figures can, however, appear somewhat stereotyped. Another noteworthy talent in this field is Pauline Alaufesen. In Holsteinsborg, there are relatively few artists, possibly because the port has a thriving fishing industry, so that most people have jobs. The young sculptor Jens Abrahamsen (b. 1951) ought, however, to be mentioned.

It is probably at Kangaamiut and Sukkertoppen that the most vigorous cultural nucleus outside the east coast is found. The unusually large painted wood sculptures by Gerth Lyberth and Johannes Kreutzmann and, subsequently, figures in sperm-whale ivory, introduced by Esra Berthelsen and Peter Rosing, became prototypes all over Greenland. The subjects were originally from daily life, but the fantastic was lying in wait and broke loose in the 1950s, when Knud Petrussen, who was at the center of the Kangaamiut school, began creating soapstone figures in a bizarre, surrealistic style that today has at least ten exponents. Particularly notable are Aron Berthelsen (b. 1933) (see fig. 131), also a teacher at the Art School of Greenland, and David Lyberth (b. 1935). David Rosing (b. 1924), Ludvig Rosing (b. 1925), Helene Villadsen (b. 1939) and Jens Villadsen (b. 1938) have created notable works. Here there is

real reason to talk of a "school," a definite Kangaamiut style, with the venerable Ole Kreutzmann (see fig. 63) as the most eminent representative. From Sukkertoppen comes the artist Laurids Jessen (b. 1917), who has lived in Denmark for many years, and who on the basis of impressions from his childhood has made noteworthy sculptures of Greenlanders in everyday situations.

Godthåb-Nuuk is the largest city in Greenland and the one most marked by cultural contrasts – a many-faceted city. It is hard to know just what is typical of the city's artists, many of whom are new arrivals. Broadly speaking, it can be said that soapstone is the principal material, and that the Kristoffersen family's style (fig. 132) has acquired imitators.

Some distinctive Godthåb artists are Isak Jessen (b. 1910), Takisunguaq Petersen (b. 1935), Nikolaj Knudsen (b. 1926), Ludvig Falksen (b. 1898), Mathias Løvstrøm (b. 1947), Alibak Johansen (b. 1925), Rasmus Thomassen (b. 1946), Ane Holm (b. 1910), and Josef Josefsen (b. 1914), who have created beautiful works in the smaller format in soapstone (fig. 133). But there are many others. Artists like Hans Lynge and the younger Frederik Holm have academic backgrounds and are pursuing their own careers entirely, and do not really belong to any one "style" or "school".

Takisunguaq Petersen works with dense, compact volumes (see fig. 100) that imply more than a little of the monumental – one can imagine the artist sooner or later attempting works of greater proportion. The

131. Dread-inspiring creature carved by Aron Berthelsen, Kangaamiut, in the 1970s. Sperm-whale ivory, about 5⅛" high. Private collection.

132. Man holding his head, carved by Kristoffer Kristoffersen, Godthåb-Nuuk, in the late 1950s. Acquired by school superintendent Christian Berthelsen. Soapstone, 4½" high. Private collection.

figures of Alibak Johansen – who variously paints, draws, and sculpts – reveal a marked sense of movement and rhythm in the form, while Ane Holm recounts a situation, tells a story. Josef Josefsen, who lives on the Godthåb Fjord and who in his time as a hunter was accustomed to making his own implements, later began carving figures out of soapstone – first humans and then animals (such as the mountain hare in figure 133), for which life on the fjord provides rich inspiration. His figure of a diver turning its egg with its beak is well known.

In Frederikshåb the Thorsen family sets the style. A kind of soapstone figure has been developed there that for many people probably stands alongside the *tupilak* as the typical souvenir from Greenland. The predominant motifs are everyday situations, such as "Flensing the Seal." But even though stagnation lurks, new and original works are now and then created in Frederikshåb.

It was in the 1950s that soapstone figures as small vignettes of everyday life began appearing in the Frederikshåb district. Elias Eigilsen (1920-60) introduced the form with thoroughly executed, realistic little effigies,

133. Mountain hare, carved by Josef Josefsen, Kapisidlit, in the 1960s. Green (in some places translucent) soapstone, 4⅝" high. Private collection.

134. The Catechist Reads from the Bible (or chants), carved by Anton Thorsen, Frederikshåb, in the 1970s. Soapstone, about 5½" high. Collection of the Queen and Prince Consort of Denmark.

whose surface showed a prodigious amount of textural treatment. It was especially Anton Thorsen (1927-77) who took up this surface treatment and soon acquired a recognizable style in the rhythm with which the wrinkles in the anorak and the folds in the clothing in general accommodate themselves to the figure. In Frederikshåb there is a municipal workshop where about ten artists are engaged in carving in soapstone, with the Royal Greenland Trading Company as buyer.

South Greenland – loosely Julianehåb, Nanortalik, Narssaq, Sydprøven, and Sletten – also has its traditions. Works carved in wood by Isak Lund have stimulated an interest in the portrait, which is also cultivated by doll carver Emanuel Thomsen and several mask carvers. Painted wood sculptures, otherwise known only from Kangaamiut in the 1920s, have for the past twenty years had several exponents in Nanortalik. The grotesque, too, has a place here, represented not only by Aron Kleist (fig. 136), but also in the works of Jokum Sikkimsen and Edvard Lundegård, the latter rendering his spirit visions in a sculpturally very sure and dramatically convoluted style. The proximity to East Greenland is the reason one sees both inlaid black eyes and the skeleton motif here, in addition to inlaid teeth in figures and masks (fig. 135).

A very great proportion of Greenlandic art is "typical East Greenland" (fig. 138). East Greenland is where the traditions are oldest and richest. From 1884-85 – when Europeans first became acquainted with the art of the Angmagssalik people – up to the present, the region has produced such a multitude of fine artists that an enumeration of them here would be impossible. Suffice it to say that the Royal Greenland Trading Company has at present a "procurement" of figures from 300 manufacturers – a state of affairs approaching that in the Canadian arctic, where up to 90 percent of the indigenous population live by making artistic works.

The vast throng of handicraft manufacturers and artists whose work is outstanding include Georg Poulsen and his sons Nuka and Pavia, who made masks in the thirties; Jacob Amángtaneq (figs. 90a and b and 117), a maker of masks and works in stone; Adam Pîvât (figs. 22 and 98); and Lunde Kúko (fig. 54a and b) – all of them now deceased. And there are many gifted families of artists, among them the Tukula, Kilimê, Qeqe, Kûitse, Bâjaqe, Singertât, and Knudsen families.

135. Dread-inspiring creature carved by Jakob Frederiksen, Nanortalik, around 1974. Dark soapstone with 6 inlaid dog's teeth, 7" long. Private collection.

136. Male figure, carved by Aron Kleist, Julianehåb, in the 1970s. Stylistically, the figure represents a transition from the Frederikshåb tradition (fig. 134) to the more grotesque style (fig. 135). Dark soapstone, 13¾" high. Qaqortoq Municipality.

There is truly a broad tradition in East Greenland, and also the realization that as an artist one has roots in the past and builds on the experiences of one's forefathers. The hunter and artist Thorvald Mikkaelsen from Kulusuk, who makes his own implements and household utensils, says of his relationship to art and culture: "It is time we Greenlanders woke up in soul and spirit. Our forefathers had the strength to protect their country in order to pass it on to us as a sacred gift, which we shall honor."

Another artist from Kulusuk, Axel Nuko (b. 1949), who also prefers to make his own implements, has a similar awareness of the worth of traditions: "My father was a great hunter. I regard it as my personal task to pass his and his forefathers' way of life on, so that people will always be able to see how they lived."

Tradition in East Greenland encompasses wooden figures showing close ties with the Thule culture, wood and ivory figures with Dorset culture traits such as skeleton motif, inlaid teeth, and black eyes, and the whole wealth of mask art with its many old cultural traits. Figures in stone arrived later, but to date they still do not play as great a role as the bone and ivory figures. The thematic material is strongly rooted in the cults and magic of olden times (see fig. 139).

To a great extent, East Greenlanders are still hunters, which is probably the reason why good craftsmanship, the beautifully carved implement, is so highly esteemed. While the boundary between art and artisanry is fluid, I would nevertheless like to draw a dividing line in the following discussion of crafts in Greenland.

137. *Fantastic creatures carved by Karl Kreutzmann of Kangaamiut in the 1950s. Gift from Otto Rosing to Christian Berthelsen. Walrus molars, 1¼" to 1⅝" high. Private collection.*

138. *Creeping* tupilak *figures acquired by Aviaja and Egon Mørk Rasmussen in Angmagssalik ca. 1949. Seal bone, 2¹³⁄₁₆" and 2" long. Private collection.*

139. *Composite being with woman's body and double head (polar bear and bladder-nose seal). Acquired by Caroline and John Jensen in Angmagssalik in the 1960s. Carved by the drum-dancer and hunter Odin Maratse, Sermiligaq. This figure with two pairs of eyes is an appropriate concluding picture for the chapter on Greenlandic sculpture. The Greenlandic sculptors have always had two pairs of eyes to see with: the eyes of the imagination, and the soberly observing. Soapstone, 5⅞" high. Private collection.*

Crafts

Art and implement culture

140. Water bucket from East
Greenland. Bottom formed from two
pieces of wood, sides from 4 broad and 4
narrow wooden staves. Decorated with
edging inlays and, on the exterior sides,
with riveted figures of seal and whales
carved from walrus ivory. On the rim, a
drinking straw leading down to the
bottom of the bucket, where the water
from thawing chunks of ice gathers.
Purchased in the Angmagssalik district
in 1924 by colony manager
A. T. Hedegaard. Driftwood and walrus
ivory; height at handle blocks, 11⁷/₁₆", top
diameter at handle, 10⁵/₈", bottom
diameter, 7¹/₂", thickness of sides, ⁷/₁₆".
National Museum, Copenhagen.

The concept "art", in the sense of non-functional decorative or art objects, was unknown in the old Eskimo society, so thoroughly were ornamentation, carving, and color integrated into daily life and connected with implement culture and use in cultic life. Only in recent times did the Greenlanders formulate a word for art: *eqqumiitsuliaat*, meaning something made that is strange. It was when Europeans began giving money for a figure or a drawing and the demand increased that this concept arose.

This chapter deals with art that is anything but strange or peculiar: the natural and beautiful shaping of implements, dwellings, boats, and clothing, everything belonging to daily living – with the perfect utilization of the materials at hand, and the imagination and creativity that have made Eskimo crafts into a perfect fusion of function and beauty.

In mentioning the association with implement culture, I am thinking of two things; one is the perfect form and artistic decoration of actual implements – throwing stick, harpoon, dog-whip – and the other is the tool itself, the implement that, together with the character of the material, determines part of the form and appearance of the art work.

The two most important tools in traditional Eskimo life were beyond question the knife and the needle. With the knife, animals were flensed, the meat cut, the skin scraped – you made your implements, your harpoon, kayak paddles, kayak and *umiak* frameworks. With the needle, skins were sewed together, not only for clothing but also for boats and houses.

With the knife and the needle, works of art were created too.

The first knives were made of stone. Needles were made from bone splinters. Curved knives with slate blades were being used as late as 1900, and even in the 1970s East Greenland artists could cut a serviceable needle from bone.

Both the Norsemen and, later, European whalers exchanged knife blades, scissors, and needles for skin and narwhal tusks on a large scale. Metal became a sought-after trade commodity. Spikes and nails were pulled out of shipwrecks and worked, and every bit of metal was exploited to the utmost. Usually, a knife blade got worn down completely. When the Danes came and the Royal Greenland Trading Company started its activities, what was wanted most was metal and subsequently firearms, sugar, coffee, tobacco, cotton cloth, and beads.

Even the shape of the knife was dependent on its function. The *ulo*, the woman's knife, with its semilunar blade, was ideal for flensing and scraping. Ultimately it became so intimate a part of women's lives that it was used for everything conceivable, both in keeping house and in sewing. The man's knife was used as a sheath knife or pocketknife, in close combat with animals, and in making implements. To protect the thumb, a fingerstall was used (fig. 142). For a time, saws were made of shark's teeth, and using the same implement it was possible to cut hair. (This was seldom done in olden times, as hair and nails were thought to have special powers, and even combings of hair had such strong properties that they were used as amulet material).

141. Ulos, *curved women's knives intended especially for flensing and for scraping skins. Consisting of grip, haft, and blade proper, ulos display local characteristics, such as the bifurcated haft and straighter blade of the East Greenland women's knives. On the west coast, the blade is curved and the haft is in a single piece. Among the Polar Eskimos, the haft is sloping, either solid or bifurcated. From left to right, top row: Ulo from North Greenland or Thule, grave find; wooden grip lashed to bone haft, iron blade so worn down that only a vestigial edge remains. Ulo from Umanaq, collected by Helge Bangsted's film expedition to West Greenland in 1925-26; grip of caribou antler, blade and haft a single piece of iron. Middle row: Ulo brought back from North Star Bay, north of Cape York, by ethnographer T. Thomsen in 1909; grip and haft of bone, iron blade. Ulo from East Greenland, purchased in the Angmagssalik district in 1911 by colony manager Johan Petersen; wood, bone, and iron. Ulo from Thule, collected by Peter Freuchen in the early 1900s; bone grip, bone haft in two pieces fastened together. Bottom row: Little* ulo *from East Greenland, collected by Gustav Holm in 1884-85; wood, bone, and iron. Ulo from Holsteinsborg, collected by colony manager J. P. Engholm in 1839. Older* ulo *type without haft, from Nagtoralik, collected by Kaj Birket-Smith in 1918. Blade of largest* ulo, $6^{1}/_{16}$" *long. The latter three* ulos *are in the National Museum, Copenhagen.*

Instead of sawing, a row of holes might be drilled in a piece of bone or wood, and it was then broken off. The much used drill had a bit made of bone or iron, and was guided by a block held in the mouth. A thong attached at both ends to a bow was given a turn around the drill, and by drawing the bow back and forth, an appreciable speed of rotation could be achieved and thus considerable drilling effect (fig. 144).

Another tool was the *ulimat*, the beautiful adze, which appears with both stone and iron blades, and was used for rough cutting. Naturally, modern tools are used everywhere nowadays, but both the *ulimat* and the bow drill are used in artisanry. The craftsmen say that they can control the bow drill (or mouth drill) better than a high-speed electric drill.

The *ulo* is still found in practically every Greenlandic home. Besides the *ulo* and the needle, sewing tools include an awl, used for piercing heavy skins; instead of a thimble, a sewing ring of bone or skin; and small bone appliances for forming folds and pleats. Previously, thread was made from the sinews of various animals, the throat sinews of caribou being especially strong (fig. 143).

The materials worked by these tools were wood, bone, stone, ivory, and skin. The women developed genuine virtuosity in the working of skins – tanning, depilating, and dyeing them, sewing shirts of gut and bird skin, footwear of bear skin and the skin of the bearded seal, and so

143. *Sewing skin, with a sewing ring holder and a holder for sinew thread, brought back by C. H. Ryder's expedition to East Greenland in 1891. Dark waterskin (depilated sealskin waterproofed with blubber and oil) with white skin strip embroidery; an iron needle has been stuck into the skin. Sinew thread holder of bone. The waterskin sewing ring (used instead of a thimble) has been attached here in order to show how beautifully carved the sewing ring holder is, with a little bird at the bottom. About $9^{1}/_{2}$" long. National Museum, Copenhagen.*

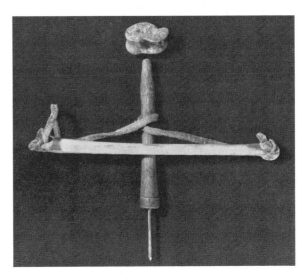

142. *Men's knives for hunting and making implements. Furthest right, a long knife with sheath, from West Greenland, collected by the merchant J. F. Molle, of Holsteinsborg, in 1817; sheath of furred and depilated sealskin, knife of iron and wood, 11" long (National Museum, Copenhagen). The little knife in the lower left of the picture is a grave find, without particulars as to date and locality; bone haft, iron point blade, 3⅜" long (private collection). All the other knives, plus a stall of embroidered depilated skin intended for the protection of the thumb, are from East Greenland, collected by Gustav Holm in 1884-85. The hafts are either of wood or bone, some of them richly decorated; the blades are of iron or slate, and one of delicately chipped flint. Many of the pommels of the knives have been carved with the sign of Toornaarsuk – the stylized seal hindquarters. National Museum, Copenhagen.*

forth. For decoration, they used skin embroidery in contrasting colors, and beads of bone or the vertebrae of fish.

144. *Bow drill from West Greenland, around the turn of the century. The mouthpiece is a particular bone from a caribou heel, the bow likewise of caribou bone; bearded seal thong; drill of wood with iron bit. Bow, 9⅞" long. National Museum of Greenland, Godthåb-Nuuk.*

145. *"Kayak Men, and* Umiak *with Passengers."*
Woodcut by Aron of Kangeq, from a drawing. From
the book Kaladlit assilialialit *(Greenlandic*
Woodcuts), published in Godthåb in 1860. 3½"×8⅝".
National Library of Greenland, Godthåb-Nuuk.

The kayak and its equipment

What was created with these tools and materials? A finely adapted culture of implements and useful articles, functioning perfectly and artistically and aesthetically of high quality.

First the kayak, the beautiful one-man craft that could penetrate a storm wave or ride it, and slip in and out of iceberg formations. So light that it could be carried long distances, the kayak represents the very foundation of the hunter culture. Without it, there was no freedom of movement and possibilities of obtaining food were very much diminished. This vital implement of the coastal Greenlanders is in itself a work of art (fig. 145). With its long, narrow, closed form, its elegant lines and movements, its perfect adaption to the man and the element, the kayak is in fact the Eskimos' purest artistic expression.

It is in the Thule period that we first find definite evidence of the kayak and its equipment, but some type of boat was probably in use before then. Unfortunately, the perishable skin and wood with which the Eskimos built their boats have made for a scarcity of archaeological remains. The heathen practice, which persisted to a late date, of sinking the kayak in the sea at its owner's death has also minimized finds of old kayaks.

There is an interesting theory that the open bark and skin canoes of the Indians spread to the Eskimos in the interior of Canada, where they were used on the big lakes, and that when the Eskimos penetrated to the coasts these vessels developed into covered skin boats. Certainly older kayaks, such as those from the 1600s, with their raking prows and sterns, are reminiscent of the shape of a canoe. Later only the stern was raked, and this composite form has persisted well into our own century, especially in Central and North Greenland.

146 a. *"Here We See Kangualiorssi alongside of*
Petrus's Walrus." Painted by Jens Kreutzmann (see
p. 188) in the middle of the 1800s. Ink drawing with
watercolors, 1⅜"×5¹⁵/₁₆". National Library of
Greenland, Godthåb-Nuuk.

146 b. "One Who is Shooting Seal from the Ice. The Other Sets Off from the Ice Floe to Retrieve the Seal He Has Shot." Painted by Jens Kreutzmann in the middle of the 1800s. Ink drawing with watercolors, 3¹/₈″×4³/₁₆″. National Library of Greenland, Godthåb-Nuuk.

147 a. "Ennissuitsok's Little Son about to Paddle a Kayak." Painted by Jens Kreutzmann in the middle of the 1800s. Ink drawing with watercolors. 1⁷/₈″×3⁵/₈″. National Library of Greenland, Godthåb-Nuuk.

147 b. "Ennissuitsok's Little Son about to Harpoon His First Seal." Painted by Jens Kreutzmann in the middle of the 1800s. Ink drawing with watercolors, 1⁵/₁₆″×3¹/₂″. National Library of Greenland, Godthåb-Nuuk.

The kayak was both transport vessel and part of the hunter's equipment. In Angmagssalik, the kayak is also known as *sarquin*, meaning "means of journeying," an exceedingly graphic designation when considering the vast distances covered with the kayak. The man went on long reconnoitering expeditions in the kayak, visited family and friends, looked for new hunting grounds. In the kayak, you fetched your bride (as seen in the film *Palo's Wedding*) or someone who was sick, delivered the mail, went to a song contest. Former national council member Ole Petersen of Sukkertoppen told me how, from the summer grounds where he and his family went salmon fishing in the thirties, he would get in his kayak and paddle the 200 miles to Godthåb-Nuuk when there was a council meeting.

But most of all, the kayak was a means of hunting sea mammals. The inland Eskimos, who hunted caribou, did not need it. Nor did Eskimos living in iced-over areas, where hunting took place at breathing holes. For dwellers beside the open or partly ice-filled sea, on the other hand, the kayak meant an enormous expansion of hunting range and a mobility that resulted in catches far surpassing anything previously known (figs. 146a and b).

Man and kayak were one, both visually – the occupant appears as though cast in his boat, encapsulated in the skin of the half-jacket and the streamlined superstructure around the cockpit – and physically, inasmuch as the kayak was built for an individual, according to his height and weight. It was an extremely personal craft, accompanying its owner through life and, as mentioned, into death.

From early childhood, boys were trained to use a kayak. First they practiced balancing and paddling movements on land, and later paddled a child's kayak in calm water (figs. 147a and b). Gradually, training took place in rougher weather, including the art of rolling the kayak. You had to overcome dizziness and lack of confidence. Throwing the harpoon and bird dart was part of the training, and to this day Greenlandic boys have incredible aim and force when knocking down a snow bunting with a stone – or breaking a window in an uninhabited house.

The building of the kayak required the combined efforts of men and women. The men built the ingeniously constructed wooden framework, reinforcing it in places with bone. The wood had to be of a certain degree of humidity, and was joined – either rabbeted and pinned or lashed – so that it would not break but would give at possible strains. It was then covered with wet, depilated sealskins, soaked just enough so that when they dried they would have the proper tautness over the wooden frame. First the skins were attached together loosely, and then they were sewed with sinew thread in a strong double seam. The sinews had the further advantage of swelling in the water and thus totally sealing the seam.

The treatment and sewing of the skins was the responsibility of the women. Naturally, it was vitally important that the kayak be impermeable and well sewn, and the technique of preparing the skins was developed to perfection. Tanning was done using urine, blood, ash, and oil, and often the skins were dyed with plant extract. Oil or blubber was constantly rubbed into the skin to keep it supple and water-resistant. Three to four sealskins, depending on their size, were required for a kayak covering. It was also important to know how the strength of the skins varied. The skin behind the cockpit had to be extra strong, as the catch was often carried there.

Like the ptarmigan, which changes its color with the season, kayaks could be made with dark skin (skin retaining the epidermal membrane) for use in the inner fjords, where it blended with the dark mountains, or with light skin for hunting among the big ice on the open sea. In recent years, with the advent of canvas-covered kayaks, it has become the practice to paint the covering with white oil paint, which serves the dual purpose of waterproofing it and making it blend in with the ice.

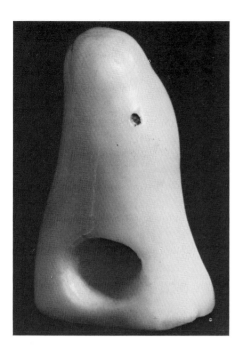

148. Qoorut, *or toggle for kayak strap. This* qoorut, *shaped like a seal on the lookout, is from the foremost strap. Collected by Ossian Elgström in 1915 in Kangaamiut. Walrus ivory, 1⅛″ high. Private collection.*

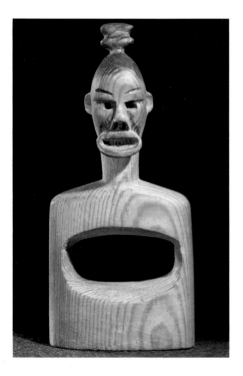

149. *Holder located on the kayak deck as muzzle support for rifle, collected by French anthropologist Robert Gessain in the Angmagssalik district in 1934-35, and described by him in* Figurine androgyne *(Paris, 1954). Driftwood, about 4¾″ high. Musée de l'Homme, Paris.*

After the covering had been stretched and sewn together, the kayak straps were made fast across the deck and lashed to the framework. These straps had to be strong, and like the harpoon line, they were made from the skin of the bearded seal. Even though they reinforced the construction as an extra lashing, their main purpose was to hold the implements. There might be eight or ten cross straps, under which the harpoon lance, throwing stick, rifle, ice scraper, bird dart, and so on, were secured, all in a definite order, so that the hunter could get at them quickly and unerringly.

On certain of the straps were small pieces of bone or wood, whose purpose was to hold the strap out from the kayak skin, enabling the implements to be easily inserted and keeping water from collecting under the strap. These bone toggles, called *qoorut*s, were now and then carved in the shape of animals and had the quality of amulets, bringing good luck in hunting. When the Swedish artist Ossian Elgström visited the west coast of Greenland in 1915, he was delighted to discover a rich tradition for such carved *qoorut*s at the Kangaamiut outpost:

> The straps of the kayak deck were everywhere furnished with *qoorut*s, but not the dull and unimaginative "checkers and halma pieces" that I had seen earlier in Godthåb and Sukkertoppen. No, here the whole of Greenland's wildlife was represented in carved figures depicting bears, seals, foxes, and naturally narwhals, halibuts, and other "wild animals" of the sea. All carved with a handsomeness and sense of form nearly reminiscent of the Japanese whittlings we can admire in all the large antique stores.

These minutely detailed and delicately finished animal sculptures varied in length from three-quarter inches to four inches, depending on whether the toggle accomodated one or two straps. In the latter case, the toggle was used to tighten the straps. On the front strap in the prow of the kayak was a small upright figure, such as a seal on the lookout (fig. 148). This *qoorut* was especially valuable as an amulet, which is emphasized by Elgström when he comments on how difficult it was to buy one of these *qoorut*s. In one case, the sale had to be cancelled when the seller's hunting luck disappeared.

On a kayak built for and given to King Frederik IX in 1968 by the inhabitants of Nanortalik, these leading toggles were shaped something like a stylized seal's hindquarters (or muzzle), but otherwise carved *qoorut*s are rare and the animal effigies from Kangaamiut are a special instance. They were used at that time and place only.

Similarly, the East Greenlandic carved figures used to support a rifle are known only from the Angmagssalik district in the 1920s and 30s. A French expedition on the east coast in 1934-35 collected a number of intriguing wooden figures, between four inches and four and three-quarter inches high, to be fastened on the kayak's front cross strap, with a hole to support a rifle muzzle (fig. 149).

The first generation of East Greenlanders to learn the use of the rifle found it natural, and in keeping with tradition, to decorate rifle holders in this special way. What is so intriguing is that as supports for the modern weapon, the wonder of the new era, the hunters chose to carve androgynous forms embodying elements of the ancient fertility cult of which we have only a murky impression – female topknot and breasts, and, at the same time, moustaches. Reminiscent of the Uaajeerteq figure and certain *mitaartut* mummers, these mysterious hermaphroditic figures – support for the gun, the effective hunting weapon of so-called civilization – are the only objects associated with the kayak's decoration that have cultic traits.

The ice knives, used for scraping ice from the kayak, might be ornamented like the haft of the work knife, with a pommel usually

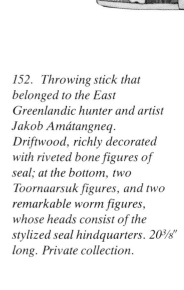

150. Harpoon points from different regions and times, and a female figure. From left to right, top: Barbed harpoon point made entirely of bone, collected by Pastor P. H. Sørensen in Jakobshavn in 1900. Female figure of indeterminate origin; driftwood, blackened with soot. Harpoon point from Hunde Eiland, collected by Kaj Birket-Smith in 1918; iron and walrus ivory, two iron rivets and three copper rivets. Harpoon point (tukaq) from Umanaq, collected by Helge Bangsted's film expedition to West Greenland in 1925-26; iron point and caribou antler, sinew thread lashing reinforcement at shaft socket. Bottom row: Harpoon point from East Greenland, collected by Gustav Holm in the Angmagssalik district in 1884-85; brass and walrus ivory. Harpoon point from North West Greenland, a grave find purchased by trading post manager Christian Olrik in the Upernavik district in 1857; delicately worked meteorite tip, bone body. Harpoon point, grave find without further particulars; bone tip and body, fastened together with bone rivets. All in the National Museum, Copenhagen, except for the last-mentioned, which is in a private collection.

151. Hunter (wearing snow goggles) harpoons seal using throwing stick. Drawn by Kârale Andreassen, 1933. Bought by Nico Tinbergen, who lived for six months in the home of Johanne and Kârale Andreassen in Kungmiut during the winter of 1933-34. Pencil on writing pad paper. Museum voor het Onderwijs, The Hague.

152. Throwing stick that belonged to the East Greenlandic hunter and artist Jakob Amátangneq. Driftwood, richly decorated with riveted bone figures of seal; at the bottom, two Toornaarsuk figures, and two remarkable worm figures, whose heads consist of the stylized seal hindquarters. 20⅜″ long. Private collection.

shaped like a stylized seal's hindquarters, the ornamentation representing Toornaarsuk, the great helping spirit (see fig. 142).

The same sense for giving things a body, so that they became creatures, is seen in the design and nomenclature of the harpoon point. The lower part is called the "tail," and the two holes for securing the line are called "nostrils." The entire configuration of the harpoon, in all stages of development, is created with equal regard for the weapon's function and its beauty of form. A beautifully carved and well-proportioned harpoon point has a sculptural value equal to that of many a figurine (fig. 150).

By and large, this double value is true of all implements and of the kayak's equipment in general. The bird dart, lances, tow line, kayak stand, float bladder, throwing stick – all are effectively and thoroughly conceived, constructed and constantly improved through the experience of generations, and at the same beautiful. That effectiveness and beauty went together in an indissoluble unity is also evidenced in the belief that the animal "would rather be caught by a beautiful harpoon."

One implement that was artistically decorated – especially on the east coast, but also on the west coast – was the throwing stick. By means of this "arm extender," the hunter could throw the harpoon sixty to seventy feet without letting go of the throwing stick – a reason for lavishing decorations on it, as the harpoon could vanish with the wounded animal (figs. 151 and 152). Certainly, the throwing stick possessed special power as amulet material, too.

The richly decorated throwing sticks of East Greenland were part of an artistic tradition of fastening bone or ivory figures with bone rivets to wooden objects like water buckets, chests, eyeshades, and kayak stands in bas-relief. The figures were the same size, around three-quarter inches to one and a quarter inches long. On throwing sticks, they were primarily seals, often close together, although effigies of humans and helping spirits might also decorate the implement.

The shape of a seal, the indispensable animal, could also form the handle of the tow thong, as mentioned in Gustav Holm's *Ethnological Sketches of the Angmagssalikians* (1888), in which he writes:

> Frequently bone knobs on kayaks are carved in shapes that are intended to represent seals. The stand of the kayak and the throwing stick for the harpoon are likewise often richly furnished with figures of ivory. Handles and cross-pieces on all sorts of straps with which the caught animal is tied, and with which it is dragged, are carved in the shape of seals [fig. 153].

A very necessary part of the kayak's equipment is the paddle – a double paddle consisting of a pole with a blade at either end. It was used for propulsion, for stabilization during embarking and disembarking, and for rolling the kayak – an exercise useful in capsizings. The paddle could also be used acoustically, as a shout along a paddle held at a certain angle to the water could be heard at a great distance. Executed in wood and with bone reinforcements on the sides and ends of the blades, the kayak paddle is both an effective and a handsome useful object. In former times, the paddle may have been decorated, if what the old legends say is true.

Many tales exist about strange tribes of people, sometimes described as being superhuman and having fabulous attributes, and sometimes as being very much human, with matter-of-fact information about hunting methods, dress, and home furnishings. Tales handed down about the habits of near or distant relations were perhaps mixed with the universal fear and suspicion of strangers, so that semi-credible imaginary beings arose – along the lines of our own terrifying stories of men from Mars.

Realistic accounts are given of the Fire People (*innersuit*) as being skilled kayak men and great hunters. Their kayaks are usually white, as

153. Handle for tow thong carved in the shape of a seal, but with scratched-in "amulet harness." Probably Thule culture. Bone, about 4³/₈" long. University Museum, Cambridge.

are their kayak jackets. Their lances are short but powerful, and their paddles are beautifully decorated with figures of seals and small whales:

> The decorations begin immediately above the paddle's end-reinforcement of bone, and they give the appearance of a swarm of animals swimming up toward the grip of the paddle. The Fire People's sorcerers had the right of decorating their paddle blades on both sides all the way to the grip. A shaman's apprentice gets away with a big haul if he manages to capture a Fire Man with his kayak paddle richly decorated on both sides, for then he obtains a really powerful helping spirit. [Knud Rasmussen, *Myths and Legends*].

Even though the Fire People appear as sorcerers, the details, like the decorated paddles, may be evidence of the material culture of former generations or related neighboring tribes.

But no decorated paddles are found in any museum. Figures and ornaments seem to be used primarily on the more permanent parts of the kayak and its equipment: the strap toggles, the kayak stand (on which the harpoon line lay rolled up), the throwing stick, and those implements that were in close association with the caught animals, such as the cross pieces of the tow thong inserted in the wound or the mouth, and wound and throat pegs.

These pegs (already discussed on page 20), were made of bone or wood and were often beautifully carved, ornamentally, with stylized seal's hindquarters, or with a face representing the peg's *inua* (its owner?). The faces on the wound plugs (fig. 154) are reminiscent of mask art. Can they be effigies of the hunter's helping spirits?

The hunter's clothes and especially the half-jacket – the skin drawn tightly around the ring of the cockpit and keeping water out of the kayak – were handsomely decorated. They will be discussed in the section on dress (see page 129), but are mentioned here because of the whole formed by the hunter, the kayak, and its equipment.

Decoration of the kayak skin itself is unknown, although there are several kayaks with waves painted on their sides in museums in the Netherlands, one resplendent with dragons and dolphins. These kayaks are from West Greenland from the period 1600-1800, centuries when the Dutch conducted a lively trade along the coasts of Greenland, where they also hunted whales. In a number of instances, Greenlanders went – more or less voluntarily – back to Holland with them. There is an account from 1625 of a Greenlander who gave performances of kayak paddling and harpooning on a lake near the royal palace at the Hague. Some of the kayaks are alleged to have been found floating and then taken aboard Dutch ships.

However that may be, the kayaks were probably painted outside of Greenland, as the style and use of color corresponds rather closely to traditional household decorative painting in Friesland and Holland at the end of the 1600s and the beginning of the 1700s. The artistic value of the kayak does not lie in painted surfaces, but in its total concept – the kayak as a phenomenon.

It has not been the aim here to describe the history and construction of the kayak, or hunting methods connected with its use, but only to point out that when functional art arrives at so refined a state, effecting a balance between scarce materials and the harsh land and climate and conditions of the hunt, and when it is carried out with such superb craftsmanship and delicately expressive detail, it is fine art.

The kayak is necessary, convincing art.

154. Throat pegs, slightly curved, pointed at one end, and furnished with transverse grooves to prevent the peg from working loose, carved on top with dread-inspiring human faces. Collected by Therkel Mathiassen in the Angmagssalik district in 1931-32. The peg is inserted firmly in the throat of the killed seal after the hunter has inflated the animal's lungs in order to facilitate towing behind the kayak. Driftwood. Longest peg, 10⅜". National Museum, Copenhagen.

The *umiak*

While the kayak was a one-man craft for men capable of hunting, the *umiak*, the women's boat, was a general purpose vessel for the rest of the family – women, children, and the aged (fig. 155).

This large skin boat, which probably also developed from the skin and bark canoes of the Indians, has different proportions from the kayak, but is built according to the same principle: skins are stretched over a wooden framework assembled by pinning or with rabbet and tenon and sewn together. As distinct from the kayak, which is decked-over, and therefore especially seaworthy, the *umiak* is open. The skins are turned over the gunwale and lashed securely to the frame.

The people of the Thule culture, who brought the *umiak* to Greenland, used it for hunting whales. Killing these huge animals required a communal effort, and for this task the men rowed the boat. Otherwise rowing was the job of the women, while a man sat in the stern and steered with an oar as a rudder. The oars were usually short and had round blades. For covering the *umiak*, the strong skin of the bearded seal was used, or skin with the epidermal membrane. Seven or eight skins were required for a boat twenty feet long. Besides human passengers, the roomy vessel transported dogs, tents, household utensils, and the family's entire belongings.

Thus loaded down, the *umiak*s sailed to and from the summer hunting ground surrounded by escorting kayaks. During the winter the boat was placed upside-down on a wooden or stone platform, and kayaks, skins, and provisions were stored under it.

The *umiak* was also used as transportation to big events, such as song contest. There is a charming watercolor by Kristoffer Kreutzmann (see page 101), "Greenlanders Sailing on a Sunday," in which the *umiak*, with a sail set, is used as a pleasure craft (fig. 156). Isak of Igdlorpait painted a watercolor showing the Danish doctor being fetched in an *umiak*

156. *"Greenlanders Sailing on a Sunday." Painted by Kristoffer Kreutzmann (see p. 201). Collected by Ossian Elgström in 1915 in Kangaamiut. Watercolor, about 5¹/₈″×7¹/₈″. National Museum of Greenland, Godthåb-Nuuk.*

adorned with a gigantic swallowtailed flag (fig. 157). As late as 1968, Queen Ingrid was passenger in a very beautifully built and sewn *umiak* built as a gift for the royal couple, which is now in the Museum of Trade and Shipping in Elsinore.

The *umiak* is no longer used, as it has been replaced by a host of motorboats and coastal passenger ships. In 1966, Jens Rosing filmed *The Last* Umiak *Voyage,* which showed how a family from Jakobshavn rowed to the salmon-fishing grounds, a trip lasting three weeks, during which the whole family worked together in catching, smoking, and drying the fish.

No decoration of the *umiak* is known, other than the decorative effect of the play of the dark and light skins. The vessel's beauty is in its construction, its impression in the terrain, and in the interplay of people and boat. Amulets were often placed in the prow, just as with the kayak. It was useful to be on good terms with the higher powers. Voyages were perilous in the frail skin boats.

Yet the kayak and *umiak,* by virtue of their very lightness, were admirable for navigating in ice-filled waters – which was demonstrated in 1884

157. *"This is the Doctor from Julianehåb." Painted by Isak of Igdlorpait (see p. 197) in the late 1800s. One of forty-four colored drawings published in Isak's Picture Book in 1969, with explanatory text by G. N. Bugge, whose family owned the original book. 6³/₄″×4¹/₈″. National Library of Greenland, Godthåb-Nuuk.*

when "Captain in the Navy" Gustav Holm, for "the Commission for the Exploration of Greenland," reached Angmagssalik with the so-called *umiak* expedition. Time and again, wooden ships had been crushed or locked in the ice, and the exploration of the east coast of Greenland had to be abandoned until Holm at length accomplished his purpose thanks to his Greenlander helpers and the *umiak*.

But he was not the first European to realize that the Greenlandic craft was the best for the purpose. Before him, in 1829, Lieutenant W. A. Graah navigated a good distance up the east coast by *umiak*, and as early as 1748 the merchant Peder Olsen Walløe wrote in his journal: "The 2nd of August. This morning I sailed in my Greenlandic women's boat, which I steered myself, as possibly the first European to avail himself of such a vessel for so long a voyage."

In his description of the nearly five years' combined trading and exploring voyages on the west and east coasts, Walløe gives several examples of the usefulness of the *umiak*. When they came into pack ice around Cape Farewell, Walløe reports: "Twice we were in mortal danger, which was averted by the skin of the boat stretching when it got jammed. Had it been a European vessel, no matter how strongly built, it would surely have been crushed to matchwood, and that would have been the end of us." Another time, a spur of ice tore the skin, but the hole was plugged with blubber, and when they got ashore one of the seamstresses sewed up the tear. It was reported that during a storm, "the only shelter or lee which we had was to crawl in under the women's boat, which we had up-ended and secured with the greatest difficulty."

The kayak and *umiak* had their place in legend and superstition too. There is terrified reference to "giant boats" and "giant kayaks," to the troll who journeys in a half kayak, and to "the crooked-mouthed one," properly a fulmar petrel but in human form always encountered in a kayak.

Many exquisite models of kayaks and *umiak*s have been made as toys or handicraft, with minute details revealing a sense of humor, such as in depicting the oarswomen. Hanging in the church at Angmagssalik there is a ship model in the form of a beautifully finished little *umiak*. Such models are made from the authentic materials, and are also used as funerary gifts.

The dog-sled

The dog-sled, too, has been the subject of model-making, although here the sled, dog-team and driver are carved from bone or ivory. It belongs in the same sphere of reference, as an important means of transportation in which function and materials, through the improvements of generations, have attained a high state of refinement. Historically, the dog-sled is the same age in Greenland as the kayak and *umiak*. We know for certain that the dog-sled has been used since the Thule period.

Three types of dog-sled are found today: the short East Greenland type (approximately four feet long) with rather wide, closed stanchions; the longer West Greenland type (approximately eight feet long); and the Thule sled, which can be as long as twelve and a half feet. Sleds are made of lumber, but formerly of driftwood, and are pinned or lashed together with enough play in the joints so the sled will give when driving in pack ice or over rocks. The runners are sheathed with strips of bone, baleen, or, on modern sleds – iron or steel. Decoration is primarily on the equipment – carved bone beads above the handle of the dog-whip and at the hitch for the traces (fig. 158).

As with the boats, the dog-sled possesses the natural artistic value of a functional and thoroughly conceived useful object. Where the boats

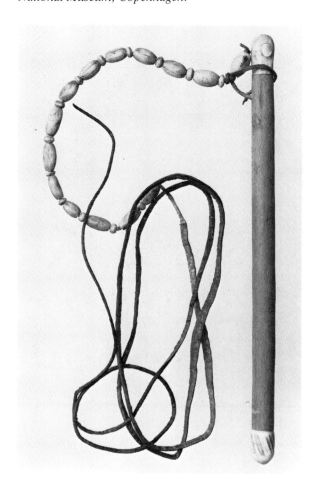

158. Dog whip from East Greenland collected by colony manager Johan Petersen in 1911 in the Angmagssalik district. Handle of driftwood with fittings and carved beads of ivory; lash, bearded seal thong. Handle about 19¾". Lash about 160" long. National Museum, Copenhagen.

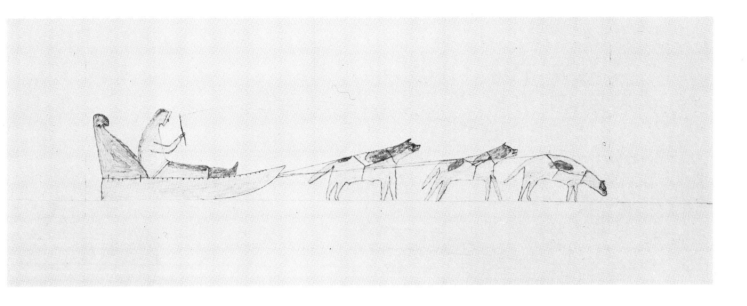

159. *Sled driver with three dogs hitched to the sled.*
Drawn by Kârale Andreassen in Angmagssalik in
1905, when he was fifteen. Acquired by William
Thalbitzer in the same year. Pencil on writing pad
paper, 4³/₄″×8¹/₂″. Royal Library, Copenhagen.

exhibit an interplay between boat and human, the dog-sled represents a unified collaboration between vehicle, driver, and animals.

The dogs, the indispensable draft animals, can be harnessed either in single rank – that is, in fan-formation (fig. 160) – or in several ranks, like a four-in-hand. Depending on the sled and the load, three or four and up to twenty dogs are used. On part of the west coast, dog-sleds are not used, but in iced-over areas it is still an indispensable and much-used mode of transportation – primarily for hunting trips, but also for carrying the mail, provisions, fetching medical help, and so on. The Danish military also use dog-sleds for patrol purposes (such as the "Sirius" dog patrol).

Many explorations have been made on dog-sled, such as the Fifth Thule Expedition, also known as "The Great Sled Journey," in which Knud Rasmussen visited all the Eskimo tribes between Thule and Siberia. The expedition took three and a half years (1921-24), covered more than 10,000 miles, and collected extremely comprehensive ethnographic material.

Knud Rasmussen relates that the sled was the first real toy of his childhood, and it was with the sled that he fulfilled his life's work. He praised the patient and hard-working dogs: "We had toiled together as only living beings can help each other, now in battle against impassable pack ice, now in the wild career of the hunting trip; but happiest when,

160. *The hunter on his way to the open sea. From the*
series "Seal Hunting during Winter Darkness from
Drifting Sheet Ice." Painted by Jakob Danielsen (see
p. 203) of the south coast of Disko Island in the
1920s. Watercolor, 3³/₄″×5³/₄″. National Museum,
Copenhagen.

161. Umiaks, *tents, dog-sleds – life in the settlement.*
Drawn in Angmagssalik in 1905 by Kattuaraje for
William Thalbitzer. Pencil on paper, 6¹¹/₁₆″×8¼″.
Royal Library, Copenhagen.

hungry and depleted with meat-craving, we caught sight of distant settlements and scented unknown people!"

With the kayak, the *umiak,* and the dog-sled, the Eskimos ranged far. They were their "means of journeying," the necessary implements for subduing vast land areas. No wonder that these three vehicles – and tools, hunting implements, and clothing – are so impressively conceived, executed, and aesthetically refined. They were the foundation of existence, the nucleus of the hunting culture (fig. 161).

House and tent

Between journeyings, people were settled, lived in sod houses, stone houses, and tents – until modern building practices caught up with the Greenlanders and society changed entirely.

All over the Eskimo area, there existed a network of settlements, which only seldom belonged to specific families over a long period of time. People traveled freely and settled where conditions were favorable. There may have been some attachment to place, but the local great hunter decided when the group should move on. Everybody pulled up stakes when he gave the word, found a house ruin somewhere else, and settled down again.

Remains of houses or tent rings from the Independence I period (2000-1700 B.C.) evidence dwellings with a circular floor plan and the hearth in the middle. Tents were presumably conical and erected on a low wall. Circular tent rings from the Sarqaq period (1200-700 B.C.) have been found, but with the hearth located at the perimeter of the space. In Independence II (600-500 B.C.), the floor plan is oval and the hearth

162. Building the igloo. The story is told in three episodes, starting at the bottom: the arrival of the family with sleds and dogs; the igloo is begun; the igloo is completed. Note the imitations of writing. Drawn by a Polar Eskimo at the beginning of the 1900s, for Knud Rasmussen. Pencil on half of a folio sheet. Jakobshavn Museum.

163. "Natives at New Herrnhut." Color lithograph
by Lars Møller (see p. 167), "Printed at the Colony of
Godthaab's Book and Lithographic Press 1863."
10¼"×18". Acquired by the zoologist M. P. Traustedt
on a journey in West Greenland. Private collection.

164. "The Doctor's Residence at Godthaab."
Painted by Mads Lynge. Signed "M. L. 1880". Pencil
and watercolor. 5¹¹/₁₆"×9⁷/₁₆" Royal Library,
Copenhagen.

oblong, and not until Dorset I (100 B.C.-A.D. 100) do we find the first evidence of an entrance passage.

Dorset I and II (A.D. 700-900) had rectangular stone houses with high walls. The building materials were the same: stones, sod, driftwood, whale bones, and, as roofing material, skins. The snow hut, or igloo, which many people automatically associate with Greenland, is a hunting and travel hut found only among the Polar Eskimos, and today is used only in Canada and Alaska. It is built up with large, firm blocks of snow around a circular floor plan and has a beautiful beehive shape (fig. 162).

The Thule culture (A.D. 900-1200) had stone houses with a pear-shaped floor plan, and during this period the sunken entrance passage was developed – an admirable cold trap. Later, single-family dwellings were combined into extended family houses in which each family unit had its bed platform – a type of dwelling that led to the common house, which was in use from the 1600s and – in East Greenland – up to the 1930s.

Up to eight families lived in the common house, each with its bed platform and each with its lamp area outside the post separating the stalls. Opposite the beds was a wall with gut windows, containing the entrance passage, a low tunnel sunken in relation to the house. Here the dogs huddled in cold weather, the children played, and various things were stored in the cool air. As warm air rises, the house space higher up was often rather hot from the many blubber lamps. There might also be a mask in the entrance passage. Otherwise these relatively rare house masks were placed on the east wall facing the direction of the sunrise. There was no decoration in the house, no carved posts or painted skins. However, the curtain skin in the summer tent was especially beautifully sewn, often in stripes of light, dark, and dyed gut. In the winter, people lived together in the common houses, helped each other with the hunting, and had a system of distributing the catch to make sure that the weak did not go hungry.

During the summer, the individual families lived by themselves in tents, and each kept its own catch. The tent was erected over an A-frame supporting a semicircle of poles. First a layer of skins was laid with the fur inside, and over it a layer of waterskins – depilated sealskin treated with oil to make it waterproof.

Settlements were established at suitable places in the terrain and close to the hunting grounds. The houses were built of native materials and

165 a-d. From a booklet af colored drawings by Isak of Igdlorpait, executed in South Greenland around the turn of the century: (a) Frederiksdal mission station and church; (b) People on their way to church; (c) Lichtenau church; (d) Greenlandic tents, and two people cooking food in the open. Pencil and watercolor. 4⅛″×6¹¹/₁₆″. The booklet is a companion piece to Isak's Picture Book *(see fig. 157). National Library of Greenland, Godthåb-Nuuk.*

thus blended in completely with the landscape (fig. 163). Indoors, the inhabitants gathered around the lamp, which provided warmth and where the cooking was done. They spent most of their time on the bed platform. Here the family slept, ate, and the women sewed or repaired skins. The flensing of animals, however, took place outside or on the floor.

The Norsemen brought their building practices with them from Iceland, and many ruins from those days are still found in Greenland. But it was with the introduction of Danish-Norwegian traditions by the merchants and missionaries following on Hans Egede's arrival in 1721 that building practices began changing in earnest (fig. 164). Lumber and builders were imported, as were nails, screws, glass, and paint, in the holds of sailing ships, steamships, and motor vessels shuttling across the North Atlantic.

The first European dwellings were whitewashed fieldstone and sometimes half-timbered houses, but mostly they were frame houses (figs. 165a-c). Most were painted in strong red and dark brown colors, but yellow, light blue, and Spanish green were also used, with white-bordered gables, windows, and doors – a style familiar in Norway, Sweden, the Faroe Islands, and on the Skaw. Anyone acquainted with the Scan-

166. *"A Great Hunter's House and the Houses of the Other, Ordinary Hunters." Painted by Isak of Igdlorpait around the turn of the century. Pencil and watercolor. 4¼"×6¹¹/₁₆". From* Isak's Picture Book. *National Library of Greenland, Godthåb-Nuuk.*

167. *"The Interior of a Destitute House during Famine." Woodcut by Rasmus Berthelsen (see p. 165), from a drawing. From the book* Greenlandic Woodcuts *(1860). 5⁵/₁₆"×8½". National Library of Greenland, Godthåb-Nuuk.*

dinavian winter darkness and fog knows that the white borders make the house visible from far away. The colors, made from dry pigments mixed with seal oil – an excellent wood preservative – gradually acquired symbolic value. Buildings belonging to the church and the Royal Greenland Trading Company were red, the salt house was white, the infirmary yellow, the telegraph department's building green, and the Greenland Technical Organization's blue.

These Scandinavian frame buildings with plank-and-lath siding, many-paned windows, and carved gable points represent an honest, solid style of building. It was often master artisans – at first Danish and later Greenlandic craftsmen as well – who designed and built churches, commercial buildings, the houses of Danish officials, the teachers' college, and so on. The Herrnhuters, or Moravian Brethren, who also evangelized in Greenland, were usually artisans, and many fine buildings are to their credit, such as the New Herrnhut mission station in Godthåb-Nuuk, which now forms part of the National Museum of Greenland.

The colonies that grew up around trading activity and the church – the start of the present-day towns – were characterized by these colorful frame structures. Often there would be a separate neighborhood of sod and stone houses, like the tent cities that mushroomed overnight for big occasions. Difference – and distance – were established between the "fine" houses of the Danes and the Greenlanders' earth hovels (fig. 166).

The imported style of building became fashionable. The sod house and entrance passage were put on top of the ground instead of being recessed into the terrain, and board walls and finished window frames were set into the sod walls inside. The bed platform was supplanted by table and

168. *"The Interior of a Prosperous House." Woodcut by Aron of Kangeq, from a drawing. From* Greenlandic Woodcuts. *5⁵/₁₆"×8½". National Library of Greenland, Godthåb-Nuuk.*

169. Wick trimmers, to arrange the moss in a blubber lamp. Here carved with a transverse pattern and topped with male and female heads. Collected in the Angmagssalik district in 1933 by Nico Tinbergen. Driftwood and iron, about 17¼" long. Museum voor het Onderwijs, The Hague.

chairs, and bought hardware, clocks, harmoniums, and pictures on the walls slowly gained a footing in Greenlandic houses.

As depicted, the prosperous house from the period of colonization has family bed platforms and blubber lamps, but it is a wooden house, and there are a table with coffee cups, a clock, a fiddle, and a picture of Christ on the Cross – a good example of the blend of cultures. By contrast, the destitute house is a picture of darkness and misery – a sod house with starving and despairing inhabitants. There is no doubt in the minds of the artists: affluence and well-being are synonymous with the new, the imported things. To be sure, the wooden houses were cold, poorly insulated, and more exposed to storms than sod houses, but nevertheless they became more and more commonplace, first in the towns but gradually in the outposts too (figs. 167 and 168).

In our century, World War II was a turning point. The Americans introduced the kerosene lamp, which replaced the blubber lamp, and gave the Greenlanders a taste for modern amenities. Since 1953 explosive development has taken place, particularly in the towns, which has given Greenland the appearance of a Western European industrialized society, with retail stores, a business life, and administration, education, and social structure that are an extension of Denmark. But the language and cultural and artistic traits are Greenlandic, so that at some time decoration and design based on Greenlandic tradition and thought will, it is hoped, make a breakthrough in the area of architecture. There is a growing consciousness of this on the part of housing associations, women's groups, and municipalities. The first efforts of Greenlandic artists at decorating buildings will be discussed in the section on painting.

Household utensils

One of the most basic objects for survival in the arctic regions was the lamp. Carved in soft soapstone, it appears in all cultural periods.

The small round and oval lamps of the Sarqaq and Dorset cultures can have been used only for lighting, while the large half-moon shaped lamps from the Thule period were used for heating and cooking as well. Seal or whale blubber was melted, and the resulting oil was the fuel. European whalers fetched cargoes of oil from the coasts of Greenland for the lamps of Europe, and during colonization, the Royal Greenland Trading Company set up a number of try works for rendering blubber. The last was closed down as late as the 1950s.

It was the man who carved the lamp, but it was the woman's property, often her dowry, and it was a matter of honor for the woman to tend the lamp, to be responsible for the perpetuation of the flame. The lamp had no decorative carvings, but had a very beautiful form. Miniature lamps have been found as toys or funerary gifts, and smaller lamps may have been used on shorter journeys.

In contrast, the wick trimmer – the stick with which the lamp moss or cotton grass was arranged as a wick – was often carved (fig. 169). Standing on a tripod of wood and with a stone pot hanging over the flame, the lamp was the center of the house or tent, around which the shivering or hungry gathered. Above the pot hung the drying rack, a wooden lattice on which wet clothes or *kamik*s were laid to dry.

Pots, also carved from soapstone, which kept the heat well, were usually deep and designed for boiling large chunks of meat – magnificent rectangular stone vessels, dark from absorbed grease and soot. Skin pots were used in earlier times. Food was cooked in them using boiling stones, which were heated in the fireplace and eased down into the water.

Spoons were made of wood, or the shoulder blade of a bear. The fish strainer was especially beautiful, with its three holes reminiscent of a little face.

Trenchers to put the meat on were carved from wood, with pieces of bone inlaid in the edges so that they wouldn't get worn down. Various cups and ladles were made of wood or baleen, or from a narwhal's jaw. Vessels were formed by pinning a wood chip around a bottom and pinning or stitching it together at the side. The handle might be decorated with bone beads, and small bone figures might be riveted around the outside. In figure 170, the little cup is covered with tiny, detailed effigies of humans and animals: a row of women with their topknots, then a row of men and three rows of animals – mostly seals, but also narwhal, bear, birds, and many whitefish. A figure resembling a pair of spectacles is a sinew thread reel. Finally, there are four mystical symbols reminiscent of a seal's hindquarters, the sign of Toornaarsuk. It is a sumptuous picture gallery to find on so small an object.

The same lavishness with riveted figures is seen on water buckets. With their exquisite sepal form and the figures on the precisely fitted staves (the Greenlanders were handy at the cooper's craft, which they further displayed in making barrels for the try works), these buckets represent Greenlandic craftsmanship as its most beautiful (see fig. 140). A refinement was to make one stave hollow, so that water from thawed snow could be drunk through a bone drinking straw fitted at the upper edge. Buckets for urine were also made of wood and handsomely carved, though not as richly decorated as water buckets. Urine was kept under the bed platform and was used for many purposes, such as washing the hair and tanning.

Wooden objects with riveted figures were made in East Greenland in particular, and there are older artists still living who are masters of the technique. Chests and boxes especially were decorated in this manner.

The chest was carved from wood, with the pieces tenoned or pinned together. Sinuate and straight bone bands divided the surface into fields on which the figures were riveted. On the lid there was generally some tableau, such as a song contest, or a situation from everyday life, such as sled-driving or hunting. House, tent, kayak, and *umiak* were also displayed. The figures were fastened upright on the lid or attached at right angles to the sides, in semi-relief, which was usually frontal, though there were no strict rules as to the configuration. In some instances human effigies lack arms, like the wooden dolls of the Thule culture, and in others both arms and feet are included. The closure was ingeniously constructed of bone, and the hinges were made from the skin of the bearded seal (fig. 171).

In our century, such chests, originally tool chests, have come to be used as fine gifts, several having been made expressly for the royal family. Obviously they are more appropriate for Danish homes than eyeshades, kayak stands, or throwing sticks.

This brings us to the subject of functional objects made for Danish use. The merely decorative object – superfluous bric-a-brac and souvenirs – was nonexistent in Eskimo culture, where everything was purpose oriented and functional. Ornamentation, color, and figures probably had an aesthetic effect, but they were always necessarily related to the hunt, survival, and religion. The new objects are basically also expressive of a functionalistic way of thinking: What do these people want? What do they need that we can carve for them?

The new values are evident in the objects the Greenlanders made for Danes. Many ashtrays were carved from soapstone, as were writing sets, paperweights, things that would look good on the polished desk of the colony manager. And the Greenlanders themselves acquired European habits, quickly becoming very partial to tobacco and carving pipes for themselves, such as the one made of walrus ivory in figure 172, where

170. Cup from East Greenland collected by Gustav Holm in 1884-85, who describes it as "Fashioned from a thin-scraped chip, bent together and pegged around the outside of a thick wooden bottom." Wood, decorated with relief figures of people, seal, whitefish, bear, birds, solar eyes, and Toornaarsuk, all of walrus ivory. Handle of sinew thread. 2¾" high. National Museum, Copenhagen.

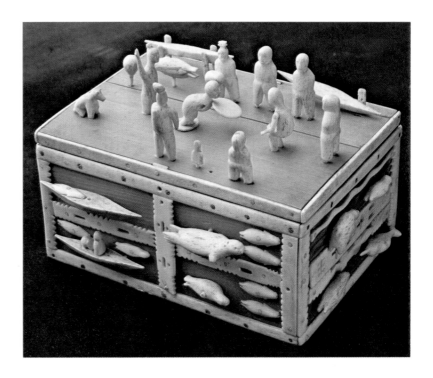

171. Chest from East Greenland acquired by the polar explorer and sculptor Eigil Knuth in the 1930s. Driftwood with riveted edging strips and relief figures of ivory; on the lid, freestanding figures, representing a drum quarrel. Such chests were the man's property, intended to contain tools and small personal belongings. They were especially beautifully decorated in East Greenland, but were in use everywhere in the country. In The Life and Living of the Greenlanders, *Lars Dalager reports: "At a death, the deceased's kayak, harpoons and arrows, along with the little chest wherein are kept knives, bits, drills, little bones, which he used daily, are placed in the grave to rot so that, according to the poor delusion of the living, they may serve the deceased in the next world." The modern chest depicted here is 4³/₈" high and 7¹/₁₆" long. Greenlanders' House, Copenhagen.*

walrus and bear are decoratively entwined around the bowl, as though the knife still preferred whittling the beloved animals.

People learned to have pictures on the wall or standing in frames, and they carved soapstone frames like the one in figure 173. The clock, too, was one of the new things the Danes appeared to set great store by, dividing their days and tyrannizing their surroundings with it. "Remember, such-and-such o'clock on the dot!" The Greenlanders had no clocks, but lived in harmony with nature and were accustomed to being guided by the rhythm of the days, the seasons, and the tides. They let the weather gods decide whether it was the right moment to begin a journey, go hunting, or stay put. At many colony complexes, a bell was set up, which the colony manager rang when the workers were supposed to meet at their jobs, and for lunch break and quitting time, just like the school bell. Later the bell was replaced by the factory whistle.

This new demand – punctuality, minding the clock, "stress" – was strange for the Greenlanders, and seemed rather ridiculous to them. The Danes, however, attached great importance to it. To arrange one's day according to the little mechanism was almost a virtue in itself.

How appropriate, then, that the Greenlander who carved a clock case for the trading post manager at Upernavik in the 1880s practically made it into a little temple for the god of the new era, constructed of wood, bone, and baleen. With lion's feet, corbiesteps, and three crosses, it almost looks like a mausoleum – but turn it around and a whale's fluke has come in by the back door (figs. 174*a* and *b*). The Greenlander, for

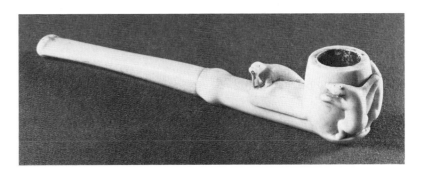

172. Pipe with carved animal figures (walrus and polar bear) carved by an unnamed Eskimo artist and given to Kaj Birket-Smith by a colleague in 1936. Walrus ivory, 6¹/₈" long, bowl 1⁵/₁₆" high. National Museum, Copenhagen.

whom cult and hunting and daily life were an indivisible unity, thought it natural that the symbol of the new religion, the cross, should decorate a box containing the divider of the white man's day.

The clock case is made with the superb, craftsmanly skill that justified the initiative taken by some of the people involved in trade in the nineteenth century. The colony managers of the northern towns proposed handicrafts production as an occupation for hunters who had moved to the colony on account of poor hunting conditions and did not have much chance of earning a living. A "sample board" was sent around (fig. 175) with a needle, an awl, initials, spoons for mustard and salt, the latter obviously copies of silver spoons – marvelously skilled carving, but from an artistic point of view disheartening, in that these things were proffered as production prototypes to a people who already possessed so sure a sense for exact and beautiful design.

What else did the Danes want? A belt buckle (fig. 176) carved with exotic excrescences for a Danish lady, perhaps copied from a fashion magazine. Other necessary articles in a Danish household, such as a cake knife (fig. 177) and a bottle opener (fig. 178), could be given beautifully carved handles and presented, as in this case, as gifts to the wife of the trading company manager.

There are those who would say that if this is not art, why deal with it here? If such objects are hybrid abortions, expressive only of cultural confusion, wouldn't it be better to pass them by in silence? I don't think so. You can't expect art and culture to remain static, as though preserved in alcohol. Art thrives on influences and development, and it is proper to call attention even to bad influences. From the earliest times, Greenlandic art has been realistically oriented. What is practical and suitable? the artist appears to be thinking. How is the material best utilized? How can I best portray the forces of evil I must propitiate? Formerly, everything had a function – implements, kayak, *umiak,* dog-sled, household utensils, masks, drums, Now a new era has arrived, with altogether different needs; with a new religion, money, hardware, imported materials. It is realistic not to carve for oneself when one can buy the things one needs. One carves for the Danes in order to get money.

173 a. *"The Prophet Habakkuk Dances around the Graves with His Followers." Drawn by Kristoffer Kreutzmann in Kangaamiut at the beginning of the 1900s. Pencil and watercolors, 4³/₄″×8¹/₁₆″. Carved soapstone frame, 12⁵/₁₆″ long, ³/₄″ thick.*

173 b. *Reverse of the above. Frame and support extending 2³/₄″ carved from a single piece of soapstone. Made for Karla Simonÿ in Sukkertoppen, ca. 1905. Private collection.*

174 a. *Clock case for a pocket watch. West Greenland, 1880s. Whalebone with edging strips and inlay of narwhal ivory, 8¹/₂″ high. Museum of Trade and Shipping, Elsinore.*

174 b. *Reverse of the above. The naturalistically carved whale's fluke is also of whalebone. The clock case is opened from above.*

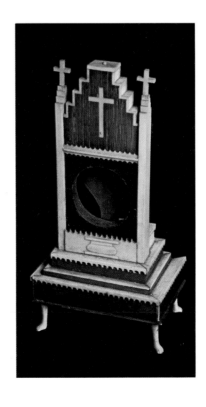

175. Sample board with needle, stiletto, initials, salt and mustard spoons. Carved by an unnamed artisan in North Greenland, where in the 1880s the trading post manager initiated an attempt at employing the Greenlanders in handicrafts. Narwhal ivory, 5¹¹/₁₆″×3⁵/₈″. Museum of Trade and Shipping, Elsinore.

176. Belt buckle carved ca. 1918 for Olga Borchersen, wife of the doctor in Sukkertoppen. Walrus ivory, 3¹⁵/₁₆″×2³/₁₆″, ³/₁₆″ thick. Private collection.

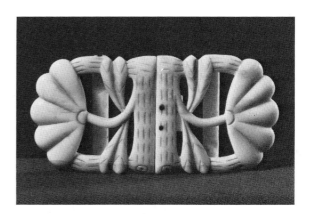

177. Cake knife. Handle carved by Ado Stach in Julianehåb, ca. 1970, for Lone Borchersen, wife of the trading-post manager. Sperm-whale ivory, 4¹/₁₆″ long, 1¹³/₁₆″ broad. Private collection.

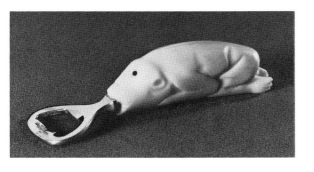

178. Bottle-opener. Handle carved by Ado Stach in Julianehåb in 1970 for Lone Borchersen. Sperm-whale ivory, 4″×1⁵/₈″. Stach noticed that the handles on Mrs. Borchersen's cake knife and bottle opener were defective, and so offered to carve new ones. Private collection.

The clock case and the soapstone picture frame are representative of a period of transition, and they are included in order to denote the new demands of art. Obviously, the boundary between art and artisanry is vague, though to the latter category belong the many models of kayaks, *umiak*s, and miniature dwellings. As handicraft, these are very successful. The artist was on home ground, knew precisely how the details should be rendered. That was how he maintained his recollection of the old culture.

But other functional household objects evidence a difficult balance between use and the new concept of art. Consider the carved board with many small mask faces in figure 179, intended to be hung on the wall – as what? A happier result is seen in a segment of a walrus's upper jaw with the tusk socket forming a neat cigarette cup and the smaller teeth carved as faces – a gift from the National Council to the governor (fig. 180).

Many candlesticks were carved from soapstone, but nearly all as copies of brass models. An ancient Eskimo fabulous monster lent its back to be an Advent candelabrum (fig. 181). Equally curious is a soapstone tobacco jar (fig. 182) whose front is a big jolly face with the cap as lid – here humor has gotten the upper hand. The Greenlandic imagination and humor frequently penetrate. Slowly, a liberated art is developed, divorced from function and from its original context, but joined as by an umbilical cord to the old culture and with the heritage of craftsmanship as secure ballast.

179. Carved board with attached relief figures in the form of tiny masks. Recent East Greenland household craft, probably from the 1950s. Board of bone, 3⅛″×8⁷/₁₆″. Masks of walrus ivory. National Museum, Copenhagen.

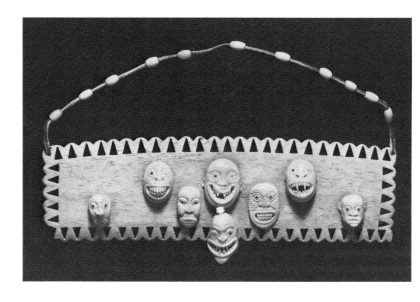

181. Advent candelabrum in the shape of an animal representing the legendary worm Quperdlugessuaq, carved by Qargutsiaq of Thule for Annelise and Ingmar Egede in 1956. Walrus ivory, about 9″ long. Private collection.

180. Cigarette cup given to district governor C. F. Simonÿ in his capacity as National Council chairman in 1946 by the artist, National Council member Karl Kreutzmann of Kangaamiut. Walrus jaw with teeth, the tusk socket forming a natural cup. 2⁹/₁₆″ high. Private collection.

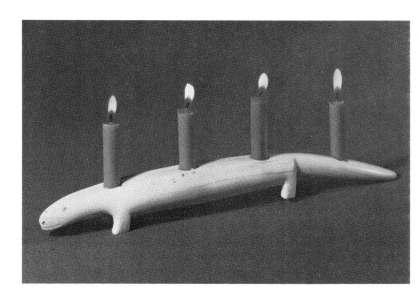

Dolls and toys

The first delicate little sculptures from Greenland that we know of are from the Dorset culture: a woman with a topknot, a man wearing a suit with a high collar – strong, taut bone figures. We have many wonderful wooden figures from the Thule culture, most without arms and feet and with flat faces, but some with facial features. All are either dolls or amulets. If I recall my own childhood rightly, some of my dolls came very much alive for me – an observation everybody has probably made. A toy figure, a doll, can easily acquire significance beyond the original intention and value appropriate to an amulet – another area where concepts are fluid and where it is most likely our eagerness to determine what is "art" that is inappropriate.

However that may be, these dolls are wonderful sculptures, and a very strong thread runs from them to modern Greenlandic sculpture. They are quite different, despite common traits, and have individual features both in face and body. The artists made much of depicting the body, though the dolls were often intended to be dressed (fig. 183).

Look at the exuberant fullness of the forms in figure 113 and notice the little differences: one is wearing *naatsit* (the tiny house briefs), another has the nipples indicated, a third a wonderful fat belly – sensual, life-affirming figures. Or see the expressive strength radiating from the buxom woman in figure 184. Women especially are portrayed with great feeling.

There are also taut, firm lines, as in the two broad-shouldered personages in figure 185 – with their unusually slender waists and pointed headgear, they almost belong to another style. Perhaps they mark a transition from the Thule culture. In its facial markings, the doll in figure

182. Tobacco jar, carved as a bust, with the cap forming the lid. Carved by Johannes Rosing in Kangaamiut, ca. 1930. Light soapstone, 3¾" high. National Museum, Copenhagen.

183. Partially dressed doll couple. Both figures without arms, but with feet indicated. No particulars to find, but probably from around the turn of the century. Wood, cloth, and skin. She, 3¼" high; he, 3⁹⁄₁₆". National Museum of Greenland, Godthåb-Nuuk.

185. *Two female figures from West Greenland. Thule culture, with pointed heads, broad shoulders, and kamiks indicated. Driftwood, about 4¾″ high. National Museum of Greenland, Godthåb-Nuuk.*

184. *Female figure with topknot resting on the neck. East Greenland. Collected in the Angmagssalik district around the turn of the century. Driftwood, 4½″ high. National Museum, Copenhagen.*

186. *Male figure, without arms and with truncated legs. No particulars as to find. Possesses points of similarity with Samoyed carvings of human figures from Siberia found driven ashore. Driftwood, about 4″ high. National Museum of Greenland, Godthåb-Nuuk.*

187. *Male figure from East Greenland collected by Pastor Kristian Rosing, who was active as missionary in Angmagssalik in the early 1900s. Driftwood, about 3⅛″ high. National Museum of Greenland, Godthåb-Nuuk.*

186 is reminiscent of finds from the Dorset period (e.g., the bottom of an amulet box, fig. 3*b*) while the truncated legs place him in the Thule era. The man with the fat belly and the decorated face in figure 187 is not immediately perceived as being a doll, but rather as a cult effigy.

But other small figures have been found wearing clothes, so one is more certain of their function – they are dolls to dress and play with. The clumsy body in figure 188 is nothing without clothes. In the couple in figure 183, the man has a delicately whittled face, while the woman has to settle for an elegant topknot.

The carved block of wood in figure 189 is packed with faces, and Gustav Holm, who collected it, termed it a toy. But in what way? With its swarm of spirit faces, it would be more comprehensible as an amulet. Maybe someone thought that an only child would find a happy pastime in this bunch of faces like a crowd of siblings.

Stiff wooden dolls without arms, totally frontal and having truncated legs and no feet – torso dolls – were long in use on the east coast. In the 1960s a man in Scoresbysund carved a wooden doll (fig. 190) for a little girl, with the words: "Now I'll make you a doll the way a real doll is supposed to be." It turned out to be very much like the Thule figures (fig. 113), but the hairdo was the saucepan cut that became fashionable around the turn of the century.

On the west coast, it is said of Johannes Kreutzmann (see page 44) that at first he carved figures as dolls for his children and only gradually came to regard them as works of art of interest to a wider public. His figures may not so much be to play with and dress as to contemplate. However, the owner of figure 191 relates that "Peter" was loved by all the children

189. Wooden block with carved faces of inersuak*s* – *supernatural beach dwellers, characterized by flat noses. A toy collected by Gustav Holm in the Angmagssalik district in 1884-85. Driftwood, 2¼″ high. National Museum, Copenhagen.*

188. *Two dolls, one without facial features, arms, or feet, and wearing an anorak of skin; the other with facial features but completely lacking limbs. Collected in the Angmagssalik district in 1933 by Nico Tinbergen. Wood and skin, 4¹³/₁₆″ and 4⅛″ high. Museum voor het Onderwijs, The Hague.*

of the family and was dragged around the lawn, brought in to enjoy the Christmas tree, and looked upon as a living being.

Most dolls are made of wood, although there is a collection of bone dolls from Upernavik from the end of the 1800s (fig. 192). Executed in a very personal style, with small, round heads and broad, flat chests, they bring to mind a modern sculptor like Henry Moore. The hands look as though they were grasping implements or oars and are delicately attached with tiny bone rivets. In one of the figures, the frontality is broken, and in another mobility has been introduced – when you rotate a stick attached to a string pulley, the man moves from side to side.

Mobility came with articulated dolls, whether they were an indigenous invention or copies of articulated porcelain dolls. The face of the drum dancer doll in figure 193 does not seem very nice for a toy for children, but his movements were probably funny. The dolls in figures 194*a* and *b* are both articulated and were made in East Greenland in the middle of this century. In spite of the flood of factory-made dolls, the art of doll

190. Doll without arms from Scoresbysund, carved by Peter Pike in 1970 as a gift for Maja Chemnitz. Wood and paint, about 9½″ high. Private collection.

191. "Peter," carved by Johannes Kreutzmann in the 1920s for Pastor Hother Ostermann in Jakobshavn. Painted wood, 26¾″ high. Private collection.

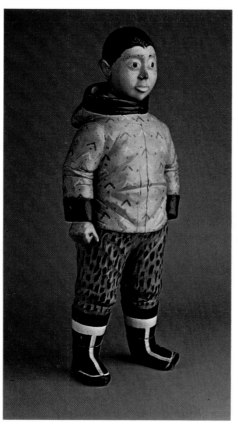

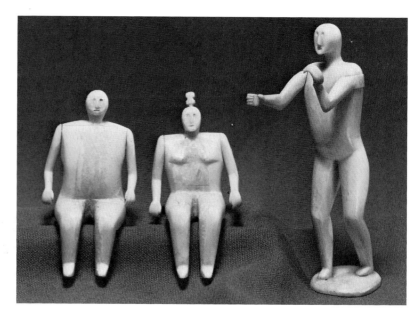

192. Sitting man and woman, and walking man. Carved by an unknown West Greenlandic artist presumably in the 1800s, and purchased for the Danish National Museum in 1881. In the museum's records, it is observed that the figures are "a breach with Greenlandic accomplishments," and indeed the style is not found in other examples. Walrus ivory, arms attached with bone rivets, eyes drilled and originally inlaid with black material. Walking man, 4⁵⁄₁₆″ high. National Museum, Copenhagen.

193. Articulated doll from East Greenland collected in the Angmagssalik district in 1924 by colony manager A. T. Hedegaard. Driftwood, 8$^{11}/_{16}$" high. Eyes of walrus ivory with lead inlay, head attached with a piece of thong, legs articulated at the hip, arms at shoulder and elbow. It is possible that the doll represents a masked drum dancer – there is space in the hands to hold a drum and drumstick, which may have been lost along with clothing. National Museum, Copenhagen.

carving has not been forgotten. In 1973, in the home of a Greenlandic artist, I saw a half-finished articulated doll, which was finished at my request – with many apologies and explanations that it was no good. In my opinion, however, it was really good and amusing, and at the same time evidenced a tradition.

Nor has the art disappeared from the west coast; and in South Greenland especially, fine examples of hand-carved dolls are to be found, often wearing the beautifully embroidered full traditional dress. The Greenlandic Folk Art Association has seen to collecting the last hand-made dolls (figs. 195a and b). A new initiative is being taken by women's associations, local groups working collectively in sewing the district's native costume for dolls. Unfortunately, the dolls themselves are not carved in Greenland but made of vinyl in Hong Kong. Today, dolls are exclusively souvenir objects, whose only value lies in the correctness of their costume.

The same thing applies to toys as a whole: traditions vanish with the advance of the modern era and factory-produced toys. But surely this is in keeping with the mission of all toys: to prepare children, through play, for the adult world and its demands. Today the demand is to adapt oneself to modern industrialized society, whose mechanization and restlessness are naturally reflected in the toys modern children use.

There is no denying that artistic excellence is in the old carved wooden figures: small seals, bears, and birds (fig. 196), perhaps used for target practice with the miniature implements the boys trained their skills in making. The most common games of the boys were hunting and kayak paddling. The girls had little *ulo*s and sewing tools, and their own little lamps. Gustav Holm writes of the daily life of the Angmagssalikians: "Sometimes there is also found a little playhouse for the children, equipped with a passageway, bed platform, etc. Here the children have their lamps burning and it is here that they stay during the winter." Even if they did not always have a playhouse, the children probably often had carved replicas of various household effects. A lot of "doll's house furniture" is thus found in Thule: tiny figures, pots, cups, and primus stoves, all carved minutely in bone.

But there are many other games: wrestling, Indian wrestling, football, cat's cradle, and various kinds of whirligigs and puzzles, all as popular among adults as among children – particularly singing games and especially the drum dance, which was known all over the Eskimo area. The

194 a and b. *Doll couple – woman in full dress, man in hunting dress – purchased in Denmark in the 1930s by the sculptor Robert Jacobsen. Driftwood, sealskin,*

195 a. *Couple in West Greenland full dress. Articulated dolls; bodies carved by Anders Nielsen, heads by Emanuel Thomsen, clothes sewn by Malene Nielsen, all of Sydprøven, in 1964. 18⅞″ high. Association for Greenlandic Folk Art, Godthåb-Nuuk.*

195 b. *Couple in North Greenland dress made in 1964 in Jakobshavn. Head and hands carved from wood, 18⅜″ and 17⅝″ high.*

drum, however, possesses a significance making it incorrect to categorize it as a toy, even though the drum dance occurred as a game and entertainment. The drum dance had a specific cultic function in song contests, which were judicial decisions, and in shamanism. The drum was thus an instrument used both in play and in earnest. It consists of a circular wooden rim over which is stretched a drumhead of skin, preferably from a bear's paunch (fig. 197). A handle, often carved with a face, is attached to the rim. The rhythm is beaten with the drumstick on the underside of the rim, and the sound varies with the tautness and humidity of the drumhead. The stick never touches the drumhead itself.

Besides the drum dance, there are two amusements related to the theme of this book by the elegance of their design. One is the cup-and-pin game *ajagaq,* which is still known and played. A bone with various indentations and holes is attached by a string to a stick. The idea is to toss the bone so that it lands lightly and elegantly with the stick through one of the holes.

cloth, and beads, about 11¾" high. Carved with articulated joints in shoulders, elbows, hips, and knees. Private collection.

196. Three bird figures and two polar bear figures from East Greenland, collected in the Angmagssalik district by Nico Tinbergen in 1933. Driftwood, 3⁹⁄₁₆" to 5⅛" long. Museum voor het Onderwijs, The Hague.

197. Two drums. The oval drum is from Thule, collected by H. P. Steensby, who traveled in North Greenland and the Thule district in 1909. Bone and polar bear paunch, about 11¾" long. The round drum is a child's drum from East Greenland, collected by colony manager Johan Petersen in 1911. Wood and polar bear paunch, about 8¼" in diameter. National Museum, Copenhagen.

The oldest known sculpture from Greenland happens to be an *ajagaq* (fig. 198), delicately carved with closely set faces. Eyes, nostrils, and ears are the holes in the *ajagaq* in which the stick is supposed to land. The total effect brings to mind the Dorset block with the many heads (see fig. 2), and this bone might very well be from the same period.

Another toy I would like to emphasize is a puzzle with an erotic point, called *pulaartut*, or "going visiting." A system of strings ending in two beads or figures – usually a crudely carved man and woman – is arranged on a frame. By the clever untying of knots, the idea is to get the figures placed together on the same side of the frame. Hence the name of the game – going visiting. Often the little figures are elegantly carved, of the same type as the concise, stylized torso figures of the Thule period.

The attitude of Greenlandic parents to their children does not appear to have changed. Gustav Holm relates: "They grow up in the most unfettered freedom. The parents feel an indescribable love for them, and never punish them no matter how recalcitrant they are." Today's Greenlandic children are allowed to do pretty much what they want. Nowhere else have I seen such universal indulgence toward children. They are regarded as real little people with a will of their own. Later, the grown-up children often feel great devotion to their parents. The love is returned.

Dress – function and materials, ornamentation and colors

Togetherness and close fellowship are expressions I have already used in describing the self-sufficient hunting society. The woman's contribution to society was just as indispensable as the man's. A woman was praised not only for her ability to bear children, but also for her skill at sewing. A great hunter must have a clever wife to take care of the catch, dress the skins, and sew impermeable, durable clothing and kayak coverings. Often he needed two wives to do the work.

With the needle (fig. 199) as her tool, the woman fulfilled her central position in the mutuality, creating such wonderful things with it that the following section really ought to be called "Artists of the Needle." In an extension of the practical, appropriate, and precise craftsmanship embodied in the sewing of kayak and *umiak* coverings, tents, gut curtains, bed skins, and so on, we will now turn to dress and the profusion of creative work flowering in connection with its history. It is the story of women artists, just as sculpture – so far as the old era is concerned – was the domain of men.

Dress is the beginning of a house, a shelter one erects around one's body. But it quickly becomes more than that – a signal to the world at large about one's gender, age, material circumstances and membership in a particular tribal group. In this way, traditions are created, and thus style. Changes occur within style – that is, fashions – and some of these phenomena are lasting and transform style.

To write about the history of Eskimo clothing with anything approaching comprehensiveness would require a separate book. Here I will make do with presenting samplings from old and modern times: from East Greenland, Thule, and West Greenland, from men's and women's dress. The aim in each case is to elucidate an artistic effect.

First, something needs to be said about the raw materials and the craft. The principle material was, and is, skin – skins of seal, caribou, bear, fox, dog, raven, auk, eider duck, and fish. Knowledge of the properties of the various skins was huge, and the art of dressing skins is still far from

198. Ajagaq – an ancient Eskimo toy. Grave find from the Upernavik district, without further particulars. Probably early Dorset culture. Caribou antler, about 4⅜" high. National Museum, Copenhagen.

199. Iron needles (stuck in a piece of cork). Manually produced, without the use of a forge. Collected in the Angmagssalik district in 1884-85 by Gustav Holm. National Museum, Copenhagen.

200. Washed and scraped sealskin stretched on the drying frame. Photograph taken by Anne Bang in 1969 in Upernavik. Everywhere in Greenland, even in apartment buildings in the largest towns, one sees sealskins stretched on a frame in this manner.

forgotten. The skin of the bearded seal was thick and strong. As its native name – belt seal – implies, it was used for belts, thongs, harpoon lines, and dog-whips; for lashing sleds and boats and for *kamik* soles. Caribou skin was light and warm but not durable, while bear skin was both warm and strong. Skins of other varieties of seal were prepared in different ways. The skin was scraped, washed, tanned, dried in the shade; bleached in frost and sun, perhaps depilated, treated with fat again, perhaps dyed (fig. 200) – in other words, variations of modes of treatment that could produce a skin for almost any purpose. The paunches of the animals were used for drumheads and float bladders, and the intestines were inflated and dried and sewed together for curtains and gut shirts. The latter served as raincoats both at sea and at home in wet weather. The sinews were used as thread, after being split, frayed, "spun" by being rolled on the palms or the thighs, and braided into a thread of whatever gauge was desired. With furred skin juxtaposed against smooth and with light against dark, effective results were created (figs. 201*a* and *b*).

As decoration, skin embroidery was used in a combination of larger or smaller dyed and appliquéd squares of skin and trimmed with beads carved from ivory or the paw bones of foxes. The vertebrae of the smelt-like little fish capelin were used for beads, now and then dyed with blood. Glass beads quickly became a popular trade object, from contact first with the Norsemen and later with the Dutch whalers (fig. 202). In addition, there were stone beads made from a kind of green stone. When

201 b. *Closeup of the border's skin mosaic, the so-called* avigtat *embroidery.* Avigtat *means "something one takes apart," and the embroidery consists simply of tiny skin squares painstakingly composed into a pattern and sewn in place as invisibly as possible. National Museum, Copenhagen.*

201 a. Trouser embroidery from a West Greenland girl's dress, 1800s. Detail from vertical borders in front. Caribou skin and dyed, depilated sealskin, sewn with sinew thread.

imported glass beads became store merchandise, it turned out that small ones the size of capelin vertebrae were preferred. Imported cloth also became very popular – cotton cloth for anoraks, brocade and checked silk ribbon for the women's full dress (fig. 203), and woollen cloth for men's trousers. Danish clothing habits became more and more common and real skin harder and harder to get. During the period of transition, droll blends of clothing styles appeared, such as when the men went around with ties outside their anoraks (see fig. 58) and the women with Danish women's underwear outside their skins – the better to see the

202. Whaler's beads, trade goods in the 1600s and 1700s. The largest bead is about 3/4″ in diameter. Length of string, about 23 5/8″. National Museum, Copenhagen.

203. West Greenland women's full dress, worn here by Cecilie and Anike Frederiksen. Photographed in Kraulshavn by Keld Hansen in 1968.

204. The upper, visible part of the inner kamik*s in the woman's full dress. Topped by a border of black dog skin, followed by Danish (or European) elements in the national costume: a piece of lace and embroidered flowers in flat stitch. Photo by Anne Bang, 1973.*

lace! The much-coveted lace, it was soon discovered, could be placed as trim at the top of the *kamik* border (fig. 204).

In modern Greenland, fashion is entirely that of the western world, and there is no lack of anything. Some of the old traditions remain, however. Just about every man owns a white cotton anorak for confirmations, weddings, and celebrations, and many have a black anorak as well, for extra ceremonious occasions. Many also wear the anorak – made of blue pepper-and-salt cloth, for example – as everyday apparel. Women's full traditional dress is still seen, but it is on the wane, both because the genuine materials are costly to obtain and because it is exceedingly difficult to sew. The Greenlandic boots, the *kamik*s, are still being sewed both for children and adults (fig. 205), but there is no denying the ubiquitousness of the rubber boot. Nowadays *kamik*s are worn mostly in connection with traditional dress. Ornamentation from the traditional dress is commonly seen on bags, cushions, and various decorative objects. It is as if decorative skin mosaic and beadwork had been removed from their context and were trying to live their own artistic life on matchboxes and coasters. Their proper function is gone, but it must not be overlooked that needlework technique and the sense of color are being maintained in this way.

The tools used in preparing dress materials were the curved woman's knife (the *ulo*) and various stones to rub, scrape, and soften the skin. Hard skin could also be chewed soft, and during scraping the skin was held taut with the teeth, so that basically they, too, were a tool.

Then there were needles, preferably triangular or rectangular in section the better to penetrate the skin. They ranged from the big, flat needles used for covering boats to delicate embroidery needles. Of the latter, the missionary Henrik Glahn, who worked in West Greenland in the 1700s, relates: "These fine embroideries such as on boots, shoes, furs, by preference where they are coated with the beards of reindeer (NB. of old bucks), require such fine sewing needles as cambric sewing."

Originally, needles made of fishbones and small bird bones were used, or needles carved from bone. Later a metal needle was a much-coveted item. Many good skins, narwhal tusks, and gyrfalcons were given in exchange for needles, knives, and beads. If you could not barter for or otherwise get yourself a needle, the metal from shipwrecks would do. Nails and barrel hoops and fittings of all kinds were hammered out and made into needles and knife blades.

In a grave from the 1400s in the Upernavik district there was found an amulet belonging to a little boy: two miniature *kamik* soles in which there was fastened an iron needle – undoubtedly a good strong amulet. Naturally, it was wished that this child would always have well-sewn *kamik*s, and the metal needle was so desirable that it was itself a valuable amulet.

A needlecase, an awl, a gathering bone, a little sharp knife, a thimble, a roll of sinew thread, and a reel to twist the thread with – those were the rest of the requisites, and the same ones are still employed for sewing skins and skin embroidery. Otherwise, the sewing machine is industriously used. The thimble is not closed like ours, but consists of a ring (of skin from the bearded seal, for example) to be placed on the forefinger. The needle is held between the thumb and the long finger, and one always sews toward oneself.

The seams are often thrown seams, sewn so as to avoid hard edges against the skin. Forestitch is also used, and a seam may be reinforced by inlaying a thread along it, or covering it with tape. With another technique, the thread is not sewn all the way through the layer of skin. This is used for embroidery and (among the Polar Eskimos) to sew the sole onto the bootleg in a way that makes the boot watertight. Otherwise the sinew threads, by swelling up, made sure seams were tight in water and wet weather.

205 a. *Women's* kamiks *with knee piece. West Greenland. Inner* kamik *of sealskin with the fur inside, outer* kamik *of dyed depilated sealskin. Collected by Helge Bangsted's film expedition to the Umanaq district in 1925-26. Yellow pair, 18¹/₂″ from heel; width of top 9 ¹/₁₆″. Blue pair, 19⁵/₈″ long.*

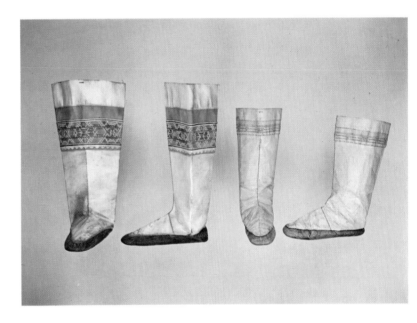

205 b. *Short outer* kamiks *with skin embroidery from West Greenland. Pair at left: gift from doctor and colony manager Christian Rudolf to the Danish National Museum, 1841. Pair at right: gift from Knud Rasmussen in 1906.*

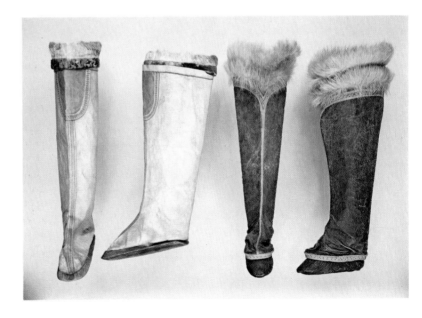

205 c. *Left: West Greenland women's* kamiks *with dyed knee pieces, predating 1834. Collected by assistant colony manager J. P. Engholm of Frederikshåb. Right: East Greenland women's* kamiks *from around the turn of the century. Note the special cut above the instep. National Museum, Copenhagen.*

206. The "jumpsuit" formerly worn when hunting whales. This example, the only one extant in the world, was collected in Frederikshåb prior to 1834 by J. P. Engholm, later colony manager in Holsteinsborg. Dark depilated sealskin, so-called waterskin. National Museum, Copenhagen.

In the beginning, clothes were simply a protection against the harsh climate of the arctic regions, in their simplest form an animal skin one crept into, and which followed the contours of the body as much as possible, allowing one to move as freely as possible. On the whole, Eskimo dress is reminiscent of an extra skin, either smooth or furred, that the person pulls on. This is especially true of the "jumpsuit," kayak jackets, and the hunter's everyday garb of furred sealskin (figs. 206 and 207).

The "jumpsuit" was a combination garment made of depilated, dark sealskin, oil-impregnated so that it was waterproof (hence the term "waterskin"). Anorak and trousers, mittens and *kamik*s were sewed together into a closed suit, something like a set of rompers with a hood. The only aperture was around the face. Of course there was an opening in the middle of the suit allowing the wearer to crawl inside, but it was tightly closed by means of a drawstring. The hood could also be drawn shut so that it closed against the face, and the wearer was completely protected against the intrusion of water. It was possible to inflate the suit through a button on the chest, making it warmer with the insulating layer of air. At the same time, it could function as a lifejacket if the wearer fell into the water.

This happened frequently. The "jumpsuit" was designed for whale hunting, and during both harpooning and flensing there was the risk of falling overboard, just as there was danger of the boat being capsized by the whale. Glahn writes of the suit: "Those who know well how to wear it can, in the most severe cold, stay in the water as long as they like."

Besides being eminently practical and functional, this total garment – which brings to mind flying suits and space suits – has its origins in a mythical-ritual past.

Many peoples have used whole animal skins in ritual functions. One vests oneself in the skin of the animal and thus takes on its soul – the costume is associated with the animal's attributes. Among the Indians of the Pacific Northwest (neighbors of the Eskimos), a whole bearskin was worn by the priest during religious ceremonies. That the "jumpsuit" was assigned special value above and beyond the practical is seen in a remark by Gustav Holm to the effect that there was still (in 1884) "one who out of superstition dresses in such a skin."

The kayak jacket – also made of waterskin – was an anorak with a hood designed to be drawn tightly around the face. The jacket could also be closed tightly around the waist and the wrists, and its bottom edge cinched around the wooden ring of the cockpit of the kayak. The jacket, which was often handsomely embroidered with tiny bits of white skin, had various drawstrings ornamented with carved bone beads, such as a cord like a decorative lanyard that held the hood securely in place. With a well-sewn and impermeable garment like this, the kayak man could roll his boat full circle without a drop of water getting in.

In summer, a so-called half-jacket was used – a kind of waistcoat or vest made of waterskin, whose bottom was cinched around the cockpit, while the upper part was secured with a drawstring up under the man's armpits. At the back, the half-jacket ended in a point continued by two suspenders with carved bone beads attached to them, which passed over the shoulders and were fastened in front. Occasionally, the hunter wore a short white anorak. White, depilated skin was the thinnest kind, as the layer of skin containing the roots of the hair was removed, in contrast to the dark and thicker waterskin.

The embroidery on the half-jacket is among the most beautiful made in Greenland. Growing organically out of the deck of the kayak, the light skin mosaics mark a culmination in the graphically effective ornamentation that flourished around the turn of the century, particularly in East Greenland. Both the half- and full jackets were strongly associated with the whole decoration of the kayak. Man and kayak, clothes and gear, constituted a unity of the man's and woman's artistic abilities.

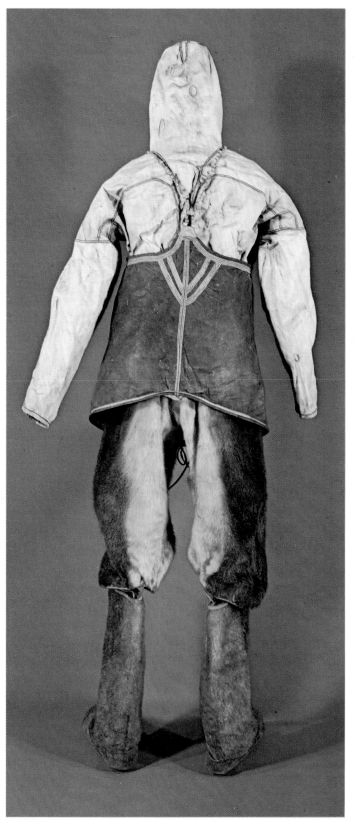 

207 a *and* b. *Back and front of a hunter's dress. Outer jacket of white depilated sealskin, embroidered with brown skin strips; half-jacket of dark waterskin embroidered with white skin strips; trousers of furred sealskin. Purchased by colony manager Johan Petersen in Angmagssalik in 1910, "by extraordinary allowance from the Administration for Greenland." National Museum, Copenhagen.*

208. *Hunter creeping in on a seal by imitating its movements when it tumbles on the ice in the spring sun. Drawn by Kârale Andreassen in the 1920s for colony manager A. T. Hedegaard, Angmagssalik. Signed "K. A." Sepia ink on paper, 4³/₄"×7¹/₂". Royal Engravings Collection, Copenhagen.*

The tight, closed, animal-like form also characterizes the man's everyday winter dress. With anorak, trousers, and *kamik*s of sealskin with the fur outside, he almost resembles a seal. The hood is close around the head, and neither neck nor waist are pronounced, so that the body forms a plump oval, which both in size, coloration, and streamlined shape is strongly reminiscent of the animal. The hunter avails himself of this resemblance in a specific hunting technique: when the seal is disporting itself on the ice in the spring sun, the hunter imitates its movements and wriggles in so close to the animal – which thinks the hunter is a member of its own species – that it may easily be harpooned or shot (fig. 208). It may be for the same reason that this dress is not ornamented, but is effective by its design and the pattern of the fur.

Just wherein lies the beauty of this everyday dress? First of all, in the use of the natural materials' own color and substance. In times like ours, with much use of synthetics – this could almost be called the age of acrylics and plastics – the color and play of the light and dark waterskin, in gut skins and furs, seems extraordinarily beautiful – nature's own colors, given shape in clothing that follows the contours of the body, gives effective protection against cold and moisture, and permits the human being to run, row, and throw a harpoon with the least possible hindrance.

The handsome cut was frequently emphasized with skin embroidery, arranged symmetrically and forming borders of miniscule geometric forms, usually squares. Borders or edgings of skin in contrasting colors accentuated the seams, and trim was applied at the cuffs, collar, and around the bottom of the anorak. In addition to their beautifying value, embroidered borders were used to connect important seams. Reinforcement of the angles formed in attaching the sleeves, or at the base of the hood was provided, for example. The vertical central seam of the half-jacket was also reinforced with embroidery that connected it with the upper edge of the garment.

In other words, the embroidery was practical and at the same time aesthetically effective, and both qualities were important for the outcome of the hunting. The practical aspect is obvious; as the Polar Eskimos say, "A man is the hunter his wife makes him." Without well-sewn and impermeable clothing, he could never succeed in the hard life of the hunter. That the handsomeness of the garb had a beneficial influ-

209. Hunting seal from a kayak, with harpoon and float bladder. Collected by Hinrich Rink in Godthåb in the years 1857-61, and pasted in a book sent to King Frederik VII. India ink and watercolors, done "by a boy at the colony of Godthaab," 3⅝″×6⅛″. The Queen's Reference Library, Copenhagen.

210. Boy and girl in present-day full dress. Photo taken in Julianehåb in 1978 by Ivars Silis.

ence on the hunting corresponds to the idea that "the animal would rather be caught by a beautifully carved harpoon" (see page 97) – in any case, Hans Egede relates that the Greenlanders dressed in their handsomest and newest clothes when rowing out to catch whales. He writes: "For whale fishing in particular they fit themselves out in their best finery, as for a wedding, lest the whale shun them, for he cannot abide uncleanliness."

Greenlandic dress is characterized by good cut, appropriate for the purpose. The half- and full jackets were designed for life in the kayak: closed snugly at face, wrists, and waist, but wide across the back and shoulders, so that forceful arm movements could be performed unhindered. The sleeves were attached at right angles to the waist, now and then slanting upwards at an even greater angle so that the hunter could execute a well-aimed throw of the harpoon without bursting his anorak. In a somewhat naive watercolor (fig. 209), we see how.

The short white anorak, which was worn together with the half-jacket, did not need to reach below the trousers' waistband, as there was not too much room in the kayak to begin with and the half-jacket prevented the entry of water. This short model was later made of cotton cloth and is now the formal dress for men and boys everywhere in Greenland (fig. 210).

The anorak had many forms, however. It was worn by children, women and men, and was made from many materials (figs. 211a – c). An anorak is a closed jacket, with or without a hood. In principle, it is a poncho – that is, a piece of whole skin or cloth with an opening in the middle for the head. But gradually, it came to be sewn together at the sides, and sleeves and a hood were added. Real anoraks are still sewn according to this principle, so that there are no shoulder seams. Closing devices are nonexistent on an anorak, apart from drawstrings with which to tighten the jacket openings.

Two skins, a front and a back, might also be used to make a shirt, in which the head of the animal formed the rear of the hood. The skins were sewed together at the shoulder, as this type of cut was used for inner jackets. But for outer jackets it was expedient that there be no shoulder seam, where water could penetrate. Points from the one skin might circle around to the other side and reinforce the base of the hood. Where the hood was attached gussets could be placed, usually of white skin (caribou paunch), and they might be reinforced by embroidery or bead trim. These gussets or points have the effect of vestiges of animal forelegs slung over the shoulder from the other skin, like the bottom flap on the front and, especially, the back of the anorak, which is reminiscent of the tail of an animal.

The latter features are especially emphasized in women's anoraks, for although Eskimo dress exemplifies what in our day is called unisex, there are differences. In principle, the same kind of clothing is worn by both sexes – women do not wear dresses, but always pants, and anoraks and *kamik*s are common to both. Nevertheless, there is strong identification as to gender, a complex of rules according to age, sexual maturity, marital status and so on, as to which colors and types of apparel are to be worn – all naturally subject to local variants.

Dress can be divided into three regions in Greenland, with clearly distinct types: the Thule district, East Greenland, and West Greenland. In each, development has assumed very different forms. Nor has steadfastness in the face of influences from European fashions been alike in the three areas – or, rather, the habits and bad habits of so-called civilization did not prevail everywhere in Greenland at the same time.

The suits mentioned here are from the period 1460 to 1960 – that is, a span of 500 years. Common to all of them is the fact that the separate elements – anorak, trousers, boots – are the same and are worn in two layers, the inner with the fur toward the body and the outer with the fur outside. As the clothes sit loosely against the body, a layer of air is formed between the two skins, which both insulates against cold and provides room for the evaporation of sweat.

Let me outline some local characteristics before delving into a few magnificent examples.

It is among the polar Eskimos of the Thule district that we encounter the community in modern Greenland that both racially and as regards livelihood is closest to the original Eskimos. Of approximately 800 individuals, most by far live from hunting. The kayak and the dog-sled are in use, as are many old hunting techniques. Virtually all the inhabitants are Greenlanders and some are said to be of pure descent.

The Thule district is centrally located in relation to the Eskimo immigration routes, but extremely isolated in relation to Denmark and Europe. It was here that the last mission station was established, as late as 1909. A year later, it was expanded to become a combined mission and trading station, under the leadership of Peter Freuchen, and at the energetic initiative of Knud Rasmussen the area was linked up with the rest of Greenland and Denmark. For many years, there was only one postal connection a year, but since the introduction of air transportation in Greenland and the American military association with Thule, contact has been lively.

The first contact the Polar Eskimos had with Europeans was in 1818, when the Englishman John Ross, in his search for the Northwest Passage, anchored his ship at the edge of the ice in Prince Regent Bay. As his interpreter, Ross had with him the West Greenlander Hans Zakæus, whom he had met in Scotland. The meeting with the Polar Eskimos took place on the ice, and with Zakæus as his intermediary Ross was successful in achieving communication of a kind and in exchanging gifts. The event was painted by Zakæus (see fig. 248), and in the picture we see that the Eskimos wear the familiar boots, trousers, and anorak with hood. The anoraks are edged with soft skin and have flaps both front and back, but it is difficult to distinguish further details of their dress.

In 1829, Ross again encountered a hitherto unknown group of Polar Eskimos and became good friends with them. From this expedition, Ross drew three Eskimos. The women wore anoraks with high, peaked hoods (having a median seam), a tongued flap in front, and an even longer one at the back. The bottom of the anorak is decorated partly with a border and partly with fringes all the way around. The boots are interesting, in that they end high up around the thigh in front, in a kind of skin stocking ornamented with a triangular pattern.

After Ross's visit – about which the Thule people could tell Knud Rasmussen stories when he encountered them for the first time in 1903 – whaling ships and several scientific expeditions came to the region. It was

211 a. *Gut skin anorak collected by catechist Jacob Olsen in 1924. Made by an old woman, born in Holsteinsborg but living in Fiskenæsset, who had sewn many anoraks of this kind. Gut skin sewn together in longitudinal stripes, edged with depilated sealskin. Back, with hood, 39⅜″ long. Breadth from cuff to cuff, 59″.*

211 b. *Child's anorak. Inner jacket of bird skin with the feathers inside, mittens of polar bear skin. Thule, early 1900s. Collected by the manager of the trading station in Thule, author Peter Freuchen.*

only during that period, when the American explorer Robert Peary visited the region (1891-1909), that the Eskimo way of life began to change. Peary made the Thule people dependent on firearms and on consumer goods such as sugar, coffee, tobacco, and cotton cloth, and considered setting up a trading station. But others had similar plans. It was Knud Rasmussen, with private support, who got a grip on this no-man's land, and among other things used it as his sallying-out place for the famous Thule expeditions. It was only in 1937 that the Danish government officially took over administration of the Thule district.

In this arctic land area, close to the North Pole, with four months of total winter darkness and so much cold and ice that the kayak can be used no more than two months of the year, the dress is the opposite of the conditions – light colored, lightweight, and warm. With an inner jacket made of skins of the little auk, guillemot, or eider duck; trousers of blue fox; outer jacket of seal or fox; inner *kamiks* of seal edged with polar bear skin, the Polar Eskimo woman was dressed beautifully and very warmly. The man, too, wore inner clothing made of bird skins, but the trousers were of polar bear skin. The children were copies of the adults, but chiefly wore fox fur.

The suits are admirable for wearing on long dog-sled trips, and with their sled-driving expertise and their practical clothing, many Polar Eskimos have been of great help to various scientific dog-sled expeditions.

The colors of the clothing are nature's own. Polar bear skin, sealskin, and arctic fox impart a noble, delicate color scheme, with white-gold, silver-gray, chalk-white, and light bluish tints. Most characteristic of the dress are the long women's *kamiks*, which cover the whole leg all the way to the hip and are made of depilated sealskin, bleached completely white in the frost and decorated on top with a gracefully waving fringe of long polar bear hair. In the years following 1930, when Thule acquired a large trading store, the upper part of the women's dress was replaced by a hoodless anorak of flowered cotton cloth, bordered on top by tiny nee-

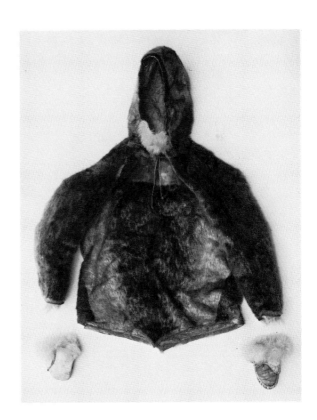

211 c. *Man's anorak. Outer jacket of sealskin. Note chin protector of polar bear skin. Point in front, seam longitudinal with sleeve; a type worn in Thule well into this century (see fig. 215). National Museum, Copenhagen.*

212. Two young women from Thule. Photograph taken in 1909 by botanist and physician T. Krabbe. Arnaruniak, about twenty one, standing; and Inadtliak, about twenty four, sitting. Both are wearing amaut, *apparent from the long straps to be tied around the back to prevent the infant from sliding down. According to Dr. Krabbe, Arnaruniak had to wear her hood up as expiation for an unfortunate childbirth. Note the hip-length* kamiks *of bear skin, the one pair with long knee gussets. Photo archive of the National Museum, Copenhagen.*

dlepoint embroidery or an edge of white dog skin – really pretty with the long white boots and trousers of blue or white fox. But for a long time an outer jacket with the old characteristics was used: flaps both in front and behind, a somewhat peaked hood, and the back cut roomily so that a child could be carried in it.

In 1909 the physician T. Krabbe took a photograph of two young women (fig. 212). The seated one is wearing a bird skin anorak with the hood finished off in a point in front. On the girl who is standing, we can distinctly see the point on the front of the anorak and the peaked hood with centerline. On the whole, the dress has elegant lines. From the stripe on the hood, the eye glides down over the edgings on the sleeves and further down along the long gussets in the central seam of the front of the *kamik*s.

This latter characteristic is also seen on the women's *kamik*s from the earliest Greenlandic dress found to date, the mummies found in 1978 in the Umanak district, which goes back to ca. A.D. 1460 (fig. 213). Also on the dress from this find are points on the bottom of the anorak, plus a somewhat peaked hood, so some elements of dress have maintained themselves through the centuries.

In another comparison with old dress – namely the furred sealskin anorak in the earliest painting of Greenlanders (fig. 214), which was painted in Bergen in 1654 – there are areas of similarity to the type of dress worn by the Polar Eskimos. We see in the painting both the transverse piece across the chest, the pointed base of the hood, median trim on the hood, and gussets, which are here quite long.

The suits of the Polar Eskimos are not decorated with embroidery or beads. Their design uses simple effects with beautiful materials in a delicate color scheme, and a cut with deep roots in the history of Greenlandic dress, as evidenced in figures from the Dorset period. Both the topknot – for which there was room under the peaked hood – and the hip-length *kamik*s are traits closely linked to our own time. The topknot has gone out of style in the present century, but the long *kamik*s are worn to this day in Thule.

Turning once again to the women's *kamik*s from 1460 (fig. 213) with

213. Women's kamik*s from West Greenland, from the earliest Greenlandic clothing find thus far, a grave containing eight mummified bodies, dated to ca. A. D. 1460. The find was made by the brothers Grønvold in 1972 on the Nugssuak peninsula near Umanaq. The* kamik*s are of dark depilated sealskin, topped by edgings of light sealskin. The sole is attached to the leg with a close gather of a kind still used. There is a long gusset from the knee to the instep, as on the Thule* kamik *in figure 212. National Museum of Greenland, Godthåb-Nuuk.*

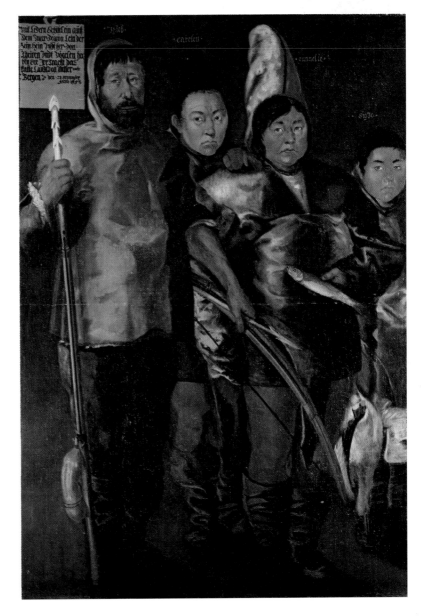

214. The oldest portrayal of Greenlanders, painted in Bergen in 1654 by Salomon von Hauen. The four Greenlanders had been abducted by an exploration ship under the command of Dutch-born David Dannel, sent out by King Frederik III. The adult women are tattooed on their faces. One is wearing her hair in a topknot and the other has her peaked anorak hood up. Note the median seam on the hood (as in fig. 212) and the long point in front. Oil on canvas, 47¼"×31½". National Museum, Copenhagen.

their long gusset – which on occasion was seen on Thule women's *kamik*s from 1909 – we see a border on top in skin of a contrasting color. It describes an arc down toward the middle in front, which brings to mind another *kamik* – the East Greenland woman's *kamik* as it appeared in 1884, when Gustav Holm wrote that "the boots go up over their knees and are shaped like large riding boots with very wide legs with a notch on top in front." Later, this type of *kamik* from East Greenland was supplanted by the familiar west coast type of mid-length with a short broad gusset covering the kneecap. Anyone suffering from arthritis of the knee would appreciate this fashion!

The kneecap *kamik* was already beginning to prevail on the east coast in the 1880s (fig. 205). It was described by Gustav Holm, who mentions that it was used on the south east coast. A reciprocal influence has always taken place between the cultures of the East Greenlanders and that of the West Greenlanders living on the south coast around Cape Farewell and the Julianehåb district. Apart from this – not lively intercourse, but rather happenstance encounters in which trade took place – the East Greenlanders were out of contact with the rest of the country.

To be sure, the legends contain accounts of meetings, especially in the form of quarrels with "inland-dwellers." Perhaps these were Indian tribes who drove the Angmagssalikians away to the east. There are also accounts of "big ships" that would come and avenge earlier clashes – perhaps Norwegian whaling ships.

All in all, we can consider the 135 people whom Holm met on the south east coast as being in contact with West Greenland, while the 413 Greenlanders living in the area around Angmagssalik were isolated from the rest of the world.

Through Holm's and Hanserak's (the catechist Johannes Hansen, who was along as interpreter) thoroughgoing accounts of the meeting with the Angmagssalikians, we know precisely what the cultural pattern looked like – close to the Thule culture and still with remnants of traits from the Dorset culture (such as the use of skeleton motif on masks).

Even though the East Greenlanders, in their isolation, had maintained life styles, traditions, and beliefs from older periods, the cultural pattern must surely have developed on its own. It was simultaneously untouched by influences from foreign cultures and cut off from contact with the tribe's origins. That is why we find a blend of old traits and local innovations, as in the dress.

Let us consider the East Greenlandic dress in its entirety as it was at that point in time – 1884. The hunter's beautifully decorated waterskin anoraks for use in the kayak have already been discussed – the full jacket, the half-jacket, and the short white anorak (fig. 210). The man might also have a bearskin anorak or a furred sealskin anorak for dog-sled driving and hunting on the ice; a handsomely embroidered gut anorak as rainwear; a gut anorak with sewn rows of fox skin; and a bird skin anorak as an inner jacket. All had the same form, with a hood, and were usually cut off at the bottom, except the furred sealskin anorak, which had a little point. The cut was so capacious that the arms could be withdrawn from the sleeves and held against the body when it was cold. Besides embroidery, the jackets might be decorated with edgings of bear or dog skin.

The headgear was an art in itself. Caps were made both of smooth white skin and embroidered with sinuous lines and concentric circles, and white fox skin caps had the fox's brush hanging down the neck. The cap visor, which was often worn separately, had edgings and a pattern with two circles reminiscent of eyes (fig. 216a) – although they could be sun signs, as the visor protects against the sun, and the large eyeshade, which protects the eyes against snow blindness, does not have these circles.

These cap visors and eyeshades (see fig. 36) are some of the most

215. Three hunters from Thule. Photograph taken by T. Krabbe in 1909. The men are wearing sealskin anoraks with points, broad transverse cut across the chest, and several seams longitudinal with the sleeves. There is a bear skin flap for the protection of the chin. The trousers are of polar bear skin, which is still used, although dog skin – formerly used only by the poor – is chiefly seen today. Photo archive of the National Museum, Copenhagen.

216 a. *Cap with visor collected by Henrik Lund, who was active as a missionary in East Greenland from 1900 to 1909. This type of cap was common in East Greenland around the turn of the century and was already in use when Gustav Holm encountered the isolated group of East Greenlanders at Angmagssalik in 1884 – although they can not have been totally isolated, inasmuch as they had cotton cloth. Cotton cloth stretched across a wooden hoop with ribbon attached. Visor of dark depilated sealskin embroidered with white skin. Diameter of crown, 11¾". National Museum of Greenland, Godthåb-Nuuk.*

beautifully decorated articles of men's dress. The eyeshades were carved from a single piece of wood, and were closely ornamented with riveted figures of a stylized nature. Visors were made either of wood with riveted bone figures or of skin with corresponding figures sewn on in a contrasting color of skin. The "eyes" have two forms: one smooth and slightly oval, and obviously resembling a human eye, and the other circular with rays, which could be a form of sun symbol. The sun was probably worshipped in one manner or another. For instance, the direction of the sunrise was significant in burial ceremonies, and the course of the sun was a component in the rubbing exercises performed on stones with which an apprentice shaman was supposed to bring himself to a state of ecstasy. But otherwise it was the moon that determined the fertility of humans and animals.

A cap could also be made from a wooden hoop covered with embroidered skin, with a visor and chin strap. At Holm's arrival, the shaman Maratse was wearing a cap whose materials testified to contact with Europeans. The crown was covered with blue fabric and bore a white and red cross – much like the Icelandic flag. The visor, on the other hand, was Eskimo, with two sun eyes (fig. 216a).

As protection for the eyes, especially against the strong sunlight reflected off snow and ice, which can cause snow blindness, goggles made of wood were also worn, either formed like a little mask (fig. 216b) or simply a piece of wood whose narrow aperture functioned as a shutter against the light.

The hair was long and was worn loose, with a hair halter of thongs, embroidered and decorated with beads or the ear stones of fish. As hair possessed growth power, it was forbidden to cut it, although some individuals had from childhood had their hair clipped by means of shark's teeth that functioned as a kind of scissors. Iron must not come in contact with the hair. He whose hair was short had to wear it short all his life and must not have points on his jackets. The ears and tails of his dogs had to be amputated, and the claws of the seals he caught had to be cast into the sea. When Christianity was introduced one of the many changes brought about was that the newly baptized had their hair cut short.

Next to his skin, the man wore an amulet harness of waterskin crisscrossed over chest and back. Where the thongs joined, an amulet holder was placed to contain protective amulets of various kinds, such as bird's

216 b. *Snow goggles from East Greenland. Top: brought back in 1892 by Lieutenant C. Ryder's expedition. Bottom: collected in 1905 by William Thalbitzer. The latter goggles, in the form of a little mask, belonged to the East Greenland mask maker and hunter Akernilik, and are 5¹¹/₁₆" long and 2⁹/₁₆" wide. Both of driftwood. National Museum, Copenhagen.*

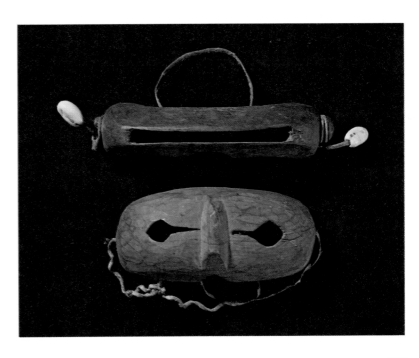

217. Portrait of an East Greenlandic man with hair halter, amulet harness, and amulet straps around his upper arms. Drawn by Kârale Andreassen in Angmagssalik, probably before 1917, as the drawing belonged to Sigrid Bugge, who was in Angmagssalik in 1916-17 as a nurse. Depicted is Erik Ali (heathen name: Angaajik), one of the principals in Knud Rasmussen's film Palo's Wedding. *Pencil on pasteboard, cut in an oval and signed "Kârale," about 11" high. Private collection.*

claws, chips, and tiny effigies. The man also wore a bead-trimmed arm band above his biceps, which gave strength to the arm and meant a long life (see fig. 217).

In the house, the tent, or in the settlement, the man wore only his hair halter, amulet harness, and house briefs. These pants were called *naatsit,* meaning "the short ones" – a striking epithet, as they barely covered the sexual organs. *Naatsit* were beautifully embroidered and were made of sealskin with the fur facing outward. Often the skin of the seal's head was used, which brings to mind Naligateq's animal head between her legs (see fig. 102). On the small number of decorated jackets found among the Polar Eskimos, there are a few points, also denoting the sexual organs, which are embroidered to resemble an animal's head.

If the man were hunting or on a journey, he wore a pair of sealskin trousers over his *naatsit,* tied at the waist outside his jacket and at the cuffs outside his boots. In winter both the outer and inner *kamik*s went above the knee, and in summer only the inner *kamik* – of sealskin with the fur inside – was long, while the richly embroidered waterskin *kamik* was short. The sole was curved sharply up around the foot, and between the two *kamik*s a layer of dry grass was placed as insulation.

The women's *kamik*s have already been discussed (see fig. 205). They were made of dark waterskin, were long, and their tops were indented in a curved vee in front, with light skin borders around the edges and down along the median seam following the shin and around the foot at the stitching. The inner *kamik* might be bordered with dog or bear skin. As mentioned, *kamik*s with kneecap embroidery were also to be found.

The woman's anorak of furred sealskin was of a somewhat different cut from the man's. The back was broader and the peaked hood larger, especially on an *amaut* – an anorak so broad across the back that there was room for a child. The top of the *amaut* was furnished with a drawstring so that the head opening could be gathered together and the child – which as an infant wore only a bonnet and was otherwise naked – could sit entirely protected and warm against its mother's warm, naked back. The jacket was so capacious that the child could be moved around inside it to the front in order to take the breast. A thong fastened under the mother's bosom went around the back pouch and back again, so that the child would not slide down (fig. 218).

The woman's jacket had points both in the front and at the back, often long enough to be tied together between the legs in cold weather. The sleeves, which were truncated at the wrists, were low-set and angled forward, making them suitable for rowing, bending down and flensing or scraping, washing clothes, and picking berries – in other words, designed for the women's work postures. The jacket was decorated with white skin at all seams, and in front with two white, narrow hood bases, which were further extended with free-hanging tapes, often decorated with beads. The bottom edge might also have a thick fringe of beaded strings.

The woman's pants were first the inner *naatsit* – like the men's, minimum covering for the sexual organs, and finely embroidered with strings of beads and skin mosaic. Over these came a pair of sealskin shorts, sitting low on the waist, and, in contrast to the man's trousers, worn under the jacket. This form of apparel cannot be called practical, as the shorts leave naked a strip of the loins and a good piece of thigh. According to reports, only when traveling in severe cold did the women bind pieces of skin around their bare thighs.

Caps or hats were worn. Holm collected two tall, pointed skin hats in which there was room for the topknot, "the way we wore them in former times," made of dark waterskin with appliquéd figures in white skin (fig. 219) – marvellous cookie-cutter scenes of everyday life – men and women, tents, *umiak*s, and kayaks.

Naturally, the hood could be turned up to protect the head. During the period of mourning following a death, it had to be turned up (see fig.

219. Conical woman's hat, for protecting the topknot. Only two examples of this type of headgear are known, both from East Greenland in the 1880s. Dark depilated sealskin with appliquéd figures in white skin. 12³/₈" high, 5⁷/₈" in diameter at band. National Museum of Greenland, Godthåb-Nuuk.

218. Woman with infant in amaut. *Collected by Hinrich Rink around 1860. As reported by him, it was "drawn by a young girl in the district of Godthaab and found by chance." Pencil on paper, 4⁵/₁₆"×2". The Queen's Reference Library, Copenhagen.*

212), sometimes for months, but otherwise one went bareheaded. The girls had long, loosely-hanging hair, but as soon as they were sexually mature, they set their hair up in a broad, flat topknot decorated with an embroidered band, from which additional beaded strings might be hung down over the forehead (fig. 220). One might also bind a kerchief of skin around the forehead, both for the warmth it provided and to conceal the temples, which among older women became bald from the extreme tension of the hair.

Setting the hair up in a topknot was enormously widespread among the Eskimos, both geographically and historically. It is found in Siberia, Alaska, Canada, and Greenland. We see it on tiny statuetes from the Dorset and Thule cultures, and it was worn by old women in South and East Greenland well into the 1950s. From the point of view of fashion, the topknot is very flattering. It makes its wearer taller and provides a nice balance in relation to the lines of the dress as a whole. Only look at the young woman in figure 221, whose topknot forms a capital from which the line descends in strings of beads, the pointed base of the hood, the tip of the point, the vee of the *kamik,* and along the *kamik* to the base of the column, the broad *kamik* sole.

The children were dressed like the grown-ups, although they did not wear the *naatsit* until puberty, but when small romped naked in the house or tent. It should be mentioned that sometimes parents deliberately dressed a child in an unsightly or ridiculous manner in order to confuse the powers, as it was believed the evil spirits would not take a ludicrous child.

It has been stated that Greenlandic artists possess a distinctive sense of form, both as sculptors and artisans, in the design of boats and implements. Their seamstresses display a not inferior sense of form in the execution of all of these skin garments. The total form is established in the cut, which adheres to the proportions of the body. The long, elegant

220. Portrait of an East Greenlandic woman drawn by Kârale Andreassen, probably before 1917. The model is Qunerseeq from the Angmagssalik district, married to Erik Ali (fig. 217). Pencil on pasteboard, cut in an oval and signed "Kârale," about 11" high. Private collection.

lines are created with embroidered borders that reiterate and emphasize the body's rhythm.

The East Greenlandic ornamentation makes use of the basic geometrical forms: the point, line, circle, oval, triangle, and square. The sphere (beads) is used as well, as is the cone or pyramid (peaked hats and hoods). The point is layed out in groups as bordered blocks, as seen in tattoos (see fig. 242), or in rows (fig. 222), and beads are strung so that they give a linear effect. The same play between straight and angled is evident in the embroidery, where the sinuous line side by side with the straight line appears time and again. Circles, sometimes concentric, are intersected perpendicularly by matching stripes, and long bands of semi-circles are fixed in place by straight lines (fig. 224). The slightly elongated triangular form is seen in the needle skin (fig. 143), in earrings of ivory or metal, and in the kneecap *kamik*. Zigzag lines, in which there appear a row of triangles, are also much used.

Whether this strict and stylistically assured ornamentation is the expression of an innate artistic sense and fulfills elementary aesthetic demands, or whether certain ornaments are stylizations of naturalistic forms, I am unable to judge. So closely connected were hunting and daily life with cult that it is natural to suppose that certain forms – such as the oval, the circle, and the triangle – were signs symbolic of the life-giving principles: the seal, the sun, and the woman's loins.

221. A young married couple, Ataqâq Ajukutôq and Saningasek Ajukutôq was the son of a shaman and was himself a shaman. Photo taken in Angmagssalik in 1884 by the Norwegian H. Knutson, an assistant on the umiak expedition to East Greenland. Published in Meddelelser om Grønland (Information about Greenland) no. 10, plate VIII.

222. *Jewelry disc (?) from East Greenland collected in the Angmagssalik district in 1901-02 by the botanist Christian Kruuse. Bone, both sides covered with drilled dots in rows radiating from the central perforation, 2¹/₁₆" × 1½". National Museum, Copenhagen.*

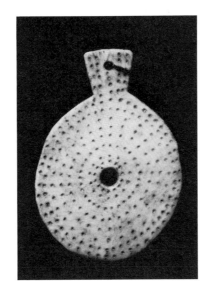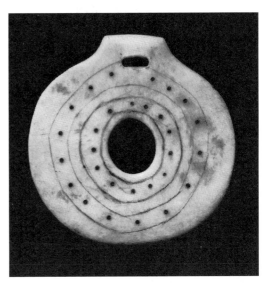

223. *A similar bone disc from West Greenland, collected in 1856 and belonging to "the finery of a Greenlanderess." 2¹/₁₆" × 2³/₃₂". National Museum, Copenhagen.*

224. *Four bags from East Greenland, all of depilated sealskin and embroidered with skin mosaic in contrasting colors. The cylindrical bag at lower right was collected by Gustav Holm in 1884-85, length about 8⁵/₈". The others were purchased by "Manager of Works" Johan Petersen in Angmagssalik in 1897. One hundred sixty seven objects in all were purchased by Petersen on the same occasion for a total of 41 kroner and 24 øre (about 5 dollars). Note the elegant closure, representing Toornaarsuk, on the bag at lower left. National Museum, Copenhagen.*

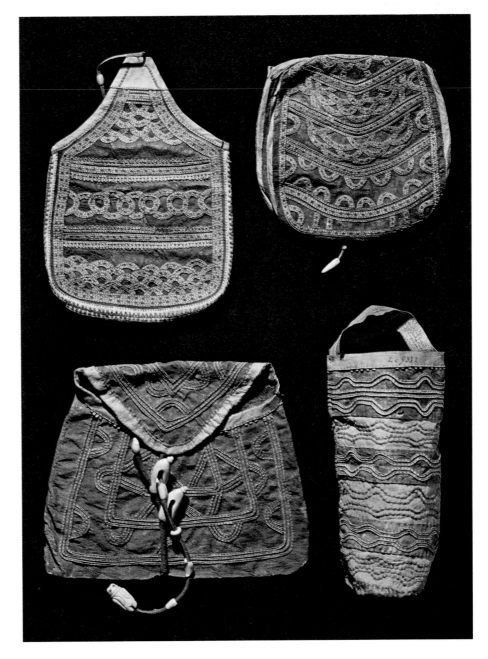

225. Figure representing a Norseman with liripipe hood. Grave find from South Greenland. Driftwood, about 1⅝" high. University Museum, Cambridge.

226. Figure representing a European with a jacket and tall hat with pompon (a military personage?). From a collection of thirteen diminutive figures found in graves and house ruins in South Greenland. Collected by C. J. Ryberg, governor of South Greenland, in the late 1800s. Driftwood, 3³/₁₆" high. National Museum, Copenhagen.

When does the change that transforms a practical arrangement into a symbol occur? The point at the bottom of the anorak protects the groin against cold – but it also denotes the pubic region, and if it has the character of an animal's head, it is no very great jump from there to the myths of the close relationship between animals and humans. We ought not to over-interpret signs, but should merely be aware that, while many early cultures *begin* by utilizing simple geometric forms, it may also be that certain figures become more and more stylized and thus *end* as simple forms. The history of pictorial art describes just such a cyclical movement between naturalistic and stylized forms.

The colors are simple in East Greenlandic dress: light and dark juxtaposed with assured graphic effect. There was some red, as beads made from the vertebrae of the capelin were now and then colored with blood, and the men's cap visors rubbed with a kind of red clay. East Greenland women still do embroidery in the traditional style with light strips of skin against the dark waterskin, though nowadays on handicrafts objects. Traditional dress as a whole disappeared rapidly when it became possible to buy store merchandise. Icelandic sweaters and Danish underwear quickly became popular, and today everybody is dressed as in Denmark. The only exception is the East Greenland *amaut,* which is still being sewn. Though it is now made of white cotton cloth with red cloth borders and decorated with glass beads, the cut is the same. Nowadays in East Greenland, West Greenland traditional dress is the national costume. Although West Greenland has had the most influence from outside, native costume turns out to have survived, though expressing a blend of cultures. Let us turn to West Greenland and see how traditional dress developed there.

Starting in A.D. 982, the Norsemen lived in Greenland for around 500 years, and there exist numerous accounts of the Eskimos' intercourse with them, both peaceful and discordant. In spite of this, Greenlandic clothing shows no influences from European fashions in the Middle Ages. In small wooden figures made by Greenlanders, we see Norsemen characterized by their dress, such as a Norseman wearing a liripipe hood (fig. 225), carved in the familiar style of the Thule period with truncated legs and no arms and a flat face. Another wooden figure depicts alien, somewhat military dress – a jacket with square shoulders, and a high bell-shaped hat with a pompon (fig. 226). When the Norsemen in Greenland died out at the end of the 1400s, approximately 100 years passed before Europeans heard about the country again.

During the long search for the Northwest Passage, the English explorer John Davis came to Greenland, and in the years 1585-87 sailed up the west coast all the way to Upernavik. Davis was on more or less good terms with the Greenlanders, traded with them, and made many observations during his visit of characteristics we recognize from more recent times.

The Greenlanders lived in tents made of skins, he relates, had great quantities of furs, had sealskins in tanning vats, ate capelins, made fishing nets from baleen, made fire by means of a drill, and carried many idols of wood and amulets on their persons and in their boats, which he called "canoas." Davis assumed that the Greenlanders were sun-worshipers, and obtained their confidence by imitating what they did – extending their arms to the sun, shouting "*Ylayoute,*" and beating their breasts. Of their dress he writes:

We bought the clothes from their backs, which were all made of seales skins and birdes skinnes: their buskins, their hose, their gloves, all being commonly well dressed: so that we were fully persuaded that they have divers artificers among them. Wee had a paire of buskins of them full of fine wool like bever. Their apparell for heate, was made of birdes skinnes with their feathers on them. We saw among them leather dressed like glovers leather, and thicke thongs like white leather of a good length.

227. *Copperplate of Greenlander brought home by the Dutch whaling captain Nicolai Tune in 1656: "Savage clothing of skins in two colors, ... as regards the form of the loose jacket and the entire outer equipment of the savage, which is shown here, the engraver has rendered it so realistically in this excellent print, that further description should be deemed unnecessary." From Louis de Poincy's* Histoire naturelle et morale des Îles Antilles de l'Amérique *(Rotterdam, 1658).*

In the following centuries, contact with European explorers, whalers, and traders became increasingly lively. Many of the strange ships took Greenlanders back to Europe with them, usually against their will. Paintings were made of several of these kidnapped Greenlanders, and so we have a rather good impression of what their dress was like. The anorak with the peaked hood has already been discussed (fig. 214). In another picture, which a Flemish artist made in England, we see the man dressed in a jacket with broad shoulders, a point in front, and a tall anorak hood cut off flat on top (fig. 227) – much like the shape of the head of a wooden figure from the Thule culture (see fig. 185).

Many place names – like Ritenbenk, Hunde Ejland, and Rodebay – recall the preponderance of Dutchmen who came to the west coast, and their brisk trade with the Greenlanders eventually meant changes in the dress. In return for skins and narwhal tusks, the Greenlanders got European trade goods, usually of poor quality, like knives and porcelain, glass beads, mirrors, woven fabrics, and above all, firearms.

Here the ground was laid for the slow transformation of the Greenlanders' way of life, and the self-sufficient Greenlandic society was never returned to. In the 1700s, the population shifted south and further out toward the open ocean, and new settlements arose along the coast. Hunting techniques changed too. Dog-sledding disappeared south of Kangaamiut, while kayak equipment evolved to still greater perfection. It was at this time that the full and half-jackets were improved, enabling the kayak man to move about not only in the fjords but on the open, agitated sea as well. The population increased, and people started living in the large common houses.

Greenland was thus in a time of convulsion when Hans Egede arrived in the country in 1721 on an errand for the king of Denmark-Norway. Egede was looking for the vanished Norsemen, but his task became instead to convert the Greenlanders to Christianity.

Many exhaustive descriptions – partly of the work of the mission, and partly of the country, fauna, and the Greenlanders' manners and customs – came out of Egede's fifteen years in Greenland. In his *The Old Greenland's New Perlustration,* published in 1741, he writes: "Their clothes consist for the most part of reindeers' skins, seals' skins as well as birds' feathers, very daintily dressed and made."

In the further description, the familiar elements appear: "jumpsuit," waterskin jacket for use with the kayak, gut jacket ("which helps to keep the water out from the inner jacket"), and anorak with hood ("some have a point front and back"). The inner jacket had the fur inside for the sake of warmth. The influence of the Dutch was even then seen in the Greenlanders' dress, as Egede writes that many had shirts of striped linen or red and blue cloth, "though made according to their own manner," likewise outer trousers of cloth.

Red or blue stockings were preferred, but otherwise inner *kamik*s of caribou skin, and "shoes and boots they have of black, yellow, or red dressed and scraped seal skin, very daintily sewed though without heels, but gathered front and back, and which look very handsome on their legs and feet." The half-jacket is mentioned too, as is the short white anorak, which, as Egede writes, is necessary in order that "the seals shall not flee from them." If there was any hunting magic associated with the short white anorak, it is easy to understand why it became the men's formal dress.

The woman's suit is different from the man's in being wider, with broader shoulders and taller hoods, and especially with the *amaut,* "inasmuch as they carry their little children there on the back and use no other cradle or swaddling clothes for them." The women wore two pairs of trousers, first the house pants to the middle of the thigh, and over them a pair of knee-length trousers. The inner jacket was of caribou skin, the outer jacket of "thinly furred and beautifully colored reindeer skin, or lacking that seal skin, trimmed and bordered with white between the seams, which has a pretty effect."

The *kamik*s were like the men's but had wide tops. The hair was put up in a topknot, and the hood was put up only in rain or snow. At a death in the family, the women went into mourning by letting their hair hang down over their faces and "as often as they go outside they must always have their hood on, when otherwise it isn't used, and they do it, according to their delusion, lest they die." Again, magic was associated with certain elements of dress. Letting the hair down was also ritual at a childbirth, and the woman who took the first stitch in sewing the skins together for an *umiak* did so with her hair let down.

The women's delight in colored glass beads – which were hung from the ears, around the neck and arms, and sewn on footwear and clothing – is described by Egede as resulting from the bartering with whalers and traders.

Of tattooing, it is related that the Greenlandic women "make themselves black streaks in the skin with a sewing needle and blacked thread" between the eyes and on the chin (see figs. 214 and 242), arms, hands, legs, and thighs. Egede thought it looked hideous, but the women claimed that "she who wasn't thus trimmed, her head would become an oil pot which would be put under the lamp when they got to heaven or the land of souls." That tattooing possessed magical significance we also know from East Greenland, where the Moon Man became angry and spoiled the hunting if the women were poorly tattooed.

In the engravings illustrating Egede's books, Johanne Fosie, presumably after Egede's originals, depicted Greenlandic life nearly ballet-like, both in hunting scenes and portrayals of drum dances and ball games (fig. 228). Among the details of the dress, we notice the white edging down along the sleeve (as in the Thule suit), the *kamik*s are white-topped and have a notch in front as on the east coast and like the *kamik*s from 1460. For the entire length of the back, the women's anoraks have a vertical insert of dark skin that emphasizes the effect of the flap.

Not long afterwards, in 1758, the merchant Lars Dalager – colony manager in Frederikshåb and later in Godthåb-Nuuk – published his *Greenlandic Relations* as a kind of continuation of the publications of Hans Egede and his sons, and with considerably more regard for the Greenlandic culture than the Egedes, who as missionaries considered it their task to overthrow the native faith and attitude to life.

Dalager writes that the rich Greenlanders' best outfits were of furred caribou skin, the darker the handsomer. The soft skin of the calves was used for children's clothing and the clothes of the young girls. The poor had to make do with dog skins and bird skins, if they had even that. Furthermore, "womenfolk as well as men of means find it in their taste to wear foreign clothes made of cloth, articles of uniform, and linen." It was especially in the colony and its environs that European fashions held sway. "The men began wearing linen stocks, and buckles on their shoes and pretty garters. It is now also common to see them with pockets in their trousers to keep their snuffbox and handkerchief in." "One sees womenfolk, on the other hand, with a kind of neck linen, which is probably called a modest, and the rest sewn over from top to toe with bows of broad silk ribbon."

Red cloth and silk materials, formerly the most popular, were now worn only by people coming from the south (or the south east coast). Further north, dark blue and white were the preferred colors. In missionary Glahn's journals from the 1760s, there is a very exhaustive account of the various types of skin – *umiak* skin, sole skin, waterskin, black bootskin, white skin, and red skin, the latter produced by the ancient method of chewing bits of bark into the skin and treating it with urine. Detailed knowledge of the exceedingly complex techniques of dressing skins was fortunately kept alive among the Greenlandic women, and it has still not

228. *Eskimo ball game. Copperplate in Hans Egede's* The Old Greenland's New Perlustration *of 1741. Engraving made by Johanne Fosie, probably from a drawing by Poul Egede. Note the long points on the women's anoraks, and the median seams on the hoods.*

entirely been forgotten, in spite of nearly 300 years of contact with European fashions.

Generally speaking, in these three centuries from whaling times to today, we trace a struggle between old traditions and new impressions that to a great degree has left its mark on the present-day national costume, so that in it we see elements from both cultural spheres. Consistent through all stages of its development are the knowledge of the materials and joy in color.

Where the Polar Eskimos and East Greenlanders kept to a subdued color scheme based on natural materials and exploited the contrast between light and dark with great refinement, the West Greenlanders display a passion for color. It was not merely born of the whalers' colored beads and silk ribbons, for there was already indigenous production of colors through vegetable dyeing. Although the colors are faded on the extant clothing from West Greenland of the 1880s (fig. 229), we sense the red, yellow, dark blue, and green yellow in the elegant borders edging the points of the anorak, the base of the hood, the trouser seam down the front and inside of the thighs. The favorite colors were red, white, and black, which both on caribou skin and sealskin provide vivid ornamentation in the vertically-running borders, especially at the base of the hood and on the thigh.

 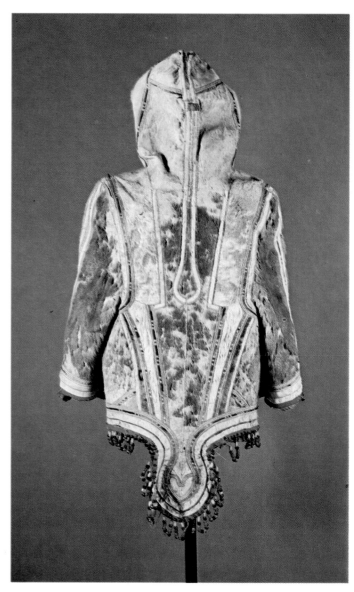

229 a and b. Front and back of a woman's anorak from the 1800s. West Greenland. "A Greenlandic woman's costume" acquired by the Danish National Museum in 1846. The upper part, shown here, is described as "a jacket of caribou skin, lined with seal skin, and richly adorned below with glass beads." Note the sophisticated and beautiful embroidery. National Museum, Copenhagen.

The men's dress was more circumspect in the use of colors, and the costume with points and edgings seen in the illustration to Hans Egede's *New Perlustration* (see fig. 228) disappeared. Apart from the kayak man's gear and the skin clothing necessary for hunting on the ice, the men wore European clothes. In a watercolor painted by Gormansen at the beginning of the 1800s, we see men wearing sailor hats, navy trousers, and vests with buttons. Still, something remained steadfast – the anorak, and today the short white anorak, in combination with Danish navy-issue or other trousers made of dark woollen material and short black *kamik*s, is the men's national costume (as shown in fig. 210).

Women's traditional dress took two forms in the 1800s, as we see from Rasmus Berthelsen's woodcut in the book *Kaladtlit assilialiait* (Greenlandic Woodcuts) from 1858. They were the "festive dress" of young women and of married women with children (figs. 230 and 257).

The young woman in the illustration is wearing a white hoodless anorak with a raised collar of dark skin, on which there is sewn a descending border of rows of beads. It is from this hoodless anorak with bead collar that present-day formal dress has developed. The point and bead fringe at the bottom have been replaced by a broad, checked band of taffeta, but the wrist embroidery and woolly wristlets are still there (fig. 231). The knee-length pants of furred skin have embroidery parallel

230. *"A girl from Godthaab in Festive Costume." Hand-colored woodcut by Rasmus Berthelsen, made from a drawing. From Greenlandic Woodcuts (1860). National Library of Greenland, Godthåb-Nuuk.*

to the femur and transversely on the inner thigh. In this case, the pants have become shorter, retaining only the vertical embroidery. The white short outer *kamik*s for young girls are the same, while the inner *kamik* has changed. Nowadays, it has a broad, black skin border, black skin edgings, lace, and Danish floral embroidery on white linen (see fig. 204).

The married woman wears a dark sealskin *amaut,* from the hood of which the little one peeps out. The *amaut* is embroidered in red, black, and white at the base of the hood, down at the point (which is also trimmed with rows of beads), and at the edge of the sleeve up to the elbow. The sleeve length has varied. Among the young women it is quite short – today only elbow-length. With married women, the *kamik*s are long, red, and with embroidery parallel to the shinbone and around the kneecap insert. The style in which short white *kamik*s are sewn for confirmations and long red *kamik*s for weddings is still used.

The women wear a ribbon around their topknot, and their marital status can be read in its color – a custom widespread in the 1800s, and introduced by the Moravian missionaries. The physician T. Krabbe wrote in 1895:

> One notices the different wreaths of beads composed of variously colored beads arranged in tasteful patterns. The topknots of the Greenlandic women in that part of the west coast which was colonized a long time ago are wound about with a broad colored ribbon, which according to old custom is red on the unmarried and blue on the

232. *Figure of married woman (recognizable by the blue ribbon around her topknot) with a child in her* amaut, *carved by Johannes Kreutzmann in the 1920s. Painted driftwood, about 15¾" high. Education League of Greenland, Godthåb-Nuuk.*

231. *Detail from the woman's full dress of today, including the checked taffeta ribbon that finishes off the upper part, the trouser embroidery along the femur, and the bead embroidered cuff at the wrist. Photograph taken by Anne Bang in 1973.*

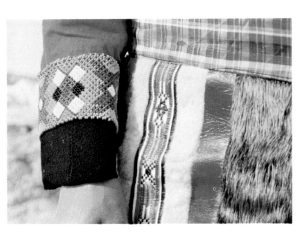

233. *Figures of two women carved by Johannes Kreutzmann in the 1920s. One though unmarried (indicated by the green ribbon around her topknot) has a child in her* amaut. *(Note the embroidery finished with large checks, like that in figure 201.) The other is carrying a burden to or from the summer settlement: tent poles, rolled-up skins, and so forth. (Note the long inner* kamik, *in this case the outer* kamik *is short.) Painted driftwood, about 15¾" high. Greenland Technical Organization.*

234. *Woman's pants from Napassoq, photographed in 1915 by Ossian Elgström. Dyed depilated sealskin and caribou skin. Here the* avigtat *embroidery follows not only the femur but also the inner thigh, so that the sex is delineated.*

married women (fig. 232), black on the widow and green on the unmarried woman who has borne a child. In recent years, this old custom has been on the decline, and is now seen nearly only in South Greenland, and there nearly only in the more isolated settlements.

The hair band could also be embroidered, as seen in figure 218 – a delightful drawing, which incidentally reveals the wide cut of the *amaut* and the elegant lines of the West Greenland woman's dress in the 1800s. Ossian Elgström, in 1915, made many observations on dress. The *amaut* of sealskin or caribou skin with the ornamentation seen in the woodcut from 1858 was still being worn. Johannes Kreutzmann includes it on a figure from the 1920s as well, and the photographer Jette Bang recorded it in use in Umanak in the thirties. By that time it was already on its way out, although it was not until the 1950s that the baby buggy made its entrance in earnest. The formal dress of the Greenlandic woman of today has its origins – as far as the upper part is concerned – in the young woman's outfit in figure 230. The rows of beads worn at the collar in the 1700s and 1800s evolved into today's large bead cape.

The ornamentation of the kneecap *kamik*s has given rise to the interesting theory that the femur, kneecap, and shinbone borders originated in remnants of the skeleton motif of the Dorset culture. In my opinion, the triangular insert covering the kneecap is a gusset whose seam is edged in order to cover the stitching as much as possible. All embroidery in Greenlandic garments follows either an edge or a seam. When the suit follows the natural contours of the body, the seams do too. It therefore follows that certain seams denote anatomical construction.

Red was for young married women, dark blue or violet for older ones, and yellow or brown for very old women. Ossian Elgström writes that when his ship was coming in at Godthåb harbor, his first impression was one of color:

Round about me stood long rows of Greenlandic women, whose variegated "anoraks" and colorful boots all shouted for first place in the retinas of my eyes. There were yellow, red, blue, and green *kamik*s (fig. 205), with white inserts and edged with dog skin. Their thigh embroideries shone and flamed in crimson and green against the speckled gray of the sealskin trousers, and the bead collars of the anoraks seared my vision.

From Holsteinsborg, Elgström gives an account of imaginative hair decorations: one woman had a string of Danish flags in a circle around her head, and another had a Christmas star in her hair and "shone from afar." Concerning the embroidery on women's trousers, Elgström observes that the Danes thought the transverse border on the inner side of the pants (fig. 234) was indecent – and that the Greenlanders therefore gave it up. This kind of embroidery on pants does indeed outline the sex, but so does the point.

When King Christian X visited West Greenland in 1921 on the first royal visit to the country, a newspaper account of a dinner aboard the royal yacht has it that "the great hunters were in elegant white or black silk anoraks, with handsome black trousers stuffed into sealskin *kamik*s, delicately kamiuted (softened) and embroidered according to the latest Greenlandic fashion. Their ladies were radiant in all the daring colors of the rainbow, with bead stitching and the finest embroidery on their silk anoraks, short fur trousers, and high red *kamik*s."

Colors on skins were originally obtained by vegetable dyeing, and later by dipping the skin in an extract of colored silk ribbons or by painting it with oil paint. The latter, however, made the skin stiff, and the paint tended to flake off. The bright colors of both skins and beads are part of the women's dress (fig. 235).

235. *Bead collar from modern-day full dress. Imaginativeness and delight in colors characterize the individual patterns in Greenlandic women's bead collars of today. Photograph taken by Anne Bang in 1973.*

The first beads were the large whaler's beads, trade goods that, when placed around a woman's neck, bespoke her husband's skill as a hunter and were a kind of status symbol. They were big and beautiful, up to one and a quarter inches long – some oblong, others round, and still others long and slender, so that when strung they formed a zigzag pattern, as shown in fig. 235. This pattern is also the basis for the very large bead collar that today covers most of the shoulders and bosom of the full traditional dress. Only old women are unostentatious, and instead of the big collar make do with a silk anorak, on the collar flap of which they pin a little brooch.

In saying that the zigzag pattern is predominant, I mean both that the colors follow that form, and that the sewing technique is to build on a series of loops in the middle of which a new loop is started – in other words, a staggered zigzag line. The patterns are individual, but all are symmetric, and the range of colors is very large. Beads were selected from a sample card in the store, and beadwork became immensely popular.

Accessories – bags, tobacco pouches, belts, and so on – were also

236. *Small bag or purse once owned by geodesist and artist Andreas Kornerup, who journeyed on the west coast of Greenland in 1876-79. Outstretched waterfowl feet and blue-dyed smooth sealskin with* avigtat *embroidery, 4³/₈" × 1". Museum of Trade and Shipping, Elsinore.*

237. *Two belts and a bag flap. The bead belt, made in 1968, is from Julianehåb, and is 32³/4″ long and 1⁹/₁₆″ broad. The skin belt and bag flap are from the region around Nanortalik, dating from the 1920s; both are embellished with* avigtat *embroidery on black-dyed depilated sealskin. Belt, 33¹/2″×2³/16″. Bag flap, 12¹/4″×5¹/4″. Private collection.*

decorated with skin mosaic and beadwork, and naturally these objects were in keeping with the local style. In East Greenland, bags are still being sewn in dark waterskin and with sinuate white skin strips, and the shape of the bag is derived from skin bags formerly used to gather lamp moss in (fig. 224). Often the skin of birds' feet was distended and used with extremely decorative effect. Birds' feet were used on the west coast as well, sometimes in combination with skin mosaic (fig. 236), and gifts and souvenirs were decorated with the sewing techniques and materials found in traditional dress.

The same thing happened with skin and bead sewing as with sculpture: the original function of the work of art altered with the arrival of influences from outside, new needs and requirements arose, and new objects were created using traditional techniques and materials – candle holders, napkin rings, desk blotters, matchbox holders, cushions, bags, table centers, and much more. Among these are the belts, in beadwork and skin mosaic respectively, shown in figure 237. The fine old art of working bird skin has not been forgotten. Although the light, warm bird skin shirts that were worn next to the skin are no longer made, the skins of the eider duck and ice diver may be assembled into a blanket to put over the baby, or to hang on the wall as a decoration (fig. 238).

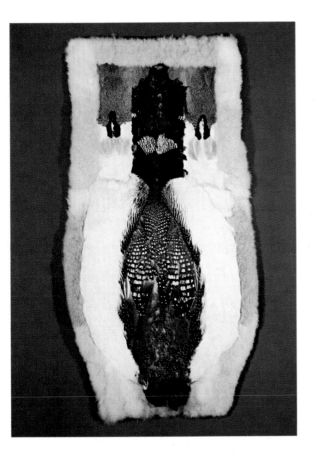

238. Bird skin blanket. Probably sewn by Benigne Jessen, Godthåb, in the 1960s. Ice diver and eider drake, with eiderdown border, 37½"×18½". Association for Greenlandic Folk Art, Godthåb-Nuuk.

239. Box sewn by Helga Rosing, Narssalik, in the 1960s. Avigtat *embroidery on black-dyed depilated sealskin, white skin strips braided into the edges. 4½" in diameter, 2³/₁₆" high. Private collection.*

As a consequence of the fact that borders and bead collars no longer had to follow the lines of the body, compositions became less bound by the frieze, the band, and the border. But most free creations in beads or skin are fortunately still characterized by geometric and symmetrical patterns. The zigzag line is still there, as in bead center cloths made in the form of a star. When modern bags, boxes, and the like are decorated with skin mosaic, it is usually done with a fixed center and strict geometrical construction.

The long traditions of line and color in Greenlandic art are in the hands of the many anonymous women artists. It is natural to turn from their endeavors to the art of painting in Greenland.

Painting

240. *Portrait of East Greenlandic man with hair halter. Painted by Peter Rosing, Angmagssalik. Oil on canvas, handmade driftwood stretcher, 19⁵/₁₆″×14³/₁₆″. Signed "P. Rosing 1926." National Museum, Copenhagen.*

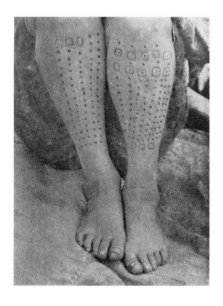

241. *Engraved drawing of a caribou. Ground find, late 1950s, from Qeerqertaussaq near Nordre Strømfjord. Caribou antler, sawed square at ends, 3½″×2″. Private collection.*

242 a *and* b. *Tattooed woman's legs photographed in Angmagssalik in 1906-7. Ornamented seal figures from same time and place.*

Sign and image

It was with the knife and the needle that the greenlanders first began creating works of art. Not only sculpture and necessities were produced with these tools; pictures were made as well. The first pigment used was lampblack. Using a knife, an image was engraved in a tusk or bone, and then soot mixed with oil was rubbed into the scratches so that a picture appeared. The masters of this technique were the Eskimos of Alaska, who have left us a picture gallery of scenes of daily life and the hunt, engraved on drill bows, pipes, and tools.

The technique is familiar in Greenland and it has numerous exponents, especially in West Greenland, so that although no old Greenlandic pictorial engravings are known to exist, I am of the opinion that it was used in the same manner as on an undated earth find, from the area around Holsteinsborg, in which the fleeting image of a caribou has been preserved on a length of bone (fig. 241).

We also find black dots on old objects made by Canadian Eskimos, and from more recent times in Greenland. The techniques are related: a depression is made using a mouth drill, and then a mixture of lampblack and oil is rubbed into it. A little figure of a bird or seal was outlined with

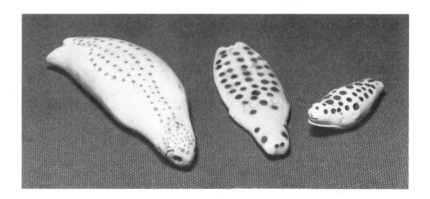

these dots, or lines of dots were inscribed on a comb, a knife, or an *ulo* (fig. 242*b*).

Eskimos also drew on their skins with tattoos – not naturalistic motifs, but rather lines and points. These either denoted important events in the individual's life, had cultic significance (see page 60), or were simply for aesthetic effect. Now and then, men had a few lines tattooed on their upper arms to give them strength, or – as related in the legend of "The Man Who Killed His Wives" (Knud Rasmussen, *Myths and Legends*) – they had lines tattooed at the temple that indicated the number of people they had killed. But for women, who were often tattooed on large areas of the body and the face, designs made with a soot-blackened needle on the skin were an element in the concept of beauty. Apart from their cultic purposes, it was considered beautiful to be profusely and skillfully decorated with points, circles, and lines (fig. 242*a*).

243. Skin figure for a silhouette show against the tent wall or placed against a translucent gut tent curtain. Collected in the Angmagssalik district 1905-6 by William Thalbitzer. Depilated sealskin, about 5½" high. Thalbitzer archives, Royal Library, Copenhagen.

244. Graphs of "Woman's Thoughts" and "Dog's Thoughts" drawn ca. 1908 by the hunter and shaman Ajukutôq (see fig. 221). Collected by colony manager Johan Petersen in 1909 in Angmagssalik. Pencil on writing pad paper. Royal Library, Copenhagen.

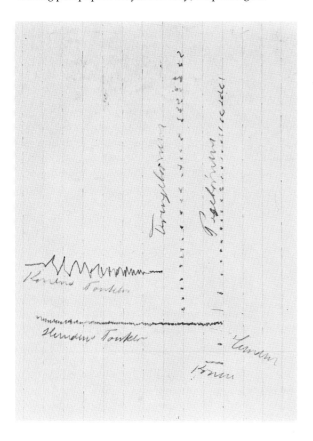

Soot mixed with oil could also be rubbed into the face, as is still done for the Uaajeerteq figure and by the *mitaartut* mummers (see figure 30). The fingers were used as brushes, and so deeply rooted is this tradition that present-day mask carvers – to whom brushes are available in any store – still apply the black pigment (acrylic paint as a rule nowadays) with their fingers. With the hands forming the shapes, images were also created on the walls of tents or against gut curtains – shadow shows with the lamp as the source of light; and simple skin figures, cut out in flat patterns, were used as silhouette puppets (fig. 243). We may also suppose that pictures were drawn with a stick in the snow, or in sand.

These simple skin figures might also be appliquéd onto other objects of skin and thus form a picture world, as seen on peaked hats (fig. 219) and on a long strip of skin (fig. 46). Apart from these stylized representations of people, *umiak*s, kayaks, and tents, all of the compositions whose material is skin are of a nonfigurative character. This is true of black-and-white embroideries, of *avigtat* embroideries with colored skin pieces, and of bead stitching. Greenland's abstract artists are its women, who with the needle and countless beads or tiny patches of skin have conceived and created innumerable constructivist works of art, with an assured sense of both composition and color combination, as seen in many of the illustrations in the chapter on crafts.

Parallel with the production of skin and beadwork art, a figurative pictorial art gradually arose with the arrival of new materials from Europe. Just as the women obtained – and still obtain – release for their imaginations and delight in color through embroidery, so painting has been the domain of men right down to our own day. It was the men who were accustomed to using the knife for scratching signs and images into bone and ivory, and it was they who first had paper and pencil put into their hands and were asked to draw by explorers and ethnologists.

One of the initiators of this experiment was Knud Rasmussen. In East Greenland, West Greenland, and among the Thule people, he set many individuals to drawing – sometimes explanations of hunting techniques, but also illustrations of myths and legends, which we shall return to later. From the east coast, whose population has been the object of great interest on the part of ethnologists ever since their first meeting with Europeans, there are many exciting records of the mentality of a people using the pencil as a tool for the first time.

In the years 1905-11, with the help of Angmagssalik's colony manager, Johan Petersen, the ethnologist William Thalbitzer collected a large number of fascinating drawings made by children and adults with ordinary pencil on scraps of paper (figs. 245 and 246a). Without the use of perspective, the people, houses, tents, and boats of the settlement are spread out over the whole surface of the paper. Houses are viewed from above or from the side, people from in front or sideways, *umiak*s as though with x-ray vision (fig. 246b) – things are explained the way they *are*, not the way they *seem*.

We see the same unsophisticated mode of expression in Ajukútôq's drawings of thoughts – an experiment that seems advanced and that will surely interest today's artists. That thinking has a continuity approaching the character of writing, and that it oscillates in a pattern of heights and depths, seems immediately and completely comprehensible. I don't think I've ever seen a truer picture of "Woman's Thoughts" or "Dog's Thoughts" than Ajukútôq's (fig. 244).

From the west coast, no drawings have been preserved from the earliest contact with Europeans. Development was different here, and was marked much earlier by merchants and missionaries who, with a few exceptions, wanted to exploit and change the Greenlandic culture. But the correspondingly earlier influx of new materials meant that painting, whose history is a mixed bag of originality and influences, came to be associated most strongly with West Greenland.

245. Tents, kayaks, umiak, and houses – settlement life depicting hunting and flensing. Collected in the Angmagssalik district in 1905-6 by William Thalbitzer. Pencil on paper, 4¹/₈″×6⁵/₈″. Royal Library, Copenhagen.

246 a and b. Details from early East Greenlandic drawings: (a) Drum dance and a common house viewed from above, drawn by Kattuaraje; (b) Umiak drawn by Kasper · Frederiksen at the age of fourteen. Collected in the Angmagssalik district by William Thalbitzer in 1905. Pencil on scratch pad paper. Royal Library, Copenhagen.

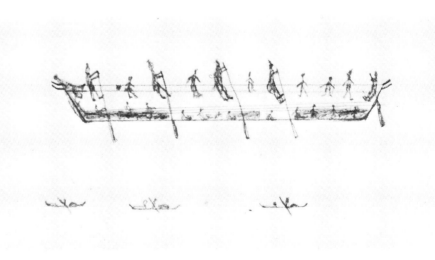

It had perhaps already begun with the Norsemen, but certainly with the English explorers. When John Davis sailed along the west coast in 1585, he found at one place a few small objects such as a bird made of bone, a toy kayak, and "a piece of wood made like an image." At several places, he traded with the Greenlanders, mostly for skins, but for other things as well: "The people had great store of darts and oares, which they made none accompt of, but gave them to us for small trifles, as poynts and pieces of paper." Whether the paper was used to draw on, we naturally don't know, and in any event several centuries were to pass before paper and pencils, canvas, brushes, and paints became commonplace.

That materials were scarce is practically a leitmotif in the history of painting in Greenland. Even after the colonies were established, the allotments of paper the managers got were measured out with an eye to thrift. Among the artists who were truly productive, it is said of Aron that he was furnished with materials by Governor Rink. As late as the 1920s, it was reported of the artists in Sukkertoppen that for want of brushes, they made their own, using the hair of their heads. Jakob Danielsen, who was immensely productive in the twenties and thirties, obtained his materials from Governor Rosendahl, and we know of other artists who painted on skin and scraps of building materials. The lack of materials is perhaps one reason why Greenlandic pictorial art was of very small dimensions until this century. It was necessary to be sparing and to utilize every scrap of paper and canvas.

The confrontation with Europe and the new norms

Not only new tools and materials came to Greenland from Europe, especially after the 1600s, but also new norms, other concepts of art, and a totally different attitude to the function of art. Practically all art forms were deeply integrated in the life of the Greenlanders. Song, dance, and mime were intermediaries in cultic life, a judicial process, and entertainment. Narrative tradition maintained recollection of ancestral beliefs, and thus preserved cultural patterns. The visual arts, in particular, both served religious purposes and formed the basis for everything the individual surrounded himself with: clothing, implements, boats, and dwellings.

In opposition to this stood the Europeans' attitude to art as something exalted. Belonging originally to the church and the court, and later penetrating to the walls of affluent burghers, art was regarded by Europeans as a trade one could be apprenticed to and become a specialist in. As the new-coined Greenlandic term expressed it, art was "something made that is strange." The artists of the new era made pictures that were supposed to be lifelike, to *represent* something – and not simply *be*. At the same time, named artists came into being – detached from its context, art could no longer be anonymous. The aims of pictorial art in Europe were associated with a cultivated public and with the lifestyles of the rich. The artist was expected to draw or paint scenes from classical mythology or the Scriptures, or dignified family portraits to be hung on the wall as part of the furniture.

The Greenlanders did not automatically assimilate these norms. People who hunted caribou and made their livings from kayaks had no use for paintings. That belonged to the wealthy, permanently settled in big houses of stone or lumber.

Just as the Danes had for centuries thought that the habits and culture of Italy, France, and Germany were finer and better than their own, so European and Danish culture was considered by the Greenlanders as

247. The Ascension. Presumably painted by Mathias Fersløv Dalager in Jakobshavn in 1792. Oil on wood (table top), 41″×28¾″. Described by Finn Gad in the journal Grønland, *no. 1 (1977). Church of Zion, Jakobshavn.*

being worthy of emulation. At the same time, many mixed families arose, deriving cultural traits from both sides.

The dilemma is plain in the first Greenlander to acquire formal schooling as an artist, Mathias Fersløv Dalager (1770-1842), who in 1789-92 studied at the Academy of Art in Copenhagen. The education he received could not be used for anything in Greenland, and as a Greenlander he did not feel at home in Denmark.

The son of the Danish merchant C.C. Dalager and a Greenlandic woman named Juliane Marie, Mathias grew up in the home of relations in Elsinore. There he revealed artistic ability and was taken out of school and admitted to the Royal Academy of Fine Arts, whose most notable professors at that time were Nicolai Abildgaard and Jens Juel. Apparently it was difficult for Mathias to make a living as an artist, as his father applied to the managers of the Royal Greenland Trading Company for either economic support for his son or a position for him in the company. From the application, it is clear that the father did not have much feeling for Greenlandic art and culture. He says of his son: "He is a native Greenlander on his mother's side, and the first who could possibly do that poor and despised nation any honor and show that even Greenlanders can have talent and mental ability as well as other nations … It would much grieve me were this young and hopeful person to bury both genius and talent alongside the dust of his parents in this cheerless country."

He goes on to say that during a stay in their home in Jakobshavn, the son painted a "limning" and gave it to the church there. Nothing is said about the size or theme of the picture, but in point of time it could well be the oval oil painting depicting the Ascension that hangs in Jakobshavn church (fig. 247). The picture is unsigned, and is painted on the top of a tilting table whose edge forms the frame. In its whole composition and style, it is typical of Danish academic painting at the end of the 1700s – recognizable in the Academy of Art's collection of gold and silver medal works. The heroic style, of which Abildgaard was the most distinguished representative, had many practitioners. In the characteristic oblique section, groups of figures in various planes are placed one behind the other, some of them in shadow but with the main figures strongly lighted and in dramatic postures – often kneeling and with the faces in profile, the arms and fingers spread in expressive, supplicatory gestures. The subjects were taken almost exclusively from the Old and New Testaments.

That Mathias himself was skeptical about his work as a painter is apparent in the job interview he had with the Royal Greenland Trading Company management, who were of the impression that "it wasn't right for the young Dalager to endeavor to cultivate his art." Dalager was not hired, but was instead offered a wretched allowance. Later he went to Trondheim, in Norway, where he obtained a position as "teacher of the art of drawing" at the secondary school.

To become an artist is not only a question of education. It is a process that presupposes a cultural deep-rootedness from which development can take place. To blindly assume another view of art is not development, but superficial copying. It must have been hard for Dalager to come from the Greenlandic hunting society of the 1780s to Copenhagen – and to feel as relevant the instruction at the Royal Academy of Fine Arts. No wonder his correspondence with the company concerning an allowance, a job, or his wild plans for hunting whales on his own, discloses uncertainty and restlessness, sometimes aggressively expressed. What is essential in the letters is that Mathias regards himself as a Greenlander, wants to return and work for his countrymen, and feels that he – who has gotten an education into the bargain – has the right to a position in his own country. But the company refused, and Mathias ended his days in Trondheim in 1842, a bitter and disheartened man, even though he at times had many commissions and was lionized by Norwegian society.

That Mathias Dalager's story moves me so strongly is probably because the pattern has repeated itself all the way down to our own day: the belief that an education in Denmark leads to advancement and happiness, followed by confused disappointment at the alienation that is often the result. The value of attending art school probably lies mostly in the feeling of being among colleagues, of being accepted on the grounds of one's artistic endeavors, of having one's personality corroborated rather than obliterated. It was unquestionably easier for young Greenlanders to learn to be midwives and coopers, schoolteachers and nurses. Art as a profession is difficult in a different way, and the teachers at the Academy of Art in Copenhagen knew nothing of Greenlandic art and culture. What one might reproach them for is that neither were they interested in learning about it until recently.

The thirst for knowledge and experience marked another early Greenlandic painter from the west coast, Hans Zakæus, who died in Scotland in 1819. Zakæus, who was from the area around Disko Bay, was converted to Christianity by missionaries; and he himself relates that the longing to see the missionaries' country made him board an English ship in 1816 as a stowaway. The next year Zakæus returned with the same ship, the *Thomas and Anne,* to Greenland, but as his only relation had died in the meantime, he remained aboard and went back to England.

His goal was to learn to write and to draw. Through the Scottish painter Alexander Nasmyth, Zakæus was introduced into circles that led him to John Ross, who at the time (in 1818) was getting ready for a voyage in search of the Northwest Passage. Zakæus went along as interpreter and had a great share in the fortunate outcome of the voyage: the discovery of, and meeting with, the Polar Eskimos. Even though Ross didn't find what he was looking for, this meeting with the Cape York Eskimos was a historic event, whose success was due mainly to Zakæus's linguistic abilities and human adroitness.

The meeting itself has been depicted by Zakæus in a color lithograph (fig. 248) in Ross's account of the expedition, which was published in England in 1819. Beneath the lithograph is the statement that it was drawn by John Sackheouse, which is a close English pronunciation of the name Zakæus. The subject is presented as a panorama. The two English ships, *Isabella* and *Alexander,* are shown in detail, with flags and pennons flying, anchored to the ice in a bay. In the distance, on the great sheet of ice, there are two Eskimos and a man with a ship's boat. Closer to us are a man on a dog-sled and another wearing European clothes. The latter is proffering a shirt to two Eskimos, who are examining a mirror and some beads in amazement.

The man with the shirt is possibly a self-portrait, as the account mentions that Zakæus won the Eskimos over by giving them a shirt and telling them that it was made from the hair of an animal they had never seen. In the immediate foreground are another dog-sled with four dogs, two tall English naval officers in full uniform, and two Eskimos, who face directly toward the viewer. The objects of trade are seen clearly: knives for narwhal tusks. The scene is framed by distant mountains in several planes.

The drawing shows that Zakæus had learned perspective and composition, but also that he had a sense for rendering a situation and for telling a story. This sense of the illustrative, which is typical of Greenlandic pictorial art, thus found expression for the first time.

Everything in the picture tells of a meeting. The lines meet, the ships arriving from the left, the sleds from the right, and on the white backdrop of the ice the historic tableau unfolds. There is also play on the contrast of colors. The Eskimos' clothes and dog-teams blend with the green and yellow gray tones of the mountains, the sky and ice. In counterpoise, deep, varied colors represent the Europeans, who come from the dark green, agitated sea; the ships are dark, the flags bright, the uniforms

248. Encounter between Polar Eskimos and Europeans. Color lithograph made by Hans Zakæus in 1818-19 and included in John Ross's A Voyage of Discovery *(London, 1819). 8¼″×15⅜″. National Museum, Copenhagen.*

intense blue. The flukes of the two whales in the foreground match the officers' cocked hats: both are visiting creatures of the open ocean. There are contrasts in the mountains, too: the soft, easy rhythms of the hinterland converge in a couple of jagged, somewhat disquieting pinnacles in the middle distance. The tall masts, the pointed mountains, and the tall men with pointed hats are beautifully distributed on the surface of the picture against the low dog-sleds, the bent Greenlander backs, and the soft expanses of the landscape.

Fundamental to a good painting are tensions: hard against soft, cold against warm, light against dark – and in Zakæus's picture there is also a psychological contrast that was possibly unintended by the artist, but has a powerful effect on us today: the haughty, ambitious Europeans with their gaudy bait; and the Eskimos who, gaping in naive self-effacement, swallow the hook.

Back in Scotland, Zakæus got the admiralty to provide for his further education, but in 1819 he was struck down by "nerve fever" and died in Edinburgh.

After these two first Greenlanders to obtain training at European art schools, a long time was to elapse before others journeyed abroad in order to become artists. However, drawings and watercolors made in Greenland now began to appear. The artists were in no way professionals. Many of these works were intended as object lessons – explanations of the look of things, objects with their names written alongside them – which was natural enough in a country with diverse languages. Sign and picture language is an elementary means of communication between people whose spoken languages are very different in manner of thinking, construction, and pronunciation. Such picture dictionaries could be used by both Greenlanders and Danes.

A board with the outlines of various household objects – such as a saw, thimble, shirt, and woollen underwear – cut into it with their Danish designations was probably made for the enlightenment of a *kivfak*, or

249. Interior of a common house. Drinking coffee. Painted on the west coast in 1840 by Israil Nichodimus Gormansen. India ink and watercolor on paper, 7¹/₂" × 12¹/₂". National Museum, Copenhagen.

Greenlandic housemaid. A landscape drawing with the Greenlandic names of the mountains inscribed on it, on the other hand, was most likely used by a Dane when traveling. Likewise, drawings of implements and hunting methods were probably intended as orientation for the Danes.

Often the charm of these undemanding, perhaps somewhat naive and awkward, drawings lies precisely in their makers' lack of artistic ambitions. Examples of this genre, in which the artist simply renders familiar objects and inscribes a verbal explanation, are Israil Gormansen's watercolors from the first half of the 1800s.

We know very little about Gormansen and the other early artists whose pictures were meant to instruct and inform. A good hunter might one day be unable to work, and the Danish colony manager might ask him to draw the various kinds of hunt and houses and kayaks. Often he would be able to, even though it was not quite as easy for him as carving a figure. Perhaps he would make only this one drawing in his whole life – or this first challenge would spur latent artistic talent into flower.

Whatever the conditions were, Gormansen obviously had talent. Seven eight-by-twelve-inch drawings from his hand in India ink and watercolors are known to exist. All are now in the possession of the National Museum in Copenhagen. How they got there, who collected them, and what the artist's background was, we do not know – only that on one of the watercolors is written *Israil Nichodimus Gormansen, Aprel 22, 1840.* Details of the kayaks and dress, which provide us with considerable knowledge of daily life in West Greenland at the time, indicate that the artist must have lived somewhere on the east coast between Disko Bay and Godthåb.

Everyday life unfolds before us: the men hunting, harpoon aimed at the seal or the rifle at the grazing caribou; women at work scraping skins, flensing a bearded seal, or picking berries. The *umiak* is seen upside down on its platform; or at sea, with the oarswomen crowded in the bow, while the men catch capelins with dip nets. The visual angle varies. We are given a bird's-eye view of some things, but usually the pictures run from left to right. Some figures look directly at the viewer, but otherwise we see the *umiak*s, kayaks, tents, and trudging people from the side.

In the signed picture, we see the inside of a common house (fig. 249). Even though linear perspective has not been attempted, and the space is not bounded by walls, there is no question but that we are indoors. We see the drying racks over the bed platforms as though from above, while the suspended soapstone pots are viewed from the side, as are the figures in the foreground – who are pouring and serving coffee in elegant cups. The women on the bed platforms behind are seen frontally.

Both in this and in the other pictures, there is an effect recognizable from children's drawings and from various artists, such as Paul Klee – that of objects seen from all angles. This dissolution of central perspective lends a kind of clairvoyance to the motif – it is the actual values that are sought, the super-real. The artist shows us the *umiak* in its total form, including the part concealed by the water. The birds are spread – so that we can see what they are like; and the men catching capelins are elevated up out of the *umiak,* where they practically float on the gunwale, so that we can perceive that they are the main figures and see their work-movements (fig. 250).

The composition beautifully emphasizes the action in the pictures: the themes are depicted as progressive friezes. In the depiction of harpooning from kayaks and scenes of caribou hunting, the paper has been utilized to contain two "picture strips," which are "read" from left to right.

In "Hunting Seals from Kayaks" (fig. 251), we see the hunters with harpoons raised on the left – dominated by vertical and horizontal lines, despite the strong rake of the kayaks' prows and sterns – and on the right the inviting seal, at one with the soft movement of the waves and practically laying itself open to the harpoon.

In "The Caribou Hunt" (fig. 252), two hunters are creeping on their knees behind a stone blind, bottom left, toward the caribou, a wonderfully delicate and elegant animal drawing. With some of the same knowledge and love of animals found in cave paintings, the drawing elucidates the body and the slender legs, the throat fur, the white abdomen, and the muzzle. Although the animal is presented from the side, the rack is turned and seen from the front in its full magnificence, so that it forms a delicate oval ornament.

Above walks a line of nine people – women, men, and children – who are carrying huge bundles on their backs – tent rolls, buckets (full of berries?), and, above all, caribou meat – with tumplines across their foreheads (still used). A mother has reversed her *amaut* so that the child rides in front as a counterweight to the burden. Some of the men are wearing two-colored vests and are using staffs. Around the heads of all the figures are clouds of tiny crosses – swarms of mosquitoes.

Among the slightly bent figures, all walking in step, the gray tones of the clouds of mosquitoes billow in and out, joining them into a winding, rhythmic frieze of great beauty. The S-shaped arabesques of the bodies are held firm by the more vertical effect of the women's topknots and the two staffs. The picture is a poetic rendering of the joys of the hunting life, in spite of noticeable irritation at the mosquitoes.

In "Interior From a Common House" and "Catching Capelins from an *Umiak*" (figs. 249 and 250), the composition is different. Instead of progressing toward a goal at the right, here the action takes place in the center of the picture.

In the house interior, a fixed net of vertical and horizontal lines is formed by the drying racks, the women facing front on the bed platforms, the descending cords, the pots, and the table surface in front with the coffee cups. The central action of the picture – the coffee *mik* – is being played out with small vignettes of communal family life in the background. The participants in the action are in the foreground, and involve the whole picture surface in their soft rhythms: a woman bends down and pours coffee from a huge copper kettle; a boy holds out a cup to a man, who steps toward him. Larger than the others, the man appears to be the principal figure, here being honored with a cup of the precious and beloved coffee.

"Catching Capelins from an *Umiak*" is surely the most delightful of the compositions. In this drawing, with its crisp, delicate line and refined utilization of the picture surface, one senses a close relationship to Klee or Miró, who both sought inspiration in the art of primitive peoples and

250. *Catching capelins from an* umiak. *West Greenland. Painted in the first half of the 1800s by Israil Gormansen. Watercolor and India ink on paper, 7½"×12½". National Museum, Copenhagen.*

252. Coming home from the caribou hunt, detail.
West Greenland. Painted in the first half of the 1800s
by Israil Gormansen. Watercolor and India ink on
paper, 7½"×12½". National Museum, Copenhagen.

251. Seal-hunting from kayaks. West Greenland.
Painted in the first half of the 1800s by Israil Gorman-
sen. Watercolor and India ink on paper, 7½"×12½".
National Museum, Copenhagen.

children. A light blue wave runs the length of the picture. The *umiak* is located not in the center, but slightly to the left, partly under the wave line, with the boat's mass emphasized by vertical lines meant to represent the seams of the skins – again a net of verticals and horizontals. In compensation, the figures are concentrated in the right side of the vessel, so that balance is achieved, which is further upheld by a bird in the upper right hand corner and a decorative group of three birds at the extreme right, just above the water.

The principal elements are the fishermen, their long-handled dip nets, and the matchsticklike capelins. Activity is expressed by the slanting lines. The oars and projecting gunwales serve mainly to frame the figures, while the long poles of the dip nets, the agitated, angular movements of the fishermen, and the shimmering rhythm of the school of fish make up the crux of the action, embodied in the column of fish plummeting into the boat. The flat caps of the men form a lid over the figures and mute the vehement elbow movements.

Lines intersect in the picture. The waterline intersects the seams of the boat skins, the men's bodies intersect the dip net poles, and one of the poles intersects an oar. There are also many implied points of intersection. The diving bird intersects the paths of the others. The bow and stern projections would intersect if their lines were carried down into the boat. A boy is standing in the stern with his harpoon, whose trajectory would intersect the lines of the stern projection and oar, and, by implication, the pole behind it. Finally – and perhaps most imperatively – the two poles potentially intersect each other.

All of the pictures have outlines and verbal explanations in sepia or black India ink. They were doubtless drawn with pen and ink first and then colored using a medium fine brush, judging from the brushwork in the wave lines and blinds. The colors were applied pure: yellow, red, black, brown, gray, and blue. Gormansen did not want – or try – to mix colors, and neither green nor violet appear. The color scheme is basically the same as in the majority of skin and bead embroideries. The fact that the colors were applied unmixed and that no washes were employed – such as for sky or clouds – indicates that the pictures were drawn first and then colored in, as in a coloring book. The waves, which do not have ink outlines, represent the sea, using a single long brush stroke or two – "a line of waves." Gormansen never tackled the painting of a seascape; his largest single surface is an opening in the ice. The pictures are, therefore, not experienced as scenes from nature, but rather as refined arrangements of humans, animals, and things.

I make so much of these seven small pictures for two reasons. First, they are beautiful in their own right; and, second, they represent the first examples of a naive narrative style fundamentally important for Greenlandic art. A direct line runs from Gormansen to artists such as Isak of Igdlorpait, Pele Danielsen, and Gerhard Kleist, and to our own day's Peter Berthelsen, Amalie Heilmann, and Enok Absalonsen, with parallels in Aron of Kangeq and Jacob Danielsen.

There were many besides Gormansen who painted and drew in the 1800s, but their works have vanished, either because they were reckoned of no account, or because of the perishable nature of the materials used. In the 1850s, Hinrich Rink collected a number of drawings "that he found by chance in various dwellings," one of which is reproduced in figure 253.

The first known Greenlandic painters embraced two tendencies, as it were: an acquired European style, and a narrative, realistic style with naive features. Meanwhile, with the appearance on the scene of Rink, we have arrived at an epoch comprising a blend of Danish influence and Greenlandic distinctiveness, an era that became a golden age in Greenlandic art and literature and that therefore calls for a section of its own.

253. Wild duck. Collected by Hinrich Rink in Godthåb in 1857-61 and pasted in a book sent to King Frederik VII. The same artist as figure 209, "a boy at the colony of Godthaab." Watercolor and India ink. 3¼"×6⅛". The Queen's Reference Library, Copenhagen.

Art in the service of enlightenment

254 a and b. "Pok and His Chum Drive to the Big House of the King," and "Pok and His Chum Step into the King's Hall." Cut by Rasmus Berthelsen for the Pok *book (1857), the first book printed on Governor Rink's printing press in Godthåb. The book describes Pok's and Qiperok's journey to Copenhagen in 1724. Hand-colored woodcuts, 2³⁄₈″×3¹⁄₂″. National Library of Greenland, Godthåb-Nuuk.*

This fruitful period in the pictorial arts was associated with other significant initiatives on the west coast in the middle of the 1800s, such as the development of the written Greenlandic language, the starting of a printing works, and the founding of a Greenlandic teachers' college.

Ever since Hans Egede founded "Hope's Colony" at Nuuk (The Point) in 1728, all endeavors had been directed to changing or influencing the natives; but by the 1850s and 60s, people no longer spoke of "the wretched heathen savages." Certainly expressions like "instruction" and "enlightenment" were used, but now books and pamphlets were being published in Greenlandic; there was an interest in the Greenlandic legends, and Greenlandic culture was being shown another kind of regard.

It was a single man, the ethnologist Hinrich Rink, who as governor of South Greenland set in motion the vital work of preservation. On his memorial stone in Godthåb are inscribed the words *kalâtdlit asavai ilisimavai:* "He loved the Greenlanders, knew and defended them."

Rink was instrumental in setting up the Greenlandic Boards of Guardians (the forerunners of local government) and in establishing a printing plant, together with the newspaper *Atuagagdliutit.* By publishing a number of books on the country's geography, administration, language, and culture, he moreover brought into being a scientific Eskimology.

That there was a growing realization among Greenlanders themselves that their own culture had to be preserved is seen in the fact that as early as 1823, the nationalist pioneer Vittus Steenholdt sent in the first contribution to the collection of manuscripts from Greenland in the Royal Library – a legend from the Egedesminde district. Then, in 1858, Rink sent out an invitation to the Greenlanders to send in legends, tales, maps, and drawings.

The sentence "Also wanted are maps and drawings" was what summoned forth the Greenlandic artists. During Rink's period of office, nearly 500 manuscripts arrived, sent in by catechists and hunters from the entire west coast, along with hundreds of maps, drawings, watercolors, and woodcuts. (Catechists were native Greenlanders trained and given the combined position of schoolteacher, church deacon, and lay minister.) In Godthåb, a handful of men collated the material, published it in several languages, and supplied their correspondents with paper and artists materials. Besides Rink and his gifted wife Signe, the inner circle who got the idea of enlightenment started in earnest included the linguist Samuel Kleinschmidt; the Greenlandic teacher, poet, and artist Rasmus Berthelsen; and the young Greenlander Lars Møller. Others were involved as well, such as Godthåb's curate, C. H. Rosen, who, before Rink, had furnished the hunter and artist Aron of Kangeq with paper and watercolors.

The text of the first Greenlandic book, printed in 1857 on the press Rink had ordered, was not new. This was the *Pok* book, which in part describes the journey of two Greenlanders, Pok and Qiperok, to Copenhagen in 1724, and in part presents a conversation between a minister and a shaman (*angakok*) presumably written in the 1760s, inasmuch as Poul Egede published it as an appendix to his *Grammatica groenlandica* mentioned in *Meddelelser om Grønland* (Information about Greenland), no. 120. Both parts were taken "from old manuscripts found among the Greenlanders at Godthåb" and speak indirectly of the great difference between the two cultures and the peculiar mixture of patronage and oppression the Greenlanders were treated with.

Pok and Qiperoq were much feted during their visit to Denmark. The newspapers were full of the event, and flysheets were published with woodcuts showing pageants on the canals of the city, where the Greenlandic visitors could be seen rowing the kayak and throwing the bird dart. They were the first Greenlanders the populace had seen, and curiosity was naturally coupled with national pride at "our far colony." Pok and Qiperok also visited the king. The Danish-Norwegian playwright Ludvig Holberg (1684-1754) observed: "One can't help noticing that the Greenlanders have a special sympathy for our vagrant mendicants, as they regard them as being of the same creation as others who live in pomp and abundance. This and other things are evidence of the savage Greenlanders' natural intelligence and kindness of heart."

Conversely, Pok says of the Danes that "For the most part these great men are wise and thoughtful," but "there are some who are not as they are supposed to be and who therefore do nothing; while others are very lazy, and still others spend everything they have on the water by which one goes mad." Pok was, furthermore, genuinely impressed by inventions like the compass and cranes that could lift ships and great stones; but he nevertheless concludes by saying that "it is still not in the Danes' power to stop the tides."

Rasmus Berthelsen illustrated some of the events in the *Pok* book, such as the Greenlanders driving in a coach to the king's palace (fig. 254*a*). "When we came on land we were put in a sled with a house on it, in which there were windows on both sides, as we were supposed to go to the great king," Pok says. Of the king's palace, he observes "It was like a great chalk-white iceberg with a roof of copper. In the great front hall there was room for twenty tents, so large it was, and on either side stood a lot of armed men wearing very fine clothes" (fig. 254*b*).

Berthelsen illustrates these events in simple, frank woodcuts. The principals are placed frontally like two manikins. They face the viewer in passive amazement as life in the city goes on. The few details, such as the national coat of arms on the coach door, are lightly indicated. What interests the artist are down-to-earth things – a proper coach with proper wheels, solidly constructed buildings, a group of guards as a military unit. Once the outline has been indicated, the surfaces are filled out with vertical and horizontal hatching (except where the latter follows the contours, as in the coach and the church spire). Central perspective is used several places as though laid out with a ruler. The texture of the guards' bearskin hats and the Greenlanders' clothes is effectively rendered with tiny stipples.

The woodcuts found in various editions are colored, though always in a few, unmixed tones: bright red, yellow, ochre, and blue. In their simple, somewhat childlike style, the cut and color of the pictures go well with the drollness of the text. Generally speaking, Berthelsen had an aptitude for striking a mood with few lines and simple devices, such as in the vignettes used on the title pages of the first Greenlandic books: the little kayak man in the waves (fig. 256), and, the most well-known example, the silhouettelike rendering of "the church, the teachers' college, and the governor's residence at the colony of Good Hope" (fig. 255). For many years, from 1861 to 1899, this vignette was used as the logo of the newspaper *Atuagagdliutit*. Although the church spire is different, the town profile is still immediately recognizable.

Rasmus Berthelsen was a very important person in the multifarious work of enlightenment begun by Rink. As translator, author, xylographer, printer, and editor of *Atuagagdliutit* during the newspaper's first years, his contribution was immeasurable. For Rink, he was a mainstay, as is evident from the governor's own testimony:

The native assistant teacher at the teachers' college, Rasmus Berthelsen, who is both skilled in the Danish language and from childhood has heard the Greenlandic legends told, has for three winters helped

255. The church, teachers' college, and governor's residence at Godthåb. Woodcut made by Rasmus Berthelsen in 1859 and used as the logo of the newspaper Atuagagdliutit *from 1861-99. 4⁵/₁₆" long.*

256. Kayak man in waves. Vignette cut by Rasmus Berthelsen in 1857 and used as the emblem on the first books from Governor Rink's printing press. Woodcut, 1⁷/₈" long.

257 a *and* b. *"A Girl from Godt- haab in Festive Costume" (see also fig. 230), and "A Woman with Child, from Godt- haab." Cut by Rasmus Berthel- sen from a drawing for* Greenlandic Woodcuts *(1860). Hand-colored woodcut signed "RB," 7½″×4⅜″. National Library of Greenland, Godthåb-Nuuk.*

me with their translation; and without his help a translation would be difficult to procure, as it demands not only knowledge of the language, but also of concepts and colloquialisms that only the native is suffi- cently familiar with to interpolate in the at times highly incomplete manuscripts.

Berthelsen was born in 1827, during a family caribou hunt in the Holsteinsborg district. "I was born in an *umiak* and swaddled in a caribou skin; and so that I shouldn't freeze to death, a tent was built in the *umiak*," he tells us. "My face was supposed to have been very ugly at my birth, so that when my father saw me he gave me the nickname 'Kikîk' – meaning, 'Ugh!' – and to this day my countrymen call me by that name."

As the son of a hunter, Rasmus was destined for the same occupation; but he broke with tradition and was trained as a teacher at the college in Godthåb, later supplementing his education in Denmark. Subsequently, he himself became an instructor at the college, advanced to the position of head catechist, and was active in the service of school and church until his death in 1901. Berthelsen was also a composer and writer of hymns, and will always be especially remembered in Greenland for his beloved Christmas carol "Guterput" (Our God).

Several of the important contributions from his hand are to be found in the picture book *Greenlandic Woodcuts* (1860). Among them are two very popular prints, "A Girl from Godthaab in Festive Dress" and "Woman with Child, from Godthaab" (figs. 257a and b). With their statuesque beauty, the two figures have the effect of declarations of love for the Greenlandic woman. Although dress and hairdos are depicted with the usual thoroughness, what is felt are the poetry and womanly warmth that radiate from them.

That Berthelsen possessed a polemical temperament is revealed by another of the woodcuts in the book, "Starving Greenlanders." Accord- ing to information given by Rink in a book sent to King Frederik VII, *Samples of Greenlanders' drawings, and of woodcuts and lithographs executed and printed in Greenland in the years 1857 to 1861,* "Starving Greenlanders" was cut from a drawing. Who drew the original is not mentioned, but it was hardly a motif available in *The Illustrated Times* or in the other illustrated journals, such as *For Large and Small,* which were a frequent source of ideas. Perhaps Rink himself had indicated lines of perspective or made a sketch. Even if it is based on another source, a work of art will always bear the hallmarks of its maker, however. This woodcut may therefore be regarded as a work of Rasmus Berthelsen's.

The interior of a common house is shown in darkness – the lamps have gone out, and we can imagine that it is cold as well. The vertical posts divide the picture into three parts, and the suggestion of perspective in the ceiling leads us toward the back wall, where women and children are huddling together on the skins of the bed platform. All of the woodwork is frail, the ceiling has fallen in, and there is no sheathing on the sod walls, as it has been used for firewood (which happened if the hunting failed and there was no blubber for the lamps). The emaciated, half- naked figures are marked by the apathy and despair characteristic of wasted, immiserated people.

The point has been skillfully used to emphasize the textural differences in the sod wall, the woodwork, skins, bodies, and the gnawed bones on the floor. The object of Berthelsen's pictures was most likely the same as that of his other enterprises in the service of the intellect: to enlighten and instruct.

Most of the figures are seen from in front, their wretched faces gazing directly at the viewer with such expressive force that one feels the accusa- tion in it. Hunger and cold were concepts that were all too familiar in old Greenland. Poor hunting and disasters such as blood vengeance, in which a family's best men might be killed, meant the extinction of entire settle-

258. *"Starving Greenlanders. The Interior of a Destitute House during Famine." Woodcut by Rasmus Berthelsen from a drawing (see also fig. 167). From* Greenlandic Woodcuts *(1860). 5⁵/₁₆″×8¹/₂″. National Library of Greenland, Godthåb-Nuuk.*

ments. It was also unfortunate to concentrate the population around the mission stations, where there was far from enough hunting for everyone. Another calamitous factor was trade, which in return for the indispensable skins gave the Eskimos cotton cloth, coffee, and tobacco. Craving for the new goods was great, and the result was impoverishment. Rasmus Berthelsen could depict this situation, which persisted into our own century, because he had known it. This is one of the very few expressions of social comment in Greenlandic art history. It is only in the most recent contemporary art that polemical works are again encountered.

But another Greenlandic artist was coming into the fore in those years, who was to influence development for several generations. This was Lars Møller (1842-1926), called Arqaluk ("The Older Sisters' Younger Brother"). Møller was born and died in Godthåb. An illustrator, lithographer, and printer, he was also for many years editor of *Atuagagdliutit*. While only fifteen years old, he was persuaded by Rink to enter apprenticeship in the printing plant, and he is mentioned on the title pages of the first Greenlandic books as Rasmus Berthelsen's assistant. Even though he greatly enjoyed outdoor life and was a skilled kayak man and hunter, Arqaluk was nevertheless fascinated by the work at the type case and the printing press.

After a couple of years under the guidance of Berthelsen and Rink, Arqaluk went with the latter to Denmark in the winter of 1861-62 for a stay of eight months. There he learned printing, bookbinding, and lithography from Louis Klein, and his knowledge of Danish increased. With Rink, he attended functions in Copenhagen, and was present at an audience with King Frederik VII, which was the occasion of a famous exchange. When the king remarked, "Incidentally, this is the first time I have seen an Eskimo," the unimpressed Arqaluk responded, "Yes, and incidentally this is the first time I have seen a king."

167

259 a and b. Polar Eskimos encountering American expedition members and killing a polar bear. Lithographs by Lars Møller, used as illustrations for an article about the American polar explorer Elisha Kent Kane. In 1853-55, in mapping the coasts and endeavoring to find the vanished British explorer Sir John Franklin, Kane got as far as the Humboldt Glacier, where he encountered Polar Eskimos from Greenland. The article appeared in the first number of Atuagagdliutit *(1861). 8⁷/₁₆″×6¹³/₁₆″. National Library of Greenland, Godthåb-Nuuk.*

After returning home from this, his only visit to Denmark, Arqaluk's task became more than that of publishing books. Publication of the Greenlandic-language newspaper *Atuagagdliutit*, another of Rink's initiatives, had begun in 1861. A sample number of "a kind of journal" had been issued, with the aim of "providing the Greenlanders with in part entertaining and in part instructive reading." This sample issue was a blend of history and current events, including articles about a naval visit, the electric telegraph, explorers' expeditions, and the Norsemen in Greenland. It was declared that:

> As illustrations are assumed to be especially useful in regard to the object of the publication, every effort has been made to provide them. The three woodcuts were carved by the Greenlander Aron of Kangeq, from pictures in other publications. In addition, the native Lars Møller, who learned the art of printing here, and who has seen to all the typesetting and printing appertaining [to the publication of *Atuagagdliutit*], has now attained some practice in printing lithographs. The accompanying samples were thus printed by him, with the help of a boy to whom the plates were entrusted.

Finally, there was an invitation to send in written contributions, preferably in Greenlandic. The paper was distributed free to Greenlanders, whereas Europeans and others who did not belong under the Boards of Guardians had to reimburse the colony manager in Godthåb.

The paper was tremendously popular, and was literally read to tatters. The stories were devoured and the pictures scrutinized along the entire coast, so eager were the Greenlanders to know something about themselves (figs. 259a and b) and the world around them – about kings and emperors, discoveries, and wars great and petty. What was written about, and the manner in which the material was communicated, had an enormous influence on people's thinking and behavior.

During the first years, Rasmus Berthelsen was editor, and his assistent was Lars Møller. But gradually the latter took over more and more of the work, wrote and made lithographs, typeset, printed, bound, and distributed the publication. Møller's editorship lasted from 1874 all the way up to 1922. There was no exaggeration in the words spoken by the Greenlandic poet and composer Jonathan Petersen at Møller's retirement: "He has worked for three or four generations. In 1861 he printed reading material for my grandmother, and later for my parents and me, and now finally for my growing children. Thus he has made a limitless contribution for all of Greenland's coasts in the long winter darkness, toward true enlightenment for the entire people."

Both in the selection and translation of the reading matter and in the free copying of illustrations, the material taken from Danish journals acquired a Greenlandic slant. Still, the work of enlightenment had its price: the basis for both reading matter and illustrations was the Danish or European news; the Europeans' way of drawing, their clothes, habits, and culture predominated. That a Greenlander such as Arqaluk (who was, incidentally, of Danish-Greenlandic stock) prepared this material indeed provided it with a Greenlandic interpretation, but it was European culture that was disseminated.

Atuagagdliutit had a great deal of the responsibility for the emergence of the Danish-Greenlandic hybrid culture. It was not until Kristoffer Lynge's editorship, beginning in 1922, that the newspaper switched from carrying predominantly borrowed story material to being a real news organ that dealt with Greenlandic social and political issues.

At the time of the paper's inauguration, the general level of literacy was not high, and many learned to read through *Atuagagdliutit*, which was one reason the material was easily accessible and accompanied by many illustrations. The Greenlanders' delight in pictures was nourished

260. *Frederik VII's funeral. Lithograph by Lars Møller, used in* Atuagagdliutit *in 1864. 8¹¹/₁₆"×6¹¹/₁₆". National Library of Greenland, Godthåb-Nuuk.*

by the many lithographs in the paper, some of them in color, and certain fundamental themes were laid down.

Preferred subjects were royal events, such as Princess Alexandra's wedding or the funeral of Frederik VII. There is probably no other place in the world (perhaps with the exception of England) where interest in royalty is still so alive as in Greenland (fig. 260). Even today, clippings with pictures of the royal family are everywhere to be seen alongside family photographs or in magazine-clipping collages on board walls. Another favorite theme was war, both distant conflicts such as those in the Balkans, and the Danish-German war of 1864.

The peculiar behavior of strange peoples was good reading – and good material for illustration, as in a lithograph showing manners of greeting among the Chinese, Japanese, Indians, and Australian aborigines (fig. 261). Wild animals in Africa were depicted in beautiful color lithographs, and three luxuriant summer pictures in figures 262a-c must have appeared equally exotic. Idyllic scenes unfold in a saturated color scheme and detailed narrative line reminiscent of the Douanier Rousseau.

"Nuniagtut" ("They Who Pick Berries") reveals a sumptuously fertile landscape, where pumpkins swell in their beds and sunflowers nod over busy figures; people are depicted picking cherries and apples from trees, cutting bunches of grapes from vines, or on their way home with baskets bursting with fruit. A market scene teems with life, among booths displaying the farmer's vegetables and the potter's pots. Awnings and parasols indicate the southerly latitude. The Greenlandic caption reads: "This is what the people are like, who proffer various tempting items at Igdlorpait" [Some Houses]. Finally, there is a depiction of harvest time; the golden grain is being mowed with scythes, raked together, bound into sheaves, shocked, and driven to the gristmill – again, a gentle and verdant scene that must have seemed prodigiously alien to Greenlandic readers. No game animals – but abundance issuing forth out of the ground and from the trees.

It is not known whether there was a model for these three color lithographs, but the presence of a winepress and a donkey indicate that French drawings, for example, might have been the prototypes. Another series of pictures – illustrations to the Greenlandic rendering of the Danish *Molbohistorier* ("Ozark stories") – was obviously taken from the collection of M. V. Fausbøll, published in 1862.

Romances and serials were also carried, and the romance of Oberon and the Robinson Krusoe series (there is no "C" in Greenlandic), which first appeared in 1862 and was continued in the 1864-65 volumes, were richly illustrated (figs. 263a and b). Now and then, local news and practical information appeared, such as the list of sailings of the Royal Greenland Trading Company's nine sailing ships. Stories from the Bible alternated with legends from the time of the Norsemen, and accounts of expeditions with prospectuses from India. There were many contribu-

261. *Different peoples' forms of greeting; from Australia, China, and Japan. Section of lithograph by Lars Møller, used in* Atuagagdliutit *in 1864. 8¹/₄"×6¹¹/₁₆". National Library of Greenland, Godthåb-Nuuk.*

262 a-c. *"They Who Pick Berries," "This Is What the People Who Proffer Various Tempting Items at Igdlorpait Are Like," and "This Is What the Workers Do at Narssag." Color lithographs by Lars Møller, used in* Atuagagdliutit *in 1864. 6⅞″×9⁷/₁₆″. National Library of Greenland, Godthåb-Nuuk.*

tions by Greenlanders, however, such as an excerpt from catechist Johannes ("Hansêraq") Hansen's East Greenlandic journal from the *umiak* expedition of 1884-85; and space was given to hunters such as Ungâralak (in the 1877-84 volumes) and Jâkuaraq Eugenius (in 1934-35).

The intent was obviously to publish entertaining reading matter with corresponding pictures. That Lars Møller possessed great technical skill as a lithographer and much facility in drawing is undeniable, but generally he worked from published originals. Although his copies were often rather free renderings, and were far better pictures than the originals, one must look hard to find his own personal artistic expression. So engrossed was he in telling amusing or instructive stories that his illustrations were frequently mere commentaries, like the photographs in modern-day newspapers.

But there were exceptions; particularly during the first years of the paper, and in the color lithographs, we find an independent manner that is surely Møller's own. There is the personal style both in a few grandiose landscapes and in the pictures of ordinary life entitled "Greenlanders Outside Their Houses in New Herrnhut" (fig. 163) and "The New Church at the Colony of Sukkertoppen" (fig. 264). In all of these pictures, there is a clear division into foreground, middleground, and background; the terrain is in the proper place and reveals that the artist knows nature well and is accustomed to judging the distance in over the mountains. In contrast, the figures appear as embellishment, as dolls arranged in the living landscape. In the picture from the consecration of the church in Sukkertoppen, how beautiful and living the rocks are, emphasized by the dappled light of the unstable, clouded sky. There is an interaction between light and shadow, also recognizable in the delicate balance between the cool blue and warm reddish brown colors; the cold sky and the warm clouds; the cold patches of snow and ice against the warm earth; the warm front of the church – with the throng emerging from the house of God – contrasted with the chilly side, which is in shadow.

The center of the picture is the church, but there are no dead places in the picture surface. Both the rocks in the left foreground and the light field of sky at upper right are excellent details within the whole. On closer scrutiny, Greenlandic sod houses show up in the terrain, and small scenes between the figures unfold. In spite of the uneasy sky – which Møller was partial to – the total impression is mild and harmonic, the line soft and the colors subdued.

We find this very precise line in Møller's sketchbook from an expedition with the Swedish explorer Adolf Erik Nordenskiöld in 1883, when as correspondent to *Atuagagdliutit* he drew coastlines, rocks, and glacial formations with a razor-sharp sense of observation and much feeling for the long, rhythmic contours in the landscape. He was one of Godthåb's outstanding personalities, a central figure whose linguistic abilities, familiarity with Greenlandic conditions, and vast general knowledge many prominent visitors benefited by. Through the illustrations in *Atuagagdliutit*, he popularized and brought pictorial art to the ordinary population.

After the appearance of the *Pok* book in 1857, the picture book *A Conversation about War, Elucidated with Many Pictures* was published in 1858. The text was written by Rasmus Berthelsen in the form of a conversation between a catechist, who asks questions, and a minister, who answers and explains. The idea of war is investigated, from children's quarrels to Napoleon's wars of conquest and religious war between Christians and Mohammedans. The questions of the catechist represent the spontaneous Greenlandic astonishment at the contradiction between the Christian message of love and the realities of war. In replying to them, the minister occasionally has to manage by saying, "You ask so many difficult questions. To explain, I would have to tell you so much more that you don't know, and I don't have time for that now. I will

263 a and b. Robinson Crusoe. Color lithographs by Lars Møller. The story of Robinson Crusoe appeared as a serial in Atuagagdliutit *in nos. 8-14 in the 1862 volume, and again from no. 30, in 1864, to no. 41 in 1865. Format about 6¾"×8¼". The newspaper's format was for many years 10¼"×7⅞". National Library of Greenland, Godthåb-Nuuk.*

264. Sukkertoppen church. Color lithograph by Lars Møller, appeared in Atuagagdliutit *vol. 1, no. 5 (1861). 10¼"×9¼". National Library of Greenland, Godthåb-Nuuk.*

show you the pictures, so that you can see what happens in a war."

The pictures are xylographs – that is, wood engravings cut on hard end grain, which makes very fine lines possible. They were printed by Rasmus Berthelsen and Lars Møller, although, with the exception of a few vivid hand-colored ones, they were neither drawn nor cut by them. A large proportion are illustrations borrowed from the weekly journal *For Large and Small.* They include caricature-figures with large heads and distorted bodies (fig. 265), a dramatic robber-romance style, and panoramas with groups of figures, used as illustrations of the Crimean War (fig. 266). These xylograph blocks were shipped to the printing plant in Godthåb, and, after being used, were further utilized by Greenlandic artists, who cut their motifs on the reverse sides, although with characteristics of the foreign style.

It is apparent that the wood engraving from the Crimean War has been used by Lars Møller, and possibly also by Aron and Jens Kreutzmann, as a model of a tableau unfolding in a section of landscape, using perspective, and with the most important action taking place approximately in the center of the picture, with a group in the foreground and a subordinate situation in the background. The Eskimo pictorial concept, in which the action takes place as a frieze, with the pictorial elements of equal importance everywhere on the picture surface, now fell into disuse. Henceforth (in my opinion, too strongly influenced by Rink's examples) Greenlandic artists would let their themes unfold in three-dimensional space on a stage. Nevertheless, the old concept turned up now and then, and it still appears sporadically.

The famous *Kalatdlit ássilialiait* (Greenlandic Woodcuts), again printed by Rasmus Berthelsen and Lars Møller, appeared in 1860 in Danish, English, and French editions, presumably so that Rink could call attention to Greenlandic art by using it as a gift to foreigners. The book comprises pictorial material from the two collections of legends published in 1859-60, combined and supplemented so that it contains thirty-nine woodcuts, most of them by Aron of Kangeq, but with contributions by Rasmus Berthelsen, Jens Kreutzmann, the carpenter Markus of Godthåb, and Abraham and Apollus of Kangeq. There must have been a general collaboration among the artists, inasmuch as many of the cuts were drawn by one and engraved by another. It is as though the most important thing for the artists was to get the stories told; from the point of view of teamwork, it was unimportant who devised the motif and who executed it.

Thus far, we have discussed the men who were active during this

265. Caricatures. Woodcut made by an unknown European artist, probably for use in a Danish magazine. Shipped to Governor Rink's press, partly as a sample of woodcut technique and partly as material, as the reverse of the block was used for a woodcut by Aron of Kangeq. 3³/₈″×4¹/₂″. National Library of Greenland, Godthåb-Nuuk.

period in Godthåb, where they organized and prepared material sent in from the entire west coast – legends and tales, maps, drawings, watercolors, and woodcuts. Let us now turn our attention to the artists who arose by invitation, as it were. The ability to remember and recount, to pass legends and tales on from generation to generation, is extremely strong among the Greenlanders, and there are also very great storytellers in the pictorial arts.

266. Scene from the Crimean War. Color woodcut by an unknown European artist used in the book A Conversation about War, Elucidated with Many Pictures, *printed by Rasmus Berthelsen and Lars Møller at "the governor's printing works" (Godthåb, 1858). 5¹/₈″×8⁷/₈″. National Library of Greenland, Godthåb-Nuuk.*

Narrative pictorial art

It all started with Rink's "invitation" to send in legends (see page 164), which resulted in contributions from hunters and catechists from the entire west coast, among them Jonathan, called "Sameq," of Julianehåb; the catechist and hunter Christian Hendrik of Kangeq; and the catechist Albrecht of Holsteinsborg. Later came Hendrik's son, Aron of Kangeq, also a hunter and catechist; the outpost manager Jens Kreutzmann of Kangaamiut; Kristian of Kangeq; Kristian Rinatuse; the guardian Jeremias; Enos Boasen; Peter Justus; Amon; Pita; the catechist Eliasen of Umanak; and the hunter Johannes Poulsen from the Godthåb district. Finally, there were some legends "written down by natives in North Greenland thirty-five years ago and collected by Pastor Kragh."

The legends were part of an oral tradition, known and told by everybody, though with varying depths of interpretation. Now writers were needed, and from the list of authors it appears that many of the informants were catechists who knew the art of writing. At the same time, two of the authors began producing pictorial material. They were Jens Kreutzmann and Aron of Kangeq, who most assuredly knew how to tell a story in colors and lines, light and shadow, with a sense of rhythm and proportion, distance, space, and sequence – in other words, in the language of pictures.

The Greenlandic public did not at the outset become familiar with all the pictorial material sent to Rink. More than 200 of Aron's watercolors and around 50 of Jens Kreutzmann's remained unknown for nearly 100 years. The National Museum in Copenhagen received this unique collection for a nominal sum as a gift from Signe Rink in 1905, at the settlement of Hinrich Rink's estate. Rink himself had regarded the pictures as "quaint," and did not assign them any special significance.

In the archives of the museum, this collection remained in a state of obscurity until 1960, when Eigil Knuth called attention to it for the first time in an article in *Nationalmuseets Arbejdsmark* (The Work of the National Museum). Subsequently, articles and books about it appeared, and there were exhibits of Aron's watercolors in particular. In 1982, the collection was returned to the people of Greenland, and is now in the National Library of Greenland in Godthåb-Nuuk.

Naturally, it was impossible to reproduce these watercolors on "the Governor's press" in Godthåb, though a few were converted into color lithographs. Woodcuts were best suited for reproduction, as they could be printed directly from the block. Looking at the themes of the book *Greenlandic Woodcuts*, we see that they fall into three categories: daily life in Greenland, tales from the time of the Norsemen, and legendary figures. We have already touched on the motifs from daily life in discussing dress, the dwelling, and the kayak; and it is obvious that the subjects were dictated by Rink from an ethnographic point of view. Consider the titles:

1. A girl from Godthåb in festive dress (figs. 230 and 257*a*).
2. A woman with child, from Godthåb (fig. 257*b*).
3. The interior of a prosperous house (fig. 168).
4. The interior of a destitute house during famine (figs. 167 and 258).
5. Kayak men, and an *umiak* with passengers (fig. 145).
6. A Greenlandic house seen from outside.
7. An *umiak* before covering.
8. Implements for hunting from a kayak.
9. Various woodcuts, first attempts by beginners.

These pictures appear in the front of the book as a kind of preface or elucidation of the material culture: boats, implements, dwellings, dress. Paradoxically, these pictures were engraved from published originals – one would think that the Greenlanders themselves were well enough informed about these matters.

Numbers 1, 2, and 4 were engraved by Rasmus Berthelsen; 3, 5, 6, and 7 by Aron; and 8 by Abraham and Apollus of Kangeq – all of them drawings. Still, there were differences. Aron was distinctively a proficient wood-engraver, a hunter who knew how to use his knife to express himself artistically as well. Consider the cut of kayak men (fig. 145), the assuredness with which the mountains are rendered, and the precise rhythm of the waves against the firm lines of the boats.

Perhaps I am making too much of the question of how original these works are. Artists have copied each other in all countries and all times: the Romans borrowed from the Greeks, the Dutch from the Italians, the Danes from the French. Individual artists have frequently produced original and independent works using another work of art as a basis. Manet borrowed from Goya, Picasso from Cézanne, van Gogh from Delacroix and Millet. Rasmus Berthelsen's "Starving Greenlanders" and Aron's "Kayak Men" are effective as independent, personal productions, whatever the model may have been.

Apart from the fact that the phenomenon of artists arising out of examples from the illustrated press is remarkable, the question interests me because certain precedents were established for Greenlandic artists during those years. The small size, for instance, probably had something to do with the necessity of saving paper and with the cramped space in the houses, but also with the fact that we are referring to book illustrations. The book's format was 9½ by 27½ inches, and *Atuagagdliutit* measured 10¼ by 7⅞ inches, a format the paper maintained well into the 1900s. Individual large lithographs appeared as fold-outs in the newspaper, but otherwise one adapted oneself to the small size.

One also adapted oneself to didactic aims: the pictures were supposed to tell a story, to have a subject, to be instructive or illustrative. Absolute art, the cultivation of line and color for their own sake, was something that took place in embroideries on clothing – now one learned that art on paper was supposed to accompany a text, and it was no trouble. The small format and the narrative element are familiar features of other Greenlandic art, and they quickly found their place in drawing and painting.

The remainder of *Greenlandic Woodcuts* illustrates tales about "the fall of the old Scandinavians at Julianehaab (Østerbygden)" and at Godthåb (Vesterbygden), and contains "pictures relating to Greenlandic legendary stories." Virtually all these pictures deal with killing and vengeance, quarrels and trials of strength; with Aqigssiaq, who performed great feats; Ungilagtake, the cruel killer; and Akamilak, the savage heathen. We see Navaranaq being dragged to death by her countrymen, and the Greenlander Kaissape raising the severed arm of Oungertoq, the Norse chieftain, in triumph.

All of the events are violent, depicted either being enacted or immediately before the decisive moment. It is therefore natural that movement plays a great role in the woodcuts; with single exceptions, the action concerns people running, walking, or falling. Consider the series about Aqigssiaq's exploits, engraved by Markus Lynge (from drawings by Aron) in a frank, dramatically effective style.

In "The Seal Ball Game" (fig. 267a) – alleged by Rink to have been drawn and engraved by Aron, but a picture whose total style points to Markus as the engraver – not a single one of the more than thirty people depicted is at rest. Three have fallen in the turmoil and we see them in mid-fall, before they have touched the ground. The others are running in all directions. The picture illustrates an ancient Eskimo game played all

267 a. *"The Seal Ball Game," drawn and engraved by Aron of Kangeq. From the legend of Aqigssiaq. From* Greenlandic Woodcuts. *3¹⁵/₁₆″×6⁷/₈″. National Library of Greenland, Godthåb-Nuuk.*

the way up to our own day. The "ball" consists of a sealskin stuffed with good things. The object of the game is naturally to secure it and bring it to safety, and the winner gets the contents. Everybody can participate, but families or settlement fellows tend to form individual teams, who together try to get away with the prize. The game is very much a trial of strength, as it is necessary to run while lugging the big "ball."

The woodcut depicts all this with tremendous precision. With the coveted seal the only calm form – a reposing oval in the center of the picture – the running figures gyrate in a net of vertical, horizontal, and diagonal lines. The snow is ploughed up by the myriad footprints, whose horseshoe contours increase the agitation in the picture. So do the imaginary lines flashing as glances between the contenders everywhere in the picture, excepting only the two fallen figures, who cast looks of longing at the object of the contest.

The line of the seal follows the horizontal central axis of the picture, while the body of the man carrying the seal follows its vertical center, borne up by the intersection of the legs. The mountains in the background form a diagonal section in the upper half; and the three fallen figures, foremost in the lower half, do precisely the same. The extended rhomboid field, which opens between the points of intersection of the two diagonal sections, is filled out precisely by the center of the action: the seal, and the man who has it. The figures are very plastic; modeled forth, so to speak, from the surface of the picture by means of contoured hatching. The firm, plump forms of the men and women are shown to best advantage and enhance the impression of vitality.

As might be expected, the seal ball game was not always a harmless pastime (see also fig. 282). Old animosities could flare up, and jealousy and envy could lead to acts of violence under cover of sport – much like intentional football injuries in our own day. The entire Aqigssiaq legend has its starting point in just such an incident.

It was said that in Jakobshavn this ball game was eagerly gone in for during the winter, when "the sea was frozen, and as the days grew longer the hunting declined." The best player, who beat everybody in the game, had a daughter who married and bore four sons, to the great joy of all the family, until the eldest of them grew up and became very good at the game, when the grandfather got "spiteful in the mind" and killed his grandchild in envy. The three other grandchildren, together with their father, now began to meditate revenge, and at length they succeeded in murdering their grandfather. Afterwards they fled into the interior, where each of them took an "icecap dweller" to wife. The eldest of the wives first bore eight sons, and then, much later, an afterthought whom

175

267 b. *"Aqigssiaq's Great-Grandfather Being Killed by His Grandchildren." Woodcut by Markus Lynge from a drawing by Aron of Kangeq. From* Greenlandic Woodcuts. *$3^{15}/_{16}'' \times 7^{1}/_{16}''$. National Library of Greenland, Godthåb-Nuuk.*

they called Aqigssiaq (Grouse Chick). He became the strongest and fleetest of them all, and many legends have been handed down about his exploits.

In "The Seal Ball Game," the three fallen figures and the one with the ball may be the four brothers. In "Aqigssiaq's Great-grandfather Being Killed by His Grandchildren," the lines of the descending terrain in the background form the picture's only diagonal, against which the three active figures place themselves. All hold raised lances, which cut across the soft contours of the ground and the sod houses and sunder them like a blow. Their goal is the calm, horizontal form at the lower edge of the picture: the dead grandfather. The middle figure in particular, with its headlong dash, expresses the feeling of blind vengeance. As a kind of brake on the slanting figure, his lance is placed vertically, like a central pivot restraining the diagonals (fig. 267b).

If we look at another illustration of the Adventures of Aqigssiaq, "Aqigssiaq Throws a Pot Troll down a Mountain," we are struck by the effectiveness with which Markus Lynge realizes these stories of violence. With a single stroke, a powerful movement without superfluous details or middle shading, he makes a statement about struggle and survival. The pot troll (a supernatural filcher of catches of game) being flung off the edge of the escarpment and tumbling backward into the abyss is depicted dramatically and forcefully. Aqigssiaq still has some of the rhythm of the thrust in his body, but otherwise he stands firmly planted on the rock, and can now return to the catch that had been taken from him (fig. 268).

According to Rink, all of the stories in the book, about battles between coast dwellers and icecap dwellers, "doubtless originated in Indians, in olden times, having driven the Eskimos out of North America. In the legends, meanwhile, they are removed to what is now Greenland, and have been somewhat mixed with tales of the old Scandinavians."

Some of the first legends and tales Rink received, published in the first volume of the collection of legends in 1859, were stories about quarrels between Greenlanders and Norsemen: about "Oungortoq, the chieftain of the old Norsemen," written down from the oral account of Jonathan of Julianehåb, and "the fall of the old Norsemen in Amaraglik," written by Abraham of Kangeq. A year later, in volume two, a narrative appeared "concerning the first meeting of the Greenlanders with the old Norsemen in olden times," written down by Aron of Kangeq.

Legends of these battles were thus very much alive, 400 years after the Norsemen had vanished. As might be expected, the authors came from the districts where the Norsemen had settled: Vesterbygden (the Godthåb Fjord, at whose mouth lie the Kangeq islands) and Østerbygden (Julianehåb). There is, however, something that would indicate a fusion with stories of more distant strife between Indians and Eskimos, as Rink mentions. Thus the Eskimo girl Navaranaq, who was the cause of the hostilities, and ultimately of the Norsemen's downfall, has a parallel in a figure in legends from Labrador, in which an Indian girl sows enmity between inland dwellers and coast dwellers. In the Greenlandic variant, she has become a housemaid of the Norsemen, moves about among both groups, and sets the two peoples at odds with each other with mendacious gossip. Finally, the Norsemen attack and kill all the Eskimo women and children, whereupon the Greenlanders retaliate by burning the Norsemen's houses and killing all of the Scandinavians.

The scheming Navaranaq was then punished by her countrymen by being dragged to death, "and while they were dragging her, the flesh of her back came off, so that her bones were visible, and they asked her, 'Navaranaq, are you having fun?' and she replied, 'Certainly I am having fun!' As they now kept on dragging her, her intestines came out, even though they hadn't wounded her. Because she had destroyed the peace, they put her to death in this manner."

The illustration for this dramatic scene was both drawn and engraved by Aron (fig. 269). Where Markus availed himself of the black-white effect and gouged large areas away so that much remained in white, Aron worked with an abundance of hatchings, which resulted in a predominance of gray tones.

The pictorial effect of this woodcut is also due to the textural treatment of the surface, as seen in the sealskin clothes of the Greenlanders. The figures are "flat," and not vividly rounded as with Markus; but the sculptural element is nevertheless present in the total conception of the beautifully formed landscape, the boulderlike clouds of dust Navaranaq raises, and the knot of vengeful men.

The sympathy and psychological message are centered around this closed group, who, with grave resolve, calmly and inexorably enforce justice. There is none of the agitation of a lynching about the scene; no particular horror or pity in the depiction of the victim. If anything, the unfortunate Navaranaq is a dummy being dragged along the ground, although the picture's only element of unrest is the wake she makes in the dust or gravel. The severe, calm lines of the landscape intersect nearly diagonally with the line that begins with Navaranaq and continues in the thongs tied around her wrists and to her topknot.

268. "Aqigssiaq Throws a Pot Troll down a Mountain." Woodcut by Markus Lynge from a drawing by Aron of Kangeq. From Greenlandic Woodcuts. *Block later reduced; original format 3¹⁵/₁₆″×6⅞″. National Library of Greenland, Godthåb-Nuuk.*

269. Navaranaq being dragged to death. Woodcut by Aron of Kangeq. From Greenlandic Woodcuts. *3¾″×5⅝″. National Library of Greenland, Godthåb-Nuuk.*

Even though the procession describes a slightly oblique line inward toward the interior of the field, there is in this woodcut something of the original Eskimo pictorial style, in which the action takes place in a laterally progressing frieze. As prints are laterally reversed, Aron viewed the motif from left to right on the block starting with the principal, Navaranaq.

Vengeance is also the main theme in the woodcut of Kaissape killing Oungertoq, the Norse chieftain (fig. 270). This is the concluding picture in the series about the fall of the Norsemen – a dramatic tale of heads on stakes, incendiary killings, flight and pursuit, revenge and punishment.

The Greenlander Kaissape's brother had earlier been killed by Oungertoq, who had cut off the arm of his victim. When the Norsemen's farms were burned, Oungertoq, their chieftain, fled through a window with his little son in his arms. In escaping, he threw the child into a lake, as it was better that the child drown than it fall into the hands of his enemies. After being pursued tenaciously by Kaissape, Oungertoq was at length killed by an enchanted arrow. In retaliation for the death of his brother, Kaissape chopped the right arm off the dying chieftain, saying: "My brother's arm, which you chopped off, I have not forgotten; and as long as I live, and while you are still alive, you are not likely to forget your arm!"

The arm is the center of the picture and its vertical axis; the body of the dying chieftain blends in entirely with the terrain. Still bending slightly over the body stands Kaissape the avenger, dark and ominous. His form and long hair, together with the severed arm, comprise the only vertical lines in the picture. The mood of death and destruction is emphasized by the dark sky with two storm clouds, and the horizontal lines of the barren landscape.

Aron (1822-69) is a master of storytelling. He not only illustrates the legend's narrative, but uses landscape and weather as a backdrop for the action, so as to strike the appropriate mood precisely. His interpreter Eigil Knuth has called him "the master of Greenland's golden age." Certainly the period around the middle of the 1800s can be designated a golden age in literature and the visual arts in Greenland, and Aron contributed greatly to it during the last ten years of his life. A very skilled seal hunter, Aron was born at the Kangeq outpost near Godthåb. His father, Christian Hendrik, and his grandfather Abraham (whose heathen name was Kivioq), were catechists for the Moravians, who had established a mission station, a so-called *Vorhof,* in Kangeq. Aron also became a catechist for the Moravian Brethren, who had come to Greenland in Hans Egede's time, had considerable influence on missionary work, and remained in the country until the year 1900. On account of their connection with the work of the mission, Aron and his father had learned to write, and were among the first contributors to the collection of legends. The very first contribution was Christian Hendrik's account of the heathen Parpak, a tale Aron illustrated a number of times.

Aron sent in fifty-six legends in all, and with his knowledge of the extensive Godthåb Fjord, it soon proved that he was also able to draw maps. In addition, he made wood carvings and painted. There exist in all around 350 works from his hand, more than 200 of which are watercolors.

The reason for this large output was, first of all, that Aron – like so many others – was stricken with tuberculosis, and could not go out in a kayak. Pastor Rosen in Godthåb and Hinrich Rink paid for the pictures he sent in, and although the remuneration was modest, it meant an income for him. It was also a tremendous encouragement for him that there was a demand for his memory, knowledge, and artistic abilities. His general condition improved, and he even began to go hunting again, until the disease took hold in earnest and confined him to his bed platform.

Rink reported of the houses in Kangeq: "The houses of the Greenlanders are very wretched, with the exception of the one belonging to the very capable and enterprising catechist of the Moravian Brethren. It has a tall planked roof, and is likewise sheathed with boards on the inside." Aron's house was thus the finest in the outpost. Nevertheless, the conditions he had to work under must have been cramped. The house was a common house, in which each family unit had a bed platform and a lamp area. The floor space was approximately 12 by 18 feet, and the inhabitants – eighteen in all – included parents, aunts, and brothers- and sisters-in-law. Aron's little son died of tuberculosis, as did his three younger brothers, and his father was as badly stricken as he was.

Aron's technical training was limited to examples. Tools, blocks, and "a few older woodcuts to go by" were sent with the kayak mail to Kangeq. With the Greenlanders' great imitative skill, Aron quickly picked up the technique of wood engraving. As a hunter, he had been accustomed to using the knife, to carving his own implements, and it was an easy matter for him to copy the woodcuts sent to him.

When it came to using pencil and brush, it took him longer to get the material under control. A few early Aron watercolors were illustrations to "The Tale of Parpak," the first contribution his father had sent Rink. The story takes place in the 1700s, after Hans Egede, and subsequently the German Moravian missionaries had begun evangelizing, and at a time when there were many conflicts between heathens and Christians. The heathen Parpak, an expert hunter, turned out to be a murderer, whose victims were mostly baptized Christians, among them a man named Christian Frederik. Finally, everybody held Parpak under such close surveillance that he decided to withdraw further north. Later, it was rumored that, while on his deathbed, Parpak had repented the murder of Christian Frederik, and had said that to keep the murdered man's soul from walking abroad, he had cut the body open and split the heart, and that in the dead man's heart he had seen "the Savior's image, hanging on a wooden cross." These were said to have been the dying Parpak's last words. From that moment, the inhabitants of the Godthåb region began to convert and let themselves be baptized, relates Christian Hendrik, who in a postscript asseverates that, "Not a few but many times have I heard the story of Parpak from the old ones; and not one, but many told it in this way. Parpak was deceitful, but perhaps not in his right mind either."

Aron's illustration (fig. 271) must have been one of his earliest, judging by the uncertainty in the proportions of the figures (one senses in the large heads an influence from the example in figure 265), and in the

difficulty in dealing with foreshortening, as in the case of the rear kayak. It is possible that Aron's drawing accompanied his father's first contribution to Rink, who then pasted it into the book sent to Frederik VII (as were the three following illustrations).

In spite of its clumsiness, the drawing is amusing. Parpak is depicted as a cocksure, bloodthirsty fellow, while the unfortunate Christian – recognizable by the halo – who has been struck by a bird dart and is bleeding profusely, laments his fate.

The conflicts between heathens and Christians must still have occupied people's minds in the 1850s, for otherwise Aron would not have captioned the watercolor of the seal ball game in figure 272, "The inhabitants of Kangeq and Igdlorpait playing with a stuffed seal, according to old heathen custom, for the last time before their conversion." The qualifying "for the last time" has an apologetic effect; the game was played well into our own century, and is probably still not forgotten among older Greenlanders.

In this watercolor, there is again a tendency to give some of the figures oversized heads. The group furthest away, who are marching forth like a detachment of soldiers, may have been inspired by the pictures from the Crimean War in A Conversation About War (see fig. 266). The picture (9⁹/₁₆ by 13½ inches), one of the largest of Aron's that we know of, is full of life and movement, despite the stiff treatment of the figures; everybody is moving from left to right, in the direction of the seal. Only the glance of the man who has fallen goes contrary to the advancing rhythm.

273. "The Caribou Hunt at Godthaab." Tent encampment in the interior of the country. Painted by Aron before 1861 and sent to Frederik VII. One of five pictures in a series, not of the hunt but of the journey. Watercolor, 9³/₄" × 13¹³/₁₆". The Queen's Reference Library, Copenhagen.

There is a certain brute strength to the painting, which says a great deal about the battlelike character of the game. But if we compare it with his drawing for the woodcut on the same theme (see fig. 267*a*) and his later watercolor (see fig. 282), we see that he quickly achieved much greater artistic power in his composition, figure drawing, and use of color.

There were two categories of subject that interested Aron from the beginning: the Greenlanders' daily life and the tales handed down to them. At this early stage, he painted a whole series of pictures of "The Caribou Hunt at Godthaab" – "They carry the boats over land, in order to avoid the waterfall," "They row further into the country, on streams and across lakes," and "Tent encampment in the interior" (fig. 273).

In an autumn landscape, with fall colors in the mountains, our attention centers around life in the encampment. Smoke and steam waft up from the cooking pots, and people are carrying caribou meat down from the mountains; while around the tents and upturned *umiak*s, life unfolds with talk and flensing and play – surely a picture that evoked good hunting memories both in Aron and those who looked on while he painted it. The series continues with a picture captioned, "Ancient huts far in the interior, built with stones only, some with and some without roofs (presumably originating with the old Norsemen)." Finally, we are shown "The furthest point inland, alongside the icecap, which prevents us going any further. The hunters bring only kayaks with them. When they come to water, the women, who are along in order to carry the catch, have to sit on the rear of the kayaks."

I have enumerated all these titles in order to show how typical the series is in Greenlandic art; whether it is a hunting tale or a legend, the Greenlandic artist wants to include so many details that it would be impossible to contain them in one picture. Besides, the action – the plot – is vital. Regardless of theme, it is evident, too, that the deep tradition in Greenlandic culture is the art of narrative.

The caribou hunt must have been only a memory for Aron. He had, however, personally experienced another event in 1860 that gave rise to several watercolors and a color lithograph in *Atuagagdliutit* (vol. 1, no. 1). The caption under the latter reads, "The Big Steamer *Bulldog*, with a Transport Ship, Arrives at Godthaab, 1860. Drawn by Aron, from memory."

Aron must have traveled from Kangeq to Godthåb by kayak or *umiak* and experienced the big ships and the stir the visit caused in the town, which he depicted in the watercolor "Englishmen and Americans at Godthaab in 1860" (fig. 274). The picture imparts a vivid impression of

274. *"Englishmen and Americans at Godthaab in 1860." Painted by Aron 1860-61 and sent to Frederik VII. Watercolor and pencil. 9¹/₁₆" × 13¹³/₁₆". The Queen's Reference Library, Copenhagen.*

the degree to which the naval visit must have electrified the populace. The town was blue with sailors, talking to the children, going in and out of the sod houses, some strolling up on the hills in order to enjoy the view, one of them with an opened umbrella into the bargain – surely an Englishman. This time the movement in the picture is more complex: people are walking back and forth on the road, which slants up from the bottom of the picture, while others gather in groups at the houses or dwindle out into the terrain. The artist has captured the mutual curiosity among the promenaders and the easygoing atmosphere of the visit. The colors are gray-black and gray-green, a backdrop against which the different blues of the sailors' uniforms stand out with great effect. The few whites and reds provide vitality and excitement.

It was in the illustrations to the legends that Aron made his greatest contribution. There, useful as were his powers of observation, he was not so bound by considerations of naturalism, and greater play was given to the fantastic. In "The Legend of Kunnuk. All his relations and housefellows are attacked and killed" (fig. 275), there is the same use of rather dry colors and much black, and red provides dramatic point and the element of alarm, but the figures are freer and more expressively depicted than in the preceding examples.

"The Old Southerner Frightens His Enemies by Enlarging His Face" (fig. 276) is well composed. The huge naked face is effectively framed by the rock wall and the point of the tent. No wonder the two kayak men immediately back away – the fright is admirably expressed by the attitude of fending-off in the two raised paddles. The legend is found in the collection under the name of Augpilagtok, a South Greenlander who moved to Kangeq, where he fell out with the inhabitants, killed a man, and had to flee. The legend concludes by noting that people acquired "respect for the practices of the southerners and left them in peace." The enlarged face brings to mind the mask artists of East Greenland, who distend their cheeks with sticks in their mouths and flatten their noses with thongs (see fig. 30). There was communication between South and East Greenland, and so ingrained was the fear of sorcerers and of the distorted face that Augpilagtoq achieved his purpose of terrifying his enemies.

All of the works by Aron mentioned thus far were made before 1861. It is obvious that wood engraving came most readily to him, and that a certain angular rhythm, dryness of color, and a preference for black accompanied the change from printmaking to painting. But gradually Aron became a great painter. The colors became more and more intense and luminous, the landscapes were built up of light and shadow, and the

275. *"The Legend of Kunnuk. All his relations and housemates are attacked and killed." Painted by Aron before 1861 and sent to Frederik VII. Watercolor, 3⅝″×6¹¹/₁₆″. The Queen's Reference Library, Copenhagen.*

awkward brushwork disappeared. It may also have been a matter of working with the proper materials. The first watercolors are marked by a use of tempera second coats that close off any underlying color, which is contrary to the nature of watercolor painting. The paper got better, too. It was more absorbent, and the paints were of superior quality. Signe and Hinrich Rink, who themselves drew and painted, had presumably begun supplying Aron with better materials.

Meanwhile, Aron was settling into a particular postcard-size format, and his figures were becoming both better proportioned and of a size that permitted a situation to be played out among a group. Depictions of local events (such as the English and American naval visit) and of Greenlandic daily life were gradually abandoned in favor of themes from the Greenlandic legends, whose long epic form naturally calls for picture series to illustrate the story line. There was still room for observations from daily life, however, as woven in among fantastic events are very down-to-earth everyday episodes. Supernatural beings do entirely human things and thus take on familiarity and immediacy.

276. *"The Old Southerner Frightens His Enemies by Enlarging His Face." Painted by Aron before 1861 and sent to Frederik VII. Watercolor and India ink, 3⁹/₁₆″×6¹¹/₁₆″. The Queen's Reference Library, Copenhagen.*

277. "When they came around (a point) they saw Isigârserâk's son killed and spitted on his harpoon shaft." Painted by Aron, ca. 1867. Collected by Hinrich Rink during his governorship in Godthåb. Later sent to the Danish National Museum, whose records mention "196 sheets, colored drawings by Greenlandic hunters, purchased in 1905 from Signe Rink." Watercolor, $3^{15}/_{16}'' \times 6^{11}/_{16}''$. National Library of Greenland, Godthåb-Nuuk.

The matter-of-fact appears often, even in tragic situations, such as in the watercolor of the mourning over Isigârserâk's son (fig. 277). The picture, which possesses fully as much sorrow and tenderness as a pre-Renaissance Italian pieta, contains a detail that reveals how important a role the hunt played in the lives of Greenlanders. The caption – written in beautiful handwriting by Aron, as for all the pictures – reads, "When they came around (a point), they saw Isigârserâk's son killed and spitted on his harpoon shaft. They took him down and buried him, but first they made their narwhal fast to a rock." Obviously, a good catch like a narwhal had to be seen to first.

There are many horizontal lines in this well-composed picture: the narwhal, the rocks on the shore, the kayak, the *umiak,* and the slain man, with the bloody harpoon – which has the effect of a martyr's stake, of a cross – beside him. The landscape is rendered in a warm, golden tint that is in accord with my conception of sympathy.

In contrast, cold and despair emanate from the watercolor "Qivâqiarssuk Gets Rid of Some Women by Letting Them Remain Behind on the Skerry off Kangeq's Houses as the Water Rises Over Their Heads" (fig. 278). The mood is expressed both by the already none-too-pretty faces, which are now altogether distorted with the fear of death and by the colors. The blanched arms and black *kamik*s that poke up out of the choppy sea – cool blue, with whitecaps – practically make the beholder feel the icy water. On shore among the sod houses, where two women who have remained behind are distant, non-participating onlookers, there is warmth and security.

In "Ungneq Lets the Sea Cover Him Because He Is Being Pursued by Arnarssiniouk (the Monster Who Catches People in Her Big Bag)" (fig. 279), we also see somebody in the water, but this time with a different effect. Even though the sea is full of ice floes, for Ungneq it is a place of refuge. As in a swimming exercise, he makes the water foam, so that he may be mistaken for a fragment of ice. The monster, depicted in superhuman size and with a vigorous head of hair, frequently fell on solitary travelers and put them in her *amaut.* Here, she soars like a gigantic, menacing hawk on the lookout, horror lurking in the black hole of the bag. Her arms and body form the one powerful diagonal in the picture, and her raised right leg and a mountain in the background the other.

But grief, horror, and fear of the supernatural were not the only emotions Aron could express. There is humor, for example, in "Pernilik Feigns Illness Because Ûlajok Would Have Her as Subsidiary Wife" (fig. 280). In a beautiful landscape, in which the sky, too, plays a part in the composition as an expression of the mood of the picture, an *umiak* is

278. *"Qivâqiarssuk Gets Rid of Some Women." Painted by Aron in 1867 for Hinrich Rink. Watercolor, 3¹⁵/₁₆"×6¹¹/₁₆". National Library of Greenland, Godthåb-Nuuk.*

being rowed with resolute strokes. One of the women, however, is reclining passively, and a man in an escort kayak looks on with interest while hanging onto the stern. Her sisters appear to be in on Pernilik's playacting, which in any case will keep Ûlajok from losing face as a spurned suitor.

Also aglow with humor is "Qivâgiarssuk Speaks with the Great Merman" (fig. 281). The Merman almost looks as though he is giving advice to the hunter, as he is pointing somewhere or other – perhaps toward a good hunting place? His suit is either of feathers or of scales, with long-haired fur edging, and he is larger than human size. The weather is fair, the sea calm, and everything bespeaks a cozy chat, rendered pictorially by tranquil horizontals and the cloudless sky.

279. *"The Bag Monster." Painted by Aron in 1867 for Hinrich Rink. Watercolor, 3¹⁵/₁₆"×6¹¹/₁₆". National Library of Greenland, Godthåb-Nuuk.*

280. "Pernilik Feigns Illness," (Pernilik means "She with a special shape"). Painted by Aron in the 1860s for Hinrich Rink. 3^{15}/$_{16}$"×6^{13}/$_{16}$". National Library of Greenland, Godthåb-Nuuk.

It is obvious that Aron, through his career as a kayak hunter, had a thorough knowledge of the sea and of wind and weather. Many of his pictures are simply seascapes, and the weather plays an important role in the action of all the outdoor scenes. In the series relating the story of "The Great Hunters from Qilangait" (illustrated on the dust jacket of this book), the sea and the weather have been accorded the principal roles. The story is told in four pictures. A storm surprises a party of kayak men who are out hunting, and they are overcome one by one. Only one of the great hunters reaches land. He loses his paddle, but strikes a great auk with his bird dart and uses its body to paddle to the coast.

Aron painted these four dramatic seascapes in 1886, when he had long been prevented from going out in a kayak. The way the deep green waves break and strike a kayak was clear in the memory of the former hunter, however. The sea covers most of the picture shown, which is reminiscent of Japanese printmaking with its audacious perspective. The entire series has a powerful aura of drama, but the individual doing battle against the harshness of nature was an everyday facet of Greenlandic life.

Aron is a very great portrayer of nature, but human qualities and relations are what interest him most. He shows us the entire spectrum of human feeling, though perhaps predominantly the violent emotions connected with killing, vengeance, and flight, which the legends so often tell of (e.g., fig. 282). Aron relived a great part of his people's history from his sickbed, and passed it on to us on hundreds of small pieces of paper – most of them works as yet unknown to the public. He died in 1869. The

281. "Qivâqiarssuk Speaks with the Great Merman." Painted by Aron in 1867 for Hinrich Rink. Watercolor, 3^{15}/$_{16}$"×6^{5}/$_{8}$". National Library of Greenland, Godthåb-Nuuk.

282. Drama during the seal ball game: "While Ernerssiak stood watching his blood enemies playing ball, he felt the middle one shove him; so finally he took him by the hair and hurled him against the earth, killing him." Painted by Aron, ca. 1867, for Hinrich Rink. Watercolor, 3¹⁵/₁₆" × 6¹¹/₁₆". National Library of Greenland, Godthåb-Nuuk.

Moravian parish register reads:

> Aron. 732. A married Communion brother and long-time school teacher and aide at the meetings in Kangeq, to which he was admirably suited, as well as being a successful seal hunter and a skilled worker in wood and stone. He carved not a few pictures in wood for reproduction for Dr. Rink. He loved our Saviour, and endeavored to conduct his life accordingly. He was frequently ill, and passed away from consumption, happily and blessedly, in his 47th year.

An expressionist artist of high caliber, Aron led Greenlandic painting beyond the merely descriptive. With line and color – the language of painting – he put pictorial art on a level with the age-old art of narrative.

As noted, there was widespread collaboration among the artists in the artistic thaw that occurred in West Greenland in the middle of the 1800s. Pictures were drawn by Aron and engraved by Markus; drawn by Aron and lithographed by Lars Møller; engraved by Rasmus Berthelsen from a drawing; drawn by Jens Kreutzmann and engraved by Aron. The artists did not all live in the same place, so either they knew one another or the work was distributed from the governor's residence.

Another of the dominant contributors was Jens Kreutzmann (1828-99), outpost manager at Kangaamiut and "an in every respect distinguished and skillful entrepreneur." Kreutzmann's production was smaller than Aron's, but a number of his drawings are found in the collections of legends and in *Atuagagdliutit*, and around fifty watercolors are in the collection formerly in the National Museum in Copenhagen but now in the National Library of Greenland in Godthåb-Nuuk.

Of German-Greenlandic descent, Kreutzmann chiefly illustrated local

283. The caribou hunt. Picture surface divided into three fields. Painted by Jens Kreutzmann of Kangaamiut after 1858 and sent to Hinrich Rink. India ink and watercolor, 7¹¹/₁₆″×11½″. National Library of Greenland, Godthåb-Nuuk.

stories of cultural confrontation – either the religious clashes of the 1700s or those over trade, such as the conflicts with the whalers – or else the fall caribou hunts, rendered with a hunter's knowledge and delight (fig. 283).

Basically, all of Kreutzmann's watercolors are finished ink drawings (with sepia India ink), colored with a light hand. The preferred colors are verdigris, light blue, yellow, red brown, and white tempera. In "The Caribou Hunt," the picture surface is divided into three friezes; the upper running from left to right, the middle from right to left, and the lower from the left again – the same system as in the ivory engraving (see fig. 43), and thus in keeping with the age-old Eskimo pictorial concept.

But Kreutzmann was also capable of working with a centered composition, as in the picture captioned "The Two Old Folks Who Didn't Want to be Separated from Their Daughter (by the Suitors) Journey Away with Her" (fig. 284). Here, all the lines from the landscape and the sod houses converge in the knot of people from the settlement, who passively watch the *umiak* with the three departees directly in front of them.

Neither in this nor in the other watercolors is the sky or weather made a part of the mood of the picture as with Aron. What the artist wishes to illustrate is primarily the situation in question, and the landscape behind it is a rather serene backdrop. There are specific localities, however, as in two of the pictures where we see the characteristic jagged silhouette of the mountains at Kangaamiut. One of them is "Theemigok" (fig. 286), a

284. The old couple journey away with their daughter. Painted by Jens Kreutzmann after 1858 and sent to Hinrich Rink. India ink and watercolor, 4³/₄″×7¹/₁₆″. National Library of Greenland, Godthåb-Nuuk.

285. "The Invisible One" – a Greenlander who, with the aid of sorcery, was invisible to Europeans. A historical figure from Hans Egede's day whose legendary exploits are a favorite theme of Greenlandic artists. Painted by Jens Kreutzmann after 1858 and sent to Hinrich Rink. Watercolor and India ink, 3¹/8″×5¹¹/16″. National Library of Greenland, Godthåb-Nuuk.

286. "Theemigok." Painted by Jens Kreutzmann after 1858 and sent to Hinrich Rink. Sepia ink, pencil, and watercolor (with white tempera), 5¹¹/16″×4³/4″. National Library of Greenland,, Godthåb-Nuuk.

picture veritably popping with festive confusion, in which seven men fire blank charges from their rifles in all directions. Rink writes that they are celebrating either the birthday of a person nicknamed "Tea," or the day tea arrived in the country.

The same view of the mountains and the same two houses in their shadow are seen in the watercolor "Habakuk Draws an Arrow out of His Daughter's Face – and This Was the Beginning (of His Vocation)" (fig. 287). Habakuk and Maria Magdalene were a married couple who were involved in a religious movement in the 1780s. It was said that sorrow at losing their daughter from an accidental shot was what brought on their "revelations"; but originally it had been Maria Magdalene who "saw visions" in a transport of jealousy at her husband's debaucheries. People believed her, and the movement caught hold. Soon the couple were the leading figures in a religious fanaticism that cancelled all normal church life and affected the social order of the entire Sukkertoppen district.

Peculiar rituals were introduced, especially in connection with burials, in which the congregation, wearing their best clothes, danced in a circle around the graves. We have an excellent depiction of this in figure 288. The graves are seen from the side, and the ring of dancers from slightly above. The rearmost figures are the largest, imparting a clear feeling of the closeness of the congregation dancing their round.

Among the other rituals was "cleansing" of sin, particularly of the young women, by Habakuk. The children who were the fruit of this cleansing had, he asserted, been conceived by the Holy Ghost. This fanaticism, surely an understandable result of pietistic missionary efforts, was finally subdued around 1790 by the catechist Frederik Berthelsen of Sukkertoppen, as reward for which he was given vestments, becoming Greenland's first ordained native minister. Naturally, many stories circulated about Habakuk's escapades, and many pictorial accounts have been given of his career (see also fig. 173).

The story of "The Invisible One" was both written down by Kreutzmann for the second volume of the collection of legends and illustrated by him in a watercolor (fig. 285). (This was converted into a woodcut by Aron, so that it is possible to see how altered the copy is, even though the placement of the figures has been exactly duplicated). The point of the story is that the son of the Greenlander Kenake is made invisible by sorcery, and invulnerable to the European whalers. He avails himself of

287. Habakuk draws an arrow out of his daughter's face. Painted by Jens Kreutzmann after 1858 for Hinrich Rink. Pencil, India ink, and watercolor, 8″×5¹³/16″. National Library of Greenland, Godthåb-Nuuk.

288. "Followers of Habakuk dance around the graves in honor of the departed." Painted by Jens Kreutzmann after 1858 and sent to Hinrich Rink in Godthåb. A finished pen and ink drawing; sepia or bleached black India ink, with watercolors, 4¾"×4¾". National Library of Greenland, Godthåb-Nuuk.

this by taking all the trade goods he wants from their ships. At the same time, he goads them by placing the muzzle of a gun against his belly. The sorcery was vengeance against the whalers for having killed Kenake, and both this and the other illustrations tell us something about a time of upheaval and contention.

It is probably Jens Kreutzmann who tells us most about the events of two or three generations ago and recounts the most anecdotes and odd stories. His style survives, especially in Kangaamiut and Sukkertoppen, and his family has produced many gifted artists. Aron's family died out, however, and the Kangeq settlement gradually became depopulated.

This entire epoch, with its explosive development in literature and pictorial art, naturally contributed to an increased national awareness and pride. Rink's initiatives stimulated both the selftaught artists and those who desired a formal education. The selftaught among the hunting population were provided with support and encouragement. That what was wanted were illustrations to the legends surely contributed to the persistence of the narrative element as a universal trait in Greenlandic art.

On the other hand, there were the trained, "enlightened" artists. Rasmus Berthelsen had a burning desire to obtain a Danish teaching certificate. Lars Møller became a master printer, expert in the art of reproduction, and experimented with transferring photographs onto lithographic stone. His son Steffen followed in his footsteps. With this trend to wanting to learn, we are headed in a new direction, toward what may be called the period of revival.

289. Summer night, Egedesminde. Painted by Peter S. Dalager around 1930 for Frederik Lynge, Egedesminde. Dalager was a versatile talent. Besides discharging his duties as catechist, he wrote poetry and painted. A portrait of Dean Knud Balle, painted by Dalager, hangs in Egedesminde church. Oil on canvas, signed "P. S. Dalager," 13⅜″×18¾″. Private collection.

The period of revival

In many countries, painting has gone through periods during which national awareness has been strengthened by depiction of the nation's scenery and its citizens. Thus, in connection with Holland's first war of independence in the 1600s, there was a reaction against the Italian, French, and Spanish concepts of art, and painters like Frans Hals and Rembrandt created marvellous portraits of ordinary people. Vermeer van Delft, Herkules Seeger, and Willem Kalf painted interiors from Dutch houses and still lifes incorporating the country's own products, while the brothers van Ruisdael and de Koninck (the Elder and the Younger) painted magnificent panoramas of the flat countryside of Holland, with canals, windmills, and cattle in the fields. This national-romantic painting was very much expressive of Holland's independence and progress.

In Denmark, a corresponding wave of interest in Danish scenery arose in the 1800s. P. C. Skovgaard painted the Danish beech forests, and Hans Schmidt the moors of Jutland, while Dankvart Dreyer, Christen Købke, and Johan Thomas Lundbye depicted the hills, the sunken roads, the bluffs, and the coast. In 1842, Lundbye wrote in his diary: "What I have set as my life's goal as a painter is to paint my beloved Denmark, with all the simplicity and modesty that are so characteristic of her." In the middle of the 1800s, when the wars against Germany took place, Denmark needed a strengthening of the national consciousness. It was at that time that the constitution was introduced, N. F. S. Grundtvig was active, and the folk high schools and the cooperative movement got started. During this period of awakening, art too became a mirror of all that was Danish. Realism became a mode of expression in the national-romantic style of painting. People and scenery were painted precisely the way they were, were conceded as being, and loved.

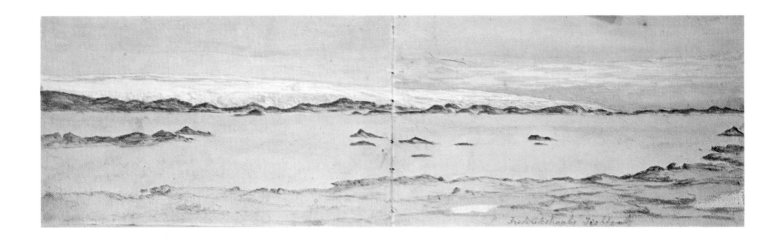

290. *From Lars Møller's sketchbook on an expedition with the Swedish polar explorer Adolf Erik Nordenskiöld in 1883. Shown here: Frederikshåb ice gleam. Watercolor over pencil, 4½"×15¹⁄₁₆". Royal Engravings Collection, Copenhagen.*

The same thing occurred in Greenland. The extremely precise rendering of people and scenery characteristic of such painters as Henrik Lund, Niels Lynge, and Peter and Otto Rosing was nurtured by a profound love for Greenland's mountains and fjords, weather and changing light, and for her people (figs. 289 and 240). Though all were deeply religious, and three were also missionaries in East Greenland, these painting pastors elected not to paint biblical themes. Instead, nature became the grand subject of their art.

Naturalistic landscape painting began, properly speaking, with Lars Møller, in whose sketchbook from the expedition with Nordenskiöld in 1883, the coastline, glaciers, and weather are depicted with great precision (fig. 290). Møller's two sons took up his artistic heritage. Remarkable powers of observation, precision, and thorough study were traits shared by both John Møller (1867-1935), who was a brilliant photographer and head of the Godthaab Photographic Works, and Steffen Møller (1882-1909), who before his premature death achieved distinction as a gifted artist.

In 1905-06, Steffen Møller underwent training in Denmark with the wood engraver Johan Pauli, and was afterwards engaged as clerk to the governor in Godthåb. At the same time, he made drawings and painted in watercolors and oils. In a photograph taken by his brother John, Steffen and his wife are seen in a studio with easel and paint box. The walls are crowded with paintings, all of them nature scenes. Ossian Elgström, who in 1915 had the opportunity of seeing these paintings, comments, "His pictures were distinguished by snug, well-balanced composition, and a deep, serious palette." In the small winter scene in figure 291, the impression of snow and cold is conveyed by harmonic construction, with the main emphasis on coloristic expression.

But it is Steffen Møller's illustrations for the Greenlandic ABC (the ABD in Greenlandic), which first appeared in 1910, that are known and loved by everybody in Greenland. Møller made many sketches for these illustrations – a girl counting on her fingers, a boy reading, children playing in the snow – which reveal the way he put his powers of observation to use and his passion for detail (fig. 292).

It was not only as an artist that Steffen Møller wished to serve his country (he bequeathed the ABD drawings to the Greenlandic people). He also founded the national Christian society *peqatigîngniat* (The Mutuality), which acquired the character of a great intellectual and religious revival. The movement simultaneously had a spiritual and a decidedly national posture, resulting in the writing of many hymns and religious songs. Another well-known figure in *peqatigîngniat* was the pastor Niels Lynge (1880-1965), who was also active as a painter. The mountains around Godthåb were his oft-repeated motif, depicted with minute precision, exact draughtsmanship, and somewhat dry coloring (fig. 293).

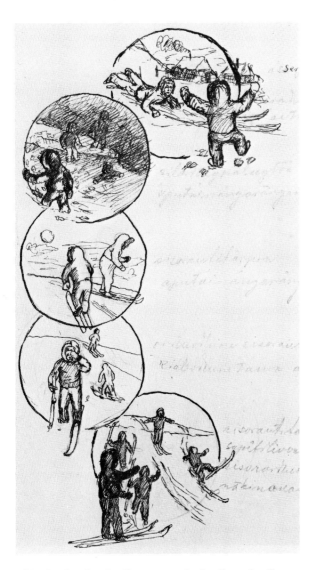

292. Studies for the illustrations in the Greenlandic ABD drawn by Steffen Møller in Godthåb in 1906-7. The story of the boy who breaks one of his skis while playing. Pen and India ink over pencil, 7¹³/₁₆"×4¹³/₁₆". Arctic Institute, Copenhagen.

As in the Greenlandic golden age around the middle of the 1800s, the new impulses emanated from Godthåb. Centered around the church and the teachers' college was an intellectual life that left its mark on the attitude of several generations toward music, poetry, and pictorial art. One of the dominant personalities was the hymn writer, composer, organist, and head catechist Jonathan Petersen (see Hans Lynge's bust, fig. 71, and fig. 72), who also taught drawing at the teachers' college. Petersen's family was of an artistic disposition. His father, Anders Petersen – head catechist in Frederikshåb – painted excellent small landscape watercolors, and his son, Pavia Petersen (1904-43), who was head catechist in Sukkertoppen, achieved importance during his short life as an author and painter. In a subdued palette, with predominantly gray and brown shades, he depicted the town of Sukkertoppen and its environs in the changing seasons.

Another great hymn writer, who graduated from the teachers' college, was the minister Henrik Lund (1875-1948), known as "Endaleraq," or Little Henrik. Seized by profound piety, Lund went to Angmagssalik around the turn of the century in order to evangelize among the heathens of East Greenland, and remained there for nine years. During this period, he began painting landscape watercolors. Delicate nature scenes, displaying painstaking draughtsmanship and softly radiant coloring, also exist from his later period as minister in Narssaq. In one instance, the figure of Christ seems to appear in the clouds, but all of the other watercolors are pure depictions of nature (see, e.g., fig. 294).

That Lund's deep love for the Greenlandic scenery acquired a religious character is seen in many of his songs, as in this verse from "The Song of Narssaq":

Narssaq, the Plain, your name evokes
Memories of my youth's beloved places,
Where the meadow is deep beside the mountain,
Sharon and Lebanon in a single embrace,
Canaan's vanished loveliness is found and recalled ...

193

293. *Landscape from the area around Godthåb, with the familiar mountain Sermitsiaq (The Saddle), painted by Niels Lynge in 1924 for his daughter Ane Holm, Godthåb. Oil on canvas, signed "NL," 24"×37". Private collection.*

or in "Amitsaurssuk Valley":

> It is as though I'm carried
> Upon the western wind
> Behind the mountain passes
> As though I inward flowed.
> As though my soul renewéd
> But hastens to the spot
> Where it shall then reveal itself
> Redeemed in flesh and blood ...

Greenland's national anthem, "Nunarput" (Our Country), was written by Henrik Lund. The final verse rouses with:

> So let the new tidings awaken the land –
> *Kalatdlit* (Greenlanders), arise! For it is day!
> A freeborn people, henceforth we shall stand
> And know the light of reason's dawning day.

294. *Angmagssalik. View north from the harbor. Painted by Henrik Lund in 1907. Watercolor, 5¹⁵/₁₆"×9¼". Royal Library, Copenhagen.*

295. *Woman at a blubber lamp in the summer tent. Painted by Peter Rosing in the 1920s in Angmagssalik. Oil on canvas, about 21¾"×16½". Private collection.*

296. *The legend of the man from Aluk. Painted by Peter Rosing in 1944. Oil on canvas, 24⅞"×35⅞". Private collection.*

In the far more complex and mixed society that Greenland was becoming at that time, Christianity and art joined hands in creating a national feeling not recognizable until then. Dominant personalities in the church, like the pietist Nikolai Edinger Balle and pastor Christian Rasmussen (Knud Rasmussen's father), took part in this, and many young Greenlanders were powerfully influenced in their Danish-Greenlandic homes.

Kristian Rosing, first a teacher and head catechist, later minister in Angmagssalik, where he completed the work of evangelizing, could report in 1921 that all of the East Greenland heathens had been baptized. He experienced the old culture at close hand and obtained immense insight into ancient Eskimo religious concepts, customs, and practices. His children grew up in Angmagssalik, and childhood experiences contributed to their positive attitude – despite acquired condemnation of heathenism – toward the old Greenlandic culture, as well as to their interest in history and their artistic imaginations. Their mother, Karoline, Jens Kreutzmann's daughter (see page 188), was said to have been gifted, and three of the sons drew and painted from their early years.

The oldest, Peter Rosing (1892-1965), displayed the greatest artistic temperament. Trained as a minister, he was active first in Godhavn, then succeeded his father in Angmagssalik, was later on the west coast again, and finally settled in Jakobshavn. He would rather have been an artist. Everywhere he lived, he painted the scenery – the sunset, the moon over a rough sea – and portraits of shamans, naturalistically, with a warmth and glow that make him Greenland's most distinctively national-romantic painter.

Even his titles indicate the emotional quality of Peter Rosing's pictures, reflecting a receptive mind's experience of the violence of nature and of the relatively unspoiled East Greenlandic people. The effect of the pictures is often related to the atmosphere that arises when two sources of light are refracted in nature, or is built up out of the contrast of light and shadow in a face, as in the picture of a woman in a tent, illuminated from below by the long flame of a blubber lamp (fig. 295). The figure is effectively framed by the tent poles, and all attention converges on the expression the light brings forth in the wise old visage. Or consider the distinguished portrait of an East Greenlander with long hair held in place by a hair halter that introduces this chapter (fig. 240). Here, too, characterization, texture, and suppleness are maintained in the contrast of cold and warm, light and dark colors.

But Peter Rosing was not content with naturalism. He was also inspired by the old Greenlandic myths and legends, and now and then peopled his landscapes with legendary figures. How natural that a legend such as "The Great Hunter of Aluk" should fascinate him (fig. 296). The legend tells of an old great hunter who allows his son to persuade him to go on a hunting trip along the west coast, but grows homesick for his beautiful abode, the island of Aluk, near Cape Farewell at the southern tip of Greenland. When he gets home, he pitches his tent as usual, with the opening facing east, so that at daybreak he can see the sun's rays over the mountains and sea. When he sees the sun rising again over the beautiful scenery, his heart bursts with feeling and gladness. Peter Rosing portrayed this profound love of the country, so deep-rooted among Greenlanders, better than anybody else.

His brother Otto Rosing (1896-1966) was also an ordained minister, and was active in Thule, Angmagssalik (as replacement for Peter), and Egedesminde. Interested in archaeology and history, he was at the same time an author and artist. He had profound respect for the history and heritage of the Greenlanders, was himself a hunter among hunters, shot polar bears, and paddled a kayak. His home contained furniture fashioned from driftwood and decorated with bone figures – all handmade by the minister himself in the same tradition as the East Greenlandic buckets and chests. Standing on the table were his small, delicate bone figures, and an exact copy of the Gardar bishop's crozier (found in the Norse ruins in South Greenland), carved from walrus ivory. On the walls hung pictures from Thule, East Greenland, and Godhavn.

Otto Rosing did research, studied, and made dissections. His sketchbooks contain a wealth of observations and studies, as in the vignettes from *umiak* voyages or dog-sled journeys, but the recurring theme is the scenery. Ice floes and the profiles of mountains are rendered with the utmost precision and fidelity in pencil, with the colors indicated in watercolor or annotated for completion later (fig. 297). "It's a question of using your eyes and being extremely critical," Rosing stated to Christian Berthelsen in an interview in *Grønlandsposten,* adding that "inner feeling and the imagination are all-determining, and you strain to the utmost to reach the limits of your performance." The latent warmth and "inner feeling" in Rosing, which may not immediately be apparent on account of the assiduously naturalistic execution of his pictures, displays itself in the choice of colors.

With a partiality for red colors in nature – whether in the reddish basalt mountains of Godhavn, the low winter sun, or the orange red magnificence of a sunset – Otto Rosing reveals himself as a romantic painter, as

297 a-e. From Otto Rosing's sketchbook. Qutligssat seen from Ujarasugssuk, painted 18 February, 1927. Watercolor over pencil, 7"×20½". Various sketches with umiaks *and kayaks made in East Greenland in the years 1934-39. Pencil and pastel, 4¾"×6¾". Private collection.*

298. *The mountains at Angmagssalik lit by the winter sun. Painted by Otto Rosing in Angmagssalik in the years 1934-39. The subject was painted in two nearly identical versions, one for Commander Louis Rostock-Jensen. The other picture is in the possession of the artist's family. Oil on canvas, handmade stretchers and frames. Shown here is a detail from the first-mentioned picture. Overall dimensions, 32⅜″×86¾″. Private collection.*

in the panorama of the Angmagssalik mountains illuminated obliquely by the low rays of the winter sun (fig. 298), a picture of unusually great size in the history of Greenlandic painting (it is more than six feet long) and audacious in its coloring. When asked why he painted, Rosing replied, "I try, in all modesty, to show the beauty of our country – the changing light and color of the clouds at their most beautiful moment."

"To show the beauty of the country" could stand as the motto of all the artists mentioned from the period of revival. They were all educated Greenlanders who believed in progress through Christianity and the acquisition of Danish culture. Even in painting, they are close to Danish tradition, though not to contemporary Danish art. The currents whose development in Europe, from the turn of the century through the 1930s, signify the breakthrough of abstract art, never reached Greenland, or only as a faint swell and in the most recent times. It was older Danish art – the painters of the golden age, the Skaw painters – that appealed to the revivalists. But love for Greenland's scenery and the Greenlandic individual was the principal element in their painting. Their national-romantic naturalism had imitators, and the movement was of such significance that their works comprise an important component in the present-day Greenlandic cultural scene.

The naive portrayers of everyday life

In the meantime, self-taught artists were flourishing everywhere. They were chiefly hunters and unlettered people – of quite a different substance from the artists mentioned above, but no less important in the cultural pattern. As a pastime, or when they weren't otherwise employed, many began to draw, especially if there was a little money in it, or if requested to. These autodidacts tended to draw themselves, their surroundings, hunting techniques – everyday life.

One of them was Isak of Igdlorpait (1866-1903), an outpost in South Greenland where the Moravians had established a mission station. As Isak had lost his right arm in an accident and was unable to support himself as a hunter, the Moravians hired him as goatherd. Isak got paper and paints at the mission station and drew and painted the life of the settlement, using his left hand. It is said that he strewed drawings about, but only a few have been preserved, among them two "picture books," sketchbooks measuring 6¾ by 4 inches, on each page of which Isak drew

299. "This is Isak, the goatherd." Painted by Isak of Igdlorpait in South Greenland around the turn of the century. The introductory picture in a little booklet of colored drawings, formerly in the possession of colony manager Ole Mathiesen in Nanortalik. 3¹⁵/₁₆″×6¹¹/₁₆″. National Library of Greenland, Godthåb-Nuuk.

300. "This is the missionary's housemaid, who is washing" and "This is the seventh day." Double opening from Isak's Picture Book, a booklet of colored drawings by Isak of Igdlorpait, painted in South Greenland around the turn of the century. The booklet, which belonged to the Bugge family, was published in 1969 in a facsimile edition. 8¹/₄″×6³/₄″. National Library of Greenland, Godthåb-Nuuk.

an object or a situation (some of these have already been shown in the chapter on crafts).

Below each drawing is written the explanation, such as "This is women, who are sewing *umiak* coverings," "This is a cod being pulled in," "This is the doctor from Julianehåb," or "This is the inhabitants on their way to divine service." The introductory picture in each book is of Isak himself. "This is Isak, the goatherd," is the legend on one (fig. 299). Here we see him in the middle of his horned flock, with the houses of the mission station in the background. In this picture, the frontality is broken by the oblique lines of the fence and the smoke from the chimney. This album of vignettes of daily life in Igdlorpait also contains an attempt at a religious subject. "This is the seventh day," we are told of a decorative Greek cross, from which the flowers of faith grow and bloom (fig. 300).

Also around the turn of the century, there is testimony of artistic endeavor at the opposite end of the west coast, some 2500 miles north of Igdlorpait, in Thule. The 1903-4 "Literary Greenland Expedition" (to collect myths, legends and folktales), led by Ludvig Mylius-Erichsen, arrived there after having driven across Melville Bay, and established communication between the separated tribes in the north and south. The drawings of the Polar Eskimos from that time reveal a close kinship with the ancient Eskimo tradition. They form a frieze, with the action running from one side to the other, as in bone engravings from all over the Eskimo area (see figs. 41-45). What interested the Polar Eskimos were hunting scenes, or friezes of their beloved animals (figs. 301*a-c*). The stationary life around the dwelling, on the other hand, was not depicted as a frieze. Here the artist spread his figures and objects out over the entire picture surface. Having neither perspective nor ground plan, they are like pieces in a puzzle laid around the central house or tent (fig. 302).

This pictorial concept is reminiscent of that characterizing the work of contemporary East Greenlandic artists far from Thule and completely without communication with the Polar Eskimos (see figs. 244 and 245). That these drawings were being made in Angmagssalik in 1905, at the same time as Henrik Lund's naturalistic landscape paintings, which had a different series of cultural influences behind them, shows how difficult it is to treat Greenlandic art as a whole chronologically. Every settlement, indeed each outpost, requires its own chronology.

The Angmagssalikians plunged very quickly into the mixed culture that the West Greenlanders had 200 years to develop. Among the contributors to William Thalbitzer's collection of drawings was a boy who displayed marked artistic abilities, and who came to be instrumental in bringing the old culture into the new era. Called Kâvkajik (Little Snow Bunting), born of Pisérajik, Kârale Andreassen (1890-1934) was from a lineage of shamans on both his father's and his mother's sides. His father was the shaman Mitsivarniannga (imperative, meaning "Suck Me!" – pertaining to *tupilak*-making, see page 67). The boy received the name Kârale in 1899, at the first baptizing of heathens in Angmagssalik, when eight people, among them Kâvkajik and his mother, took on the new faith and were given Christian names. Kârale (Karl) and Elisa were also easier to pronounce for the Danes. His father, after weighty deliberation, let himself be baptized later, under the name of Andreas.

With his knowledge, based on personal experience, of the complexities of the old faith and of the whole spirit world, and with the ability to transmit it in words and pictures, Kârale became an invaluable source for the ethnologists who worked on the east coast. William Thalbitzer (in 1905-6), Knud Rasmussen (starting in 1919), and Nico Tinbergen of the Netherlands (in 1933) are among those who used Kârale's drawings as illustrations in their scientific works.

The reader has already encountered several drawings by Kârale in this book, as it was natural to utilize them in the chapter on the old religious beliefs (figs. 10 and 23-26), and in the chapter on crafts (figs. 217 and 220).

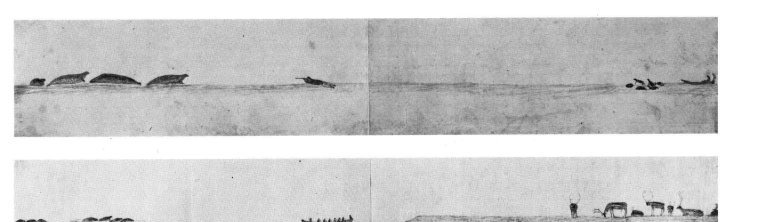

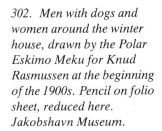

301 a-c. *Depictions of hunting and animals drawn by the Polar Eskimo Panigpak for Knud Rasmussen at the beginning of the 1900s. A number of Panigpak's drawings were used as illustrations in* Myths and Legends *(1921). Pencil on folio sheets, reduced here. Jakobshavn Museum.*

302. *Men with dogs and women around the winter house, drawn by the Polar Eskimo Meku for Knud Rasmussen at the beginning of the 1900s. Pencil on folio sheet, reduced here. Jakobshavn Museum.*

The clean, delicate line is apparent in the boy's drawing of a sled driver (fig. 159); but gradually the manner becomes closer and more "nubbly," the figures acquire shaded contour, and use is made of perspective.

The change in his drawing probably occurred in Angmagssalik. The influence may have come from Henrik Lund, or from the sculptor Ellen Locher Thalbitzer, who as William Thalbitzer's wife was in East Greenland in 1905-6, and who instructed Kârale in drawing. There were efforts being made to send the highly talented boy to the Academy of Art in Copenhagen (according to colony manager Johan "Ujuat" Petersen's journal). Nothing came of it, however, and instead Kârale went to the teachers' college in Godthåb and became East Greenland's first Greenlandic catechist. Still, he kept on drawing and, apart from a few watercolors, his production consists almost entirely of drawings. Using pencil and pen, he captured hunting techniques, shamanism, *tupilak*s, and mystical figures for us. The drawings can have an almost surrealistic effect, although the artist presumably did not intend them to. It is on account of the fantastic character of the Greenlandic spirit world that they affect us like the weird universe of the unconscious; but for Kârale they were reality, the truth. Such-and-such a *tupilak* and such-and-such a terrifying spirit actually looked like that; some of them he had seen himself, and others were drawn from his father's descriptions, or those of his maternal uncle, the shaman Ajukutôq.

These eye-witness accounts are not only exciting material for ethnographic study, they are also wonderful drawings, with a feeling for gray tones, composition and line. From the artist's large output, I have selected two more at random. One is of a hunter standing at a hole in the ice and about to harpoon what he thinks is a seal (fig. 303). We can see that it is actually a *tupilak* with bear's claws, human legs, bird's talons, and so on. X-ray vision – so that we can see what is going on under the ice – is part of the old narrative tradition, as is the ability to capture the drama, the horror, right before the catastrophe occurs. Vertical, horizontal, and diagonal lines are effectively placed, so that the viewer's attention is riveted to the center of the picture, the area of the harpoon point and the monster's soft muzzle.

Kârale provides us with a good impression of the dark side of the old era: the dread and fear of the forces of evil, and the perilous occupation of the hunter. As a Christian and a catechist, he was perhaps reluctant to depict the heathen time too positively. Perhaps the sombre appealed most strongly to his imagination. That he could also portray grief is clearly evident in a drawing of grieving parents at the grave of their son – the last he made before his death (fig. 304). It is possible, however, that this drawing, too, is about sorcery – about Ago, who was raised from the

303. Hunter about to harpoon a tupilak *with a seal's head, drawn by Kârale Andreassen and acquired by colony manager A. T. Hedegaard in Angmagssalik prior to 1927. Pen and sepia ink, 5⁵/₁₆″×8¹/₁₆″, reduced here. Royal Engravings Collection, Copenhagen.*

304. Couple mourning at a grave, drawn by Kârale Andreassen in Kungmiut in 1934. Black pastel on paper, 11¹³/₁₆″×19³/₄″. Private collection.

dead. The center of the picture is the grave. The point of land, the ice floes, and the sorrowing figures are all doubled over the pile of stones. The calm water and tranquil scenery are depicted so mutedly that one almost seems to hear the weeping. The mother's stream of tears and the father's hanging hair are the only vertical lines, and they effectively frame the grave. Emotion, drama, and narrative are the ingredients of Andreassen's seemingly serene line drawings.

Of a different character entirely were the drawings and watercolors that another head catechist, Gerhard Kleist of Godhavn (ca. 1850-1920), made with educational intent around the turn of the century, in a somewhat naive narrative style. His subject was primarily hunting techniques and animals – pleasant and instructive drawings accompanied by explanations in most fastidious handwriting. He drew and wrote a whole little book for Knud Rasmussen about the difficult art of paddling a kayak. In 1915 Kleist was given an exercise book, now in the National Library of Greenland, in which he describes the year's – though mostly the summer's – hunting pleasures (fig. 305). As a winter subject, he drew and colored a *savssat* – a kind of narwhal hunt that took place during severe winters, when, because of scarcity of breathing holes, the narwhals jammed together at the few holes in the ice. Many narwhals died of suffocation, and the hunt could practically degenerate into a massacre of the defenceless and half-dead creatures. Kleist has drawn the situation, with the gray-black figures and animals on a large ice-covered expanse, with a very delicate graphic effect.

Another artist whom Elgström met in Kangaamiut on his journey along the west coast was Kristoffer Kreutzmann (1867-ca.1920), who gave him a number of interesting watercolors. Some relate the beloved legend of the orphan Kagssagssuk, with emphasis on the boy's grotesque appearance – his outsized boots, tattered clothing, and huge nostrils. Others illustrate the (Greenlandic) prophet Habakuk's life and esca-

305. Mountain hares. Watercolor by Gerhard Kleist.

306. Savssat hunting of narwhals in breathing holes, painted by Gerhard Kleist in 1902 in Godhavn. Pencil, pastel, and watercolor on paper, signed "G. Kleist, Head Catechist," about 8¹¹/₁₆″×13¹³/₁₆″. National Museum of Greenland, Godthåb-Nuuk.

308 a and b. The story of the old bachelor's tupilak, which came to the great hunter's house to terrify him but was instead pecked in the eye by the great hunter's warning bird, a cormorant. Drawn by Gerth Lyberth for Knud Rasmussen at the beginning of the 1900s. Front and reverse of same sheet of paper. Pastels, pen and India ink over pencil, 6⅛"×9⅞". Jakobshavn Museum.

pades, employing a close, saturated palette. Kristoffer's father, Jens Kreutzmann, had also been preoccupied with the subject of Habakuk and Maria Magdalene (see figs. 173a and 288). His son's treatment of it is somewhat earthier, as it were, and more humorous and robust, although more relaxed in manner. The awkward situation appealed to Kristoffer, as in his pictures of the bird hunter who falls over backward and the woman who falls in the lake (fig. 307). With a sense of the baroque and executed in an outspoken style, Kreutzmann's pictures contributed to establishing a trait typical of some of the many artists in the Kreutzmann family, one that recurs through several generations.

The artist and colony manager Gerth Lyberth has already been discussed in the chapter on sculpture (see page 43). Radiantly colorful paintings, drawings, and pastels are also available to us from his extensive production: flower pictures, town scenes from Sukkertoppen, illustrations for *Myths and Legends* (figs. 308a and b), kayak men, interiors from old Greenlandic houses and – practically the only examples of the genre in Greenland – religious pictures with themes from the Bible. One of these hangs in Napassok church. Another is to the left of the altar in Sukkertoppen's wonderful old stone church – a large oil painting of the Virgin and Child surrounded by angels. The picture may be a free copy, and the figures are perhaps somewhat distorted, but it radiates genuine meekness and religious feeling. The colors are straw yellow, rose pink, and olive green; in delicate harmony with the church's fixtures and full of fresh, delightful details, especially among the host of angels. Lyberth apparently also recreated Danish painter Carl Bloch's "Christ in the Garden of Gethsemane" (known in Greenland from an oleograph print) and endowed it with a meekness of expression that, together with the vivid coloring, reveals his involvement in the subject (fig. 310).

A photograph was the basis for Lyberth's painting of the first East Greenlanders given permission to marry (after a difficult trial period, during which it was forbidden to swap spouses). The colors, and the artist's accentuating of the looks of discomfort on the figures' faces, make this copy of a photograph into an independent and distinguished work (fig. 309).

Lyberth often had difficulty obtaining materials. The "Gethsemane" was painted on a piece of blackboard and "The Newlyweds" on sealskin, and it was said that he used the hair of his head to make brushes for himself. Nevertheless, he became the motivator who got many artists started in the Sukkertoppen district. He himself was encouraged, and possibly inspired, by the painter Harald Moltke, who visited him with Knud Rasmussen.

Jakob Danielsen (1888-1938) of Disko Bay, probably the most signifi-

309. "The Newlyweds." Painted by Gerth Lyberth from a photo by missionary F. C. P. Rüttel that was used in the latter's book Ten Years Among the Heathens of East Greenland *(1917). Oil on depilated sealskin, 26⁷/₁₆″×30³/₄″. Danish Parliament, Christiansborg, Copenhagen.*

310. *Jesus in the garden of Gethsemane, painted by Gerth Lyberth. Oil on blackboard, about 19³/₄″×19³/₄″. Private collection.*

cant artist among the depictors of everyday life, found such a source of encouragement in Governor Philip Rosendahl. Danielsen's entire background was that of a hunter. He, his brothers, and their father were all well-known, expert hunters, and both Jakob and his brother Pele were able to pass their knowledge of the hunter's life on in the form of drawings. Danish officials and visitors such as Ossian Elgström bought their sketches and esteemed them highly. But it was not until 1924, when Rosendahl asked him to describe various hunting techniques, either in writing or in drawings, that Jakob Danielsen's artistic production got started in earnest. (As the new governor of North Greenland, one of Rosendahl's tasks was to encourage the indigenous industry of the region).

The response took the form of drawings and watercolors, with accompanying explanations written in collaboration with the interpreter Peter Dalager; for, as Jakob said, "There are letters that resemble each other, and one confuses them. If you've written a whole page and look at it, you can't see whether it's right. It's much easier to paint. If you're finished with a picture, you can look at it and see right away whether it's the way it should be." But it was not possible to include everything about a given hunting technique in a single picture. There were too many steps in the often complex and exhausting processes. Therefore Jakob worked with long series of pictures, built up like a drama. Starting with the calm and expectant prelude, in which the hunter leaves his home when the weather is right, visits the hunting grounds, and locates the game animals, the narrative continues through the climax in a thrilling chase, which usually ends with the killing of the game, to an epilogue illustrating the placid trip home and the flensing and butchering of the animal. Often as many as fifteen to twenty pictures were required in order to tell the story in all its details.

In this manner, Jakob Danielsen painted more than four hundred small pictures for Rosendahl, all measuring 3¾ by 5¾ inches. Carefully following the seasons of the year, they are a unique document of the hunter's profession in the Disko Bay area in Jakob's lifetime. The sub-

311. *Jakob's father comes home tired from the hunt. Jakob and his brother Pele run to meet their father and help by dragging the seal home. Details from the two concluding drawings in a series of sixteen pencil drawings about hunting from the edge of the ice in the month of March. National Museum, Copenhagen.*

jects include breathing-hole hunting, the crawling approach, hunting white whales from the edge of the ice, catching seals in ice nets, hunting seals from drifting ice sheets during the winter darkness, polar bear hunting, catching arctic fox in a stone trap, kayak men hunting walrus, and other techniques (figs. 311 and 312).

But Danielsen developed into a great landscape painter, who knew and could render the light of his country in the different seasons, based on the experience of generations of hunters. Just as a farmer can tell by the color of the grain whether it is ripe for harvesting, so the hunter gauges his chances of bagging game by looking at the clouds, the sea, and the color of the sky. Shown a picture painted by a Danish artist, of a hunter going out in his kayak, Danielsen conceded that it was good, but had one reservation: "He (the hunter) might as well turn around, because with that sky and that snow cover, he won't catch anything anyway."

His scenery is always the great backdrop against which the action unfolds in a calm, centered composition. Consider the watercolor of Danielsen's childhood home, which is larger than usual and for once not part of a series (fig. 313). In the middle of the picture is a sod house, with typical details of a North Greenland outpost milieu; the dogs sniffing around, the sled on the platform, the wash on the clothesline. The paths around the house reveal the habits of its inhabitants: one goes up to the lookout point, from where the weather may be assessed; one goes down to the water, branching off in two directions from which the kayak can be launched. But in spite of these narrative details – indicated, incidentally, with the only vertical lines in the picture – it is the structure of the scenery, in which tufts of grass, mountain contours, and rocks stand out

312. *Kayak men hunting white whale, Godhavn, May. Painted by Jakob Danielsen after 1924 for P. Rosendahl. The series, eight pictures in all, shows step by step how the whales are surrounded and caught. Each picture is carefully explained by the artist. Thus he writes of the first picture, upper left: "Most migrations of white whales pass along the coast in May and June, when the ice in Disko Bay has begun drifting. The pods are small, arrive from the west, pass Godhavn, and approach close by every point of land. White whales are very shy. They are easiest to get close to where silted water from streams empties into the sea and makes it opaque. Here we are lying behind the cover of ice floes off Godhavn's lookout point. The water where we are lying has been colored red by the basalt silt from 'Red Stream.' We are lying altogether silently, with white coverings over our kayak jackets, alongside an ice floe. Therefore the animals don't see us." At lower right, we see the concluding picture: after the many phases of the hunt, the seventeen-foot-long animal is towed home. Watercolor over pencil, all 3³/₄″×5¹¹/₁₆″. National Museum, Copenhagen.*

with delicate graphic effect against a light cover of snow, together with the sky and the light on that February 11th, 1925, that tells us most.

Danielsen's picture series, with their sequential action and accurately descriptive character, are an obvious continuation of the ancient Eskimo tradition of scratching a picture – such as a hunting scene in the form of a frieze – in ivory or bone (see figs. 41 to 45). Only now color has been included. Danielsen thus constitutes a link between the ancient pictorial concept and that of our own times, whose artists we shall now discuss.

Pictorial artists of the present day

That a picture tells a story or has a point is typical of Greenlandic art. It is manifest in the ancient bone engravings, in Aron, in the Kreutzmann family, in Kârale, and in most present-day artists. Nearly all Greenlandic artists are expressionists. Some, however, tell their stories as close to reality as possible, with an observant and unsentimental naturalism.

One modern narrative artist is Hans Lynge (b. 1906), whose versatility has already been mentioned in the chapter on sculpture (see page 51). In writing, color, and form, Lynge demonstrates that the ancient Greenlandic narrative skill is still alive – and not only with the legends of the past as motifs, although they are an important source of inspiration. The son of the pastor and painter Niels Lynge (see page 192), Hans grew up in Godthåb, where he knew Lars Møller and his sons (see page 192). His training was at the teachers' college, where one of his instructors was Jonathan Petersen, and his father-in-law was the minister and artist Henrik Lund (see page 193). Hans Lynge's most immediate grounding was therefore in the national-romantic revival.

From his earliest years, Lynge has had a warm and humorous affection for the old Eskimo beliefs, which he heard from the old people, when his father took him along on his pastoral rounds, and from his nannies. The tendency nascent in the works of Peter Rosing (see fig. 296) – namely the renewed interest in the former era, when it was on the verge of becoming remote – is given free play in Hans Lynge.

After several years of activity as a poet, dramatist, catechist, and public servant, he attended the school of sculpture at the Academy of Art in Copenhagen; but visits to museums in Italy and France were perhaps just as significant for his artistic development. His most impor-

313. *The artist's birthplace, painted by Jakob Danielsen in 1925. Watercolor over pencil, signed "Jakob Danielsen, Godhavn," and designated "11. Feepruar. 1925," 7¹/₂″×12⁷/₁₆″. Private collection.*

314. *Mother with children, painted by Hans Lynge in 1967. Oil on canvas, 26"×22⅞". Private collection.*

tant sources of inspiration, however, are people, nature, and the rich world of the Greenlandic legends. Written and drawn observations filled many sketchbooks; fleeting ideas were jotted down, an animal's movements were in a flash captured on paper, the mountains as experienced on a motor boat trip, a woman's profile at a sidewalk café. Later, some of these impressions were transposed onto canvas, or in watercolors or pastels. Recollection and observation worked together and, in combination with a spontaneous mode of painting and a luminous palette, comprise the constituents of Lynge's painting.

His first watercolors were somewhat cautious, done in a cordial, naturalistic style, with light colors. But gradually, as the draughtsmanship becomes more assured, it is relieved of the need to achieve simple likeness. Line and color acquire a life of their own and fill the surface. Lynge now and then plays with perspective or foregoes using it at all. An outline sinuously encompasses the figures, or else they are built up from contrasting colors. White tempera or orange are the lightest and a deep brown violet the darkest pigments.

There is humor, too, in Lynge's painting, as in the poetic picture of the mother who, according to Greenlandic custom, lets her older child taste her milk, to the little one's displeasure (fig. 314). The mother with her child is again the central point in the picture "Fear Was Our Daily Companion" in which – contrasting with the warmth of the mother and child and the burning lamp – ghastly forms are seen lurking in the darkness and under the bed platform (fig. 315). The painting "The Game Animals Come to Avenge Their Stolen Souls" (fig. 316) refers to the old belief that the animals would take revenge unless certain precautions were observed, such as throwing the bones back into the sea so that the animals could be reborn. Despite its somber motif, the picture is festive; the white whale, seal, and walrus lead off in this symphony of the animals. There are some pictures that encompass silence, and others that one associates with sounds – as in the case of the latter painting especially. In Hans Lynge's work as a whole there is shouting, laughter, weeping, the wash of the waves and the wind. With infectious joy in painting, Lynge tells us something important about life and death, idyll and drama – about the Greenlandic temperament.

Greenlandic artists are frequently versatile, expressing themselves in a number of media. This is eminently true of another great storyteller in

315. *"Fear Was Our Daily Companion." Painted by Hans Lynge in 1971. Pastel on colored paper, 16⁹⁄₁₆"×21¼". Property of the artist.*

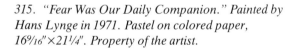

316. *"The Game Animals Come to Avenge Their Stolen Souls." Painted by Hans Lynge in 1973. Oil on canvas, 39⁷/₁₆″×39⁷/₁₆″, reduced here. Private collection.*

modern Greenlandic art, Jens Rosing (b. 1925). With the clear and constant aim of telling a story, but on a groundwork of matter-of-fact observation, Rosing has produced paintings, figures, ceramic decorations, films, illustrations, and books. Like his father Otto Rosing (see page 196), he has a vast knowledge of history, and he was for a time head of the National Museum of Greenland.

His grandfather was the minister Kristian Rosing, who zealously Christianized the heathens of East Greenland, and his father and paternal uncle Peter both did likewise. But in spite of their missionary work, all three collected information about, and legends from, the old era, took care of archaeological finds, and wrote down satirical and charm songs. It was Jens who assembled and organized the material, which was published in the books *Legend and Saga* and *Kimilik,* supplemented by his own childhood recollections from East Greenland and marked by his deep love for the ancient Eskimo heritage. He is also a lecturer and writer of articles.

As a pictorial artist, it is the clean, powerful line, simple forms, and a certain drama in the action that interest him. Study at the Academy of Art (1949-51), with Professor Kræsten Iversen, provided a familiarity with the materials, but the subsequent years in Lappland and on the Godthåb Fjord were far more significant from the point of view of art. Rosing headed a project for the moving of reindeer from the Lapps in Northern Norway to the Godthåb Fjord, where they were to restore the bygone herds of caribou there (the caribou is the North American reindeer), an experiment that happily resulted in the thriving of the reindeer. As reindeer herdsman, Rosing had ample opportunity for studying his beloved theme: the animals. He has translated birds, reindeer, dogs, bears – indeed, the entire fauna of Greenland – into paintings and watercolors, but especially drawings. With simple, precise strokes, Jens Rosing can reveal the characteristic movements of an animal, a bird in flight, a dog team before the sled, or a modern snowmobile (figs. 317 and 318).

His other theme is the ancient Greenlandic legends, but preferably fables about animals, as in "The Troll Worm Attacking the Reindeer Driver" and "The Raven Who Took a Wild Goose to Wife." With his ability to cut away the excess so that the motif stands expressed clearly in a simplified and incisive line, Rosing has created a long series of distinguished postage stamps for the Postal Department of Greenland. Their subjects are Greenlandic legends, animals of Greenland, means of communication such as the dog-sled, kayak, and *umiak,* and historic events. Converted to steel engraving, which reveals quickly whether a line is precise or not, these stamps form a wonderful picture gallery of Greenlandic motifs (fig. 319).

Engraving and drawing have always been important in Greenlandic art – in bone engraving, in illustrations for *Atuagagdliutit,* and as the grounding, so to speak, for practically all pictorial artists. Lithography was introduced by Lars Møller, and linocut far later, in the 1940s, by Kåle Rosing. Among other things, the latter executed a long series of prints for *Atuagagdliutit,* thus perpetuating the tradition of carrying original art in the newspaper. Kåle Rosing (1911-74), a younger brother of Peter and Otto Rosing's, strove to simplify the motif (fig. 320), and is stylistically a middle link between national-romantic naturalism and the pure line that – purged of superfluity and without light and shadow – is cultivated by Jens Rosing.

There are a number of artists today working in the detailed naturalistic style, both with landscapes and subjects from the past. They include Amalie Heilmann, Mads Kreutzmann, Peter Berthelsen (fig. 322), Thomas Frederiksen, Laurids Jessen (fig. 321), and Thorvald Tavnajik.

A vivid palette and audacious brushwork, on the other hand, typify Ejnar Heilmann, Karl Peter Andersen, Esaja Isaksen, and Osarqaq and

317. *The sled is started with the help of a snowmobile. Sketch from Canada by Jens Rosing (1972). Pencil and pastel, 15" long. Property of the artist.*

318. *Velvet duck drawn by Jens Rosing in 1970. Watercolor over pen and India ink. The picture field measures 16½"×15¾". Property of the artist.*

319. *Various postage stamps drawn by Jens Rosing. Engraved by C. Slania and issued by the Postal Department of Greenland. Original drawings property of the artist.*

Alibak Johansen, with action and subject as the picture's support-ideas. Landscape painting that doesn't strive for fastidious likenesses, but renders the play of light and color and the shapes of the mountains in the changing seasons, is practiced by the sensitive colorist Kîstat Lund (fig. 323). The young poet, teacher, and painter Kristian Olsen goes behind the motif to express his anguish at the situation in today's Greenland (fig. 324).

Among the younger teachers who also have artistic ability are Lars Møller Lund, Aqigssiaq Møller, Otto Lauf, Karl Kruse, who is a skillful illustrator, and Thue Christiansen, who in his linocuts brings forth rhythm and movement in simplified human figures, with fine decorative faculty (fig. 325).

An artist like Simon Kristoffersen (see fig. 67) breaks the pattern by being simultaneously a distinctive sculptor in soapstone and a fine graphic artist. In his wood and linocuts, he covers the surface closely with tones and figures, just as in his sculpture, where he stretches the form to the breaking point.

The very youngest artists express themselves chiefly in the various graphic techniques, especially as a result of the activities of the Graphic

Workshop in Godthåb-Nuuk. The workshop, which is Greenland's only art school, was for several years headed by Emil Rosing (b. 1939), the youngest son of Otto Rosing. Emil Rosing generally draws birds in a landscape of distant perspective that imparts a feeling of the vast spaces of Greenland, with assured, somewhat austere coloring (fig. 326). Many fine talents have appeared among the students at the Graphic Workshop, which in 1981 was renamed the Art School of Greenland. Figures 328-34 show a few current tendencies. The venerable tradition spanning from Gormansen to Jakob Danielsen is being perpetuated, however, in the work of the splendid graphic artist Enok Absalonsen (fig. 327) among others.

Outside the circle of workshop alumni, Arnannguaq Høegh (b. 1958), who was trained at the Eskimo workshop in Cape Dorset, Canada, the art school in Halifax, Nova Scotia, and the Academy of art in Copenhagen, has distinguished himself in a highly personal and decorative style with fantastic, somewhat surreal events, that take place in landscapes from distant planets. The spirit world, whose dread and ghastliness we see expressed in *tupilak* figures, appears again in Arnannguaq's graphic works (fig. 335). The picture surface is covered by a painstakingly disci-

320. *Black guillemot. Linocut made by Jens Rosing in the 1950s. One of a portfolio of eight linocuts published under the title* Greenlandic Prints *by Nordiske Landes Bogforlag (1968). Picture field, 6¹¹/₁₆″×5¹¹/₁₆″. Private collection.*

321. *Landscape with tent encampment in the Sukkertoppen district, summer, painted by Laurids Jessen in 1955. Oil on canvas, 14³/₈″×20¹/₂″. Private collection.*

322. *The interior of a common house, painted by Peter Berthelsen in 1971. Oil on masonite. Property of the artist.*

323. Landscape from South Greenland, painted by Kîstat Lund in 1974. Pastel on handmade paper, about 18¹⁵/₁₆″×24⅞″. Workers' High School, Julianehåb.

plined pattern, and the gray tones are built up from its varying density – a technique closely related to mosaic, a medium in which Arnannguaq has executed a number of smaller works.

What might be termed political art – rebuking established society and critical of Danish housing, economic, and cultural policy, and of Danish domination generally – has found its strongest utterances in poetry, songs of protest, and theatrical performances. Frederik Kristensen and Arnannguaq have made posters for the independence party, *Inuit Ataqatigiit;* and Anne Birte Hove, in her talented and humorous but also accusing graphic works from Godthåb, has shown us thought-provoking scenes of "progress" in Greenland, as in the lithograph of a Greenlandic woman who, in the shadow of concrete apartment blocks, seeks consolation in the contents of beer cans (fig. 336). In these times, when Greenlandic culture is struggling to stand firm, graphic art has been known to acquire an unintentional political message by virtue of its powerful content of Greenlandic identity. Inspired by some etchings, the poet

325. Dancing figure. Linocut by Thue Christiansen, 1973. 11⅝″×7½″. Private collection.

324. "Inuk and a TV Screen." Illustration by Kristian Olsen Aaju to The Ballad of Identity, *a collection of poems published by Kragestedet (1978). Linocut, 5⅞″×4⅛″. Blocks property of the artist.*

326. *Flock of guillemots taking off. One of a portfolio of three color silk-screen prints by Emil Rosing published by Nordiske Landes Bogforlag (1972). Picture surface, 12⅝"×32¾". Private collection.*

Arqaluk Lynge has, for example, written verses with unmistakable political subject matter and aim.

Probably the strongest of the young artists is Aka Høegh (b. 1947), a painter and sculptor, but above all a graphic artist. In drawings, lithographs, linocuts, and especially etchings, she has brought about a rejuvenation of Greenlandic art. Aka's talent lies in expressing her unconscious reveries, giving utterance to sorrow, joy, and mother love, as in the etchings "My Son's World" (fig. 337) and "The Wind" (fig. 338), in which a mother shields her child from the wind. In her many drawings for *Myths and Legends,* originally collected by Knud Rasmussen and published in a new edition in 1979, Aka has revivified the familiar old illustrations so that the legends come alive for us again. On a larger scale, she has made a decoration for the church at Godthåb, and an outdoor decoration for the Workers's High School in Julianehåb, where her living line – even in stone mosaic – brings salutary movement to the rather ascetic, severe Danish architecture.

327. *The orphan Kagssagssuk. Here, to the astonishment of his settlement fellows, Kagssagssuk kills three polar bears with his bare hands. Drawn by Enok Absalonsen in 1974. Lithographic chalk on stone, 8¼"×12⅝". Art School of Greenland, Godthåb-Nuuk.*

328. *The drum dancer and his helping spirits, drawn by Jeremias Karlsen in 1975. Silk-screen print, about 15³/₄″×13″. Art School of Greenland, Godthåb-Nuuk.*

329. *The woman with the iron tail, drawn by Enok Absalonsen in 1974. Cold point on copper, about 6¹¹/₁₆″×5⁵/₁₆″. Art School of Greenland, Godthåb-Nuuk.*

330. *Capelin, by Frederik Kristensen. Scratched with lithographic ink on a piece of stone, about 7¹/₁₆″ long. Art School of Greenland, Godthåb-Nuuk.*

331. Ice floe, drawn by N. Kilime in 1977. Color etching on copper, about 8¼″×11″. Art School of Greenland, Godthåb-Nuuk.

332. Ukiaq (Winter). Drawn by Anne-Birthe Hove in 1974. Lithographic chalk on stone, 23⅝″×16⅞″. Art School of Greenland, Godthåb-Nuuk.

333. Siblings, drawn by Marianne Jessen in 1976. Lithographic chalk on stone, about 12⅝″×8¼″. Art School of Greenland, Godthåb-Nuuk.

334. Sea and Mountain. Drawn by Henrik Johansen, called Arfeq, in 1977. Color aquatint, about 6¹¹/₁₆″×8¼″. Art School of Greenland, Godthåb-Nuuk.

335. "The Combatants." Drawn by Arnannguaq Høegh in 1974. Pen and India ink on paper, 9⁷/₁₆″×11¹³/₁₆″. Property of the artist.

In this book, my intention has been to illustrate a cultural pattern whose warp is the Eskimo psyche and whose weft consists of many different things: external influences, altered conditions of life, the demands of the outside world. The Greenlanders' own need for art, to express themselves creatively, is great, and their ability to do so is natural and straightforward. I have felt it incumbent on me to show how closely related the various art forms are to one another, and to the roots from which they spring. The Greenlanders are no longer a people of wandering hunters. Nevertheless, some still make their living by hunting, and the joys of the hunt and of traveling are familiar to most.

Among the Eskimos, there is no such thing as "art for art's sake." Rather, art is for the sake of people. From the Dorset period down to the folk artists and art school students of today, we are given a series of statements about inner human reality. The continuity is unmistakable. From Aron to Aka, Greenland's pictorial art shows us the reflections of the mind on a vast register of human emotions in intimate harmony with nature. The grand theme of Eskimo creativity is the human being, but set in a universal context. People, animals, and nature make up the common chord that reverberates through the art of Greenland.

336. Imiaq (Beer). Drawn by Anne-Birthe Hove in 1974. Lithographic chalk on stone, 12⁵/₈″×8¹/₂″. Private collection.

337. Ernera *(My Son). Drawn by Aka Høegh in*
1974. Cold point on copper, about $6^{11}/_{16}'' \times 12^{3}/_{16}''$.
Private collection.

338. Anore *(The Wind). Drawn by Aka Høegh in*
1974. Cold point on copper, $9^{5}/_{8}'' \times 13''$. Private
collection.

The Reason

By Moses Olsen
Drawing by Aka Høegh

You would ask me
Why I write,
Why I make songs,
Why I write poems.
Then go to the great stream
Which plunges, rushing and mighty,
Down the steep mountainside.
Bend your head down to the stream
And ask it,
"Why do you eternally rush along?"
And the stream will answer you,
"Go to the top of this tremendous mountain.
Up there,
In the eternal silence and serenity,
You will find the trickling spring
From which I come,
From which I get my water,
From which I get my power and strength.
Go up and ask that spring,
Why do you eternally flow?"

217

References

Atuagadliutit, 1, nos. 1-5 (1861). Facsimile edition, Godthåb-Nuuk: National Library of Greenland, 1962.

Berthelsen, Rasmus. *En samtale om Krig, oplyst ved mange Billeder* (A Conversation About War, Elucidated with Many Pictures). Godthåb, 1858. Reprint, Rungsted Kyst: Anders Nyborg A/S Internationalt Forlag, 1973).

Bluhme, E. *Fra et Ophold i Grønland, 1863-64* (From a Sojourn in Greenland). Copenhagen, 1865. Reprint, with an introduction by Svend Dahl. Copenhagen: Det Berlingske Bogtrykkeri, 1952.

Dalager, Lars. *Grønlandske Relationer* (Greenlandic Relations). Frederikshåb, 1752. Reprint, with an introduction by Louis Bobé. Det Grønlandske Selskabs Skrifter 2. Charlottenlund, 1915.

Davis, John. *Voyages and Works of John Davis*. The Hakluyt Society, vol. 59. London, 1880.

Egede, Hans. *Relation angaaende den Grønlandske Mission 1738 samt Det gamle Grønlands ny Perlustration eller Naturel-Historie 1741*. Relation Concerning the Greenland Mission, 1738, together with the Old Greenland's New Perlustration, or Natural History, 1741). Reprint, with postscript and comments by Finn Gad. Copenhagen: Rosenkilde og Bagger, 1971.

Elgström, Ossian. *Moderna Eskimåer* (Modern Eskimos). Stockholm: Albert Bonniers Forlag, 1916.

Glahn, Henrik Christopher. *Dagbøger for Aarene 1763-64, 1766-67 og 1767-68* (Journals for the Years 1763-64, 1766-67 and 1767-68). With an introduction by Hother Ostermann. Det Grønlandske Selskabs Skrifter 4. Charlottenlund, 1921.

Hansêraks Dagbog (Hansêrak's Journal). Edited and annotated by Signe Rink. Copenhagen: Hagerups Forlag, 1900.

Holm, Gustav. *Den østgrønlandske Expedition, udført i Aarene 1883-85, under ledelse af Gustav Holm* (The East Greenland Expedition, Carried Out in the Years 1883-85, Under the Leadership of Gustav Holm). Vols 1 and 2. Meddelelser om Grønland 9 and 10. Copenhagen: Kommissionen for videnskabelige undersøgelser i Grønland, 1888-89.

Lindow, Harald. *Kongefærden til Grønland, 1921* (The Royal Journey to Greenland, 1921). Det Grønlandske Selskabs Skrifter 16. Charlottenlund, 1948.

Lund, Henrik. "Sangen om Narssaq" (The Song of Narssaq), "I Grydedalen Amitsuarssuk" (In the Amitsuarssuk Valley), and "Nunarput" (Our Country). In William Thalbitzer, ed., *Grønlandske Digte og Danske* (Poems Greenlandic and Danish). Copenhagen: Ejnar Munksgaards Forlag, 1945, pp. 41, 42, 33.

Lynge, Hans. "Storfangeren Ujuānât" (The Great Hunter Ujuānât). In *Årbog 1976* (Yearbook 1976), edited by Henning Henningsen and Hanne Poulsen (Elsinore: Selskabet Handels- og Søfartsmuseets venner, 1976), pp. 61-72.

Olsen, Moses. "Forklaringen" (The Reason). In Mogens Jensen and Flemming Lundahl, *Læsning V* (Reading V) (A Danish textbook) Copenhagen: Munksgaards Forlag, 1978, pp. 78.

Petersen, Johan. *Ujuâts Dagbøger fra Østgrønland, 1894-1935* (Ujuât's Diaries from East Greenland, 1894-1935). Introduction and notes by B. Rosenkilde Nielsen. Det Grønlandske Selskabs Skrifter 19. Charlottenlund, 1975.

Pok og Angekokken (Pok and the Shaman). Godthåb: Inspecteurens Bogtrykkeri, 1857. Reprint, Rungsted Kyst: Anders Nyborg A/S Internationalt Forlag, 1973.

Rasmussen, Knud. *Den Store Slæderejse* (The Great Sled Journey). 1932.

Revised edition. Copenhagen: Gyldendal, 1979).

———. *Myter og Sagn* (Myths and Legends). Vol. I: *The East Greenlanders*. Vol. II: *West Greenland*. Vol. III: *The Cape York District and North Greenland*. Copenhagen: Gyldendal, 1921-1925.

Rosendahl, Philip. *Jakob Danielsen: En Grønlandsk Maler* (Jakob Danielsen: A Greenlandic Painter). 2nd edition. Copenhagen: Rhodos, 1967.

Rosing, Jens. *Sagn og Saga* (Legend and Saga). Copenhagen: Rhodos, 1963.

———. *Seminar for Husflidsproducenter* (Seminar for Handicrafters). Presented at Womens House in Godthåb, 23 to 27 November, 1976. Godthåb: Den Kongelige Grønlandske Handel, 1976.

Walløe, Peder Olsen. *Dagbøger fra hans Rejser i Grønland, 1739-53* (Journals from His Travels in Greenland, 1739-53). Edited by Louis Bobé. Det Grønlandske Selskabs Skrifter 5. Charlottenlund, 1927.

Sources

Aron of Kangeq. *Nordboer og Skrælinger* (Norsemen and "Skrælings"). Edited by Eigil Knuth. Godthåb: Det Grønlandske Forlag, 1968.

Bak, Ove. *Kujavarsiks rejse til månen* (Kujavarsik's Trip to the Moon). With a biography of the book's illustrator, Kârale Andreassen. Copenhagen: Hernov, 1977.

———. *Troldbjørnen: Også isbjørne har en sjæl* (The Wizard Bear: Even Polar Bears Have a Soul). Tales and anecdotes from Greenland, including some recollections by Kârale Andreassen. Copenhagen: Hernov, 1979.

Bang, Jette. *Grønland igen* (Greenland Again). Copenhagen: Spectator, 1961.

Boas, Franz. *Primitive Art*. New York: Dover Publications, 1955.

Bobé, Louis, and O. Bendixen. "Lars Møller." In *Det Grønlandske Selskabs Aarsskrift 1916* (The Greenland Society's Yearbook, 1916), edited by Adolf Jensen (Charlottenlund: Det Grønlandske Selskab, 1917), pp. 5-13.

Bogen om Grønland (The Book About Greenland). Revised edition. Copenhagen: Politikens Forlag, 1978.

Brandstrup, Lasse, and Hanne Josephsen. *Eskimoerne* (The Eskimos). A text collage about religion and existence. Copenhagen: Gyldendal, 1975.

Bregenhøj, Carsten. *Helligtrekongersløb på Agersø* (The Twelfth-Night Mummers on Agersø). Copenhagen: Akademisk Forlag, 1974, pp. 84-87.

Burland, Cottie. *Eskimo Art*. London: Hamlyn, 1973.

———. *Men Without Machines*. London: Aldous Books, 1965.

———. *North American Indian Mythology*. London: Hamlyn, 1965.

Continuity and Discontinuity in the Inuit Culture of Greenland, November 1976. Groningen, The Netherlands: Arctic Centre of the University of Groningen, 1977.

Dumond, Don E. *The Eskimos and Aleuts*. London: Thames and Hudson, 1977.

Erngaard, Erik. *Grønland i tusinde år* (Greenland for a Thousand Years). Copenhagen: Lademann, 1972.

Fleischer, I. P. C. von. "Af en gammel Grønlænders Liv" (From the Life of an Old Greenlander). In *Det Grønlandske Selskabs Aarsskrift 1919* (The Greenland Society's Yearbook, 1919), edited by Adolf Jensen (Charlottenlund: Det Grønlandske Selskab, 1920), pp. 90-102.

Fra Aron til idag (From Aron to Today) (Catalog for an exhibition of Greenlandic art at the Louisiana Museum, December 1969 to January

1970, with statements by Eigil Knuth, Hans Lynge, H.C. Petersen, Robert Petersen, Philip Rosendahl, Emil Rosing, and Nikolaj Rosing). Humlebæk: Louisiana, 1969.

Fraser, Douglas. *Primitive Art.* New York: Chanticleer Press, 1962.

Gad, Finn. "En fransk etnografisk skildring fra 1600-tallet" (A French Ethnographic Description from the 1600s). In *Grønland 1966* (Greenland 1966), edited by Helge Christensen, (Charlottenlund: Det Grønlandske Selskab, 1966), pp. 73-89.

———. *Grønlands Historie* (The History of Greenland). Vol. 1. Copenhagen: Nyt Nordisk Forlag, 1967.

———. "Skielderiet i Sions Kirke" (The "Limning" in the Church of Zion). *Grønland 1977,* no. 1 (1977): 1-8.

Gessain, Robert. *Ammassalik.* Paris: Librairie Ernest Flammarion, 1969.

———. "Ammassalik, trente ans aprés." *Objets et Mondes,* 7, no. 2 (1967): 133-156.

———. "Le tambour chez les Ammassalimiut." *Objets et Mondes,* 13, no. 3 (1973): 129-160.

———. "Figurine androgyne esquimaude." *Journal de la Société des Américanistes.* vol. 43 (1954): 207-217.

———. "L'art squelettique des esquimaus." *Journal de la Société des Américanistes,* vol. 48 (1959): 237-244.

———. *L'Homme-lune dans la mythologie des ammassalimiut.* Paris: Hermann, 1978.

———. "Statuettes esquimaus composites à trois personnages." *Journal de la Société des Américanistes,* vol. 44 (1955): 199-204.

Grønlandsk Kunst idag (Greenlandic Art Today) (Catalog for an exhibition of Greenlandic art at the Århus Art Association, from 7 to 22 September, 1974, with a list of living Greenlandic artists). Århus: Århus Kunstforening af 1874, 1974.

Grønlandske Folkesagn, opskrevne og meddeelte af Indfødte (Greenlandic Folk Legends, Written Down and Related by Natives). Godthåb: Inspecteurens Bogtrykkeri, 1859-61. Reprint, Rungsted Kyst: Anders Nyborg A/S Internationalt Forlag, 1972.

Gulløv, Hans Christian. *Kampen om sjælene* (The Battle for Souls). Copenhagen: Danish National Museum, 1978.

Haan, Lourens Feykes. "Beskrivelse af Straat Davids, 1720" (A Description of the Davis Strait, 1720). Translated from the Dutch and with an introduction by Louis Bobé. In *Det Grønlandske Selskabs Aarsskrift 1914* (The Greenland Society's Yearbook, 1914). Edited by Adolf Jensen (Charlottenlund: Det Grønlandske Selskab, 1915), pp. 63-69.

Hatt, Gudmund. *Arktiske Skinddragter i Eurasien og Amerika* (Arctic Skin Clothing in Eurasia and America). Copenhagen: J.H. Schultz Forlagsboghandel, 1914.

Holtved, Erik. *Contributions to Polar Eskimo Ethnography.* Meddelelser om Grønland 182, no. 2. Copenhagen: Kommissionen for videnskabelige undersøgelser i Grønland, 1967.

———. *Eskimokunst* (Eskimo Art). Copenhagen: Forening for Ung Dansk Kunst and Carit Andersens Forlag, 1947.

Isaks Billedbog (Isak's Picture Book). Introduction and notes by G.N. Bugge. Godthåb and Lyngby: National Library of Greenland and the Lyngby City Library, 1969.

Jensen, Bent. *Eskimoisk festlighed* (Eskimo Festivity). Copenhagen: Folkeuniversitetsforeningen i København, 1965.

Kleivan, Inge. "Molbohistorierne på Grønlandsk i *Atuagadliutit,* 1865" (The *Molbohistorier* in Greenlandic in *Atuagagdliutit,* 1865). *Grønland 1978,* no. 5 (1978): 156-68.

Knuth, Eigil. "Aron fra Kangeq, Grønlands Guldaldermester" (Aron of Kangeq, the Master of Greenland's Golden Age). *Nationalmuseets Arbejdsmark 1960.* (Copenhagen: Nationalmuseets Publikationsfond, 1960), pp. 45-65.

Koch, Palle, ed. *Grønland* (Greenland) (Gyldendal's regional descriptions). Copenhagen: Gyldendal, 1975.

Laursen, Dan. "Grønlændere i forsknings tjeneste: Hans Zakæus" (Greenlanders in the service of Research: Hans Zakæus). In *Grønland 1955,* (Greenland 1955), edited by Finn Nielsen and Christian Vibe (Charlottenlund: Det Grønlandske Selskab, 1955), pp. 397-400.

Lipton, Barbara. *Survival: Life and Art of the Alaskan Eskimo:* New York: Newark Museum and Morgan and Morgan, 1977.

Meldgaard, Jørgen. *Eskimo Skulptur* (Eskimo Sculpture). Oslo: Dreyer, 1959.

———. "Traditional Sculpture in Greenland." *The Beaver,* Autumn 1967: 54-59.

Miles, Charles. Indian and Eskimo Artifacts of North America. Chicago: Henry Regnery, 1963.

Nansen, Fridtjof. *Eskimoliv* (Eskimo Life). Kristiania: H. Aschehoug og Co.'s Forlag, 1891.

Nellemann, George. "Mitârneq: A West Greenland Winter Ceremony." *Folk,* 2 (1960): 99-113.

———. "Mitârtut." *Jordens Folk,* 3, no. 1 (1967): 35.

Nooter, Gert. "Mitârtut: Winter Feast in Greenland." *Objects et Mondes,* 15, no. 2 (1975): 159-168.

Oldenow, Knud. *Bogtrykkerkunsten i Grønland og mændene bag den* (The Art of Printing in Greenland and the Men Behind It). Copenhagen: Carit Andersens Forlag, 1957.

Ray, Dorothy Jean. *Eskimo Art: Tradition and Innovation in North Alaska.* Seattle: University of Washington Press, 1977.

———. *Eskimo Masks: Art and Ceremony.* Seattle: University of Washington Press, 1975.

Rink, Signe. *Fra det Grønland, som gik* (From the Greenland That Was). Copenhagen: Hagerups Forlag, 1902.

Rosing, Christian. *Østgrønlænderne: Tunuamiut, Grønlands sidste Hedninger* (The East Greenlanders: Tunuamiut, Greenland's Last Heathens). With notes and postscript by William Thalbitzer. Copenhagen: Ejnar Munksgaards Forlag, 1946.

Rosing, Jens. "Den østgrønlandske maskekultur" (East Greenlandic Mask Culture). *Grønland 1957,* (1957): 241-251.

———. "Fra åndeportrait til pind og rem" (From Spirit Portrait to Stick and Thong). *Jordens Folk,* 3, no. 1 (1967): 30-34.

———. *Kimilik: Digte fra Angmagssalik* (Kimilik: Poems from Angmagssalik). Copenhagen: Gyldendal, 1970.

Ross, John, *A Voyage of Discovery.* London, 1819.

Scavenius, Per Jensen. *Den Grønlandske Kajak og dens Redskaber* (The Greenlandic Kayak and Its Implements). Copenhagen: Nyt Nordisk Forlag, 1975.

Schultz-Lorentzen, C.W. *Det grønlandske Folk og Folkesind* (The Greenlandic Nation and National Consciousness). Copenhagen: Danish Ministry of Foreign Affairs, 1951.

———. "En Grønlandsk Kunstner" (A Greenlandic Artist) (Steffen Møller). In *Gads Danske Magasin* 1909-1910 (Gad's Danish Magazine 1909-1910), edited by Christian Gulmann (Copenhagen: G.E.C. Gad, 1910), pp. 368-371.

Sculpture/Inuit. Sculpture of the Inuit: Masterworks of the Canadian Arctic. Catalog for an international traveling exhibition of Canadian Eskimo art 1971-73. Published for the Canadian Eskimo Arts Council by the University of Toronto Press. Toronto, 1971.

Swinton, George. *Sculpture of the Eskimo.* Toronto: McClelland and Stewart, 1972.

Thalbitzer, William. *Ethnological Collections from East Greenland.* Meddelelser om Grønland 39. Copenhagen: Kommissionen for videnskabelige undersøgelser i Grønland, 1914.

————. *Language and Folklore.* Meddelelser om Grønland 40. Copenhagen: Kommissionen for videnskabelige undersøgelser i Grønland, 1921.

Acknowledge-ments

The following photographers and institutions hold the copyrights to the illustrations indicated.

Anne Bang 49, 52, 53, 76, 89a-c, 92a and b, 97a, 98, 99, 110, 116, 117, 122a, 122b, 126a and b, 127, 129, 130, 132, 138, 167, 168, 180, 200, 201a and b, 204, 231, 235, 258

Jette Bang 30, 155 (Arctic Institute, Copenhagen. The Jette Bang Foundation)

William Christensen 64, 66

Poul Dupont 217, 220, 306

Erling Irving 310

Keld Hansen 203

Erik Holm 293, 336

Mogens S. Koch 22, 90a-c, 111, 115, 131, 323, 326, 335

Lennart Larsen 2, 6, 9, 12, 13, 16, 17, 18, 20, 29, 31, 36, 46, 47, 48, 50, 57, 61, 63, 65a-e, 67, 68, 70, 73, 74, 82, 84a and b, 85, 91a, 91b, 97b, 101, 108, 112, 113, 114, 118, 120, 123, 128, 139, 140, 141, 142, 143, 144, 146a and b, 147a and b, 148, 150, 154, 158, 170, 176, 177, 178, 179, 181, 182, 183, 184, 185, 186, 187, 189, 190, 192, 193, 195a and b, 197, 199, 202, 205a-c, 207a and b, 209, 211a-c, 213, 214, 216a and b, 218, 219, 222, 223, 224, 226, 229a and b, 232, 233, 238, 239, 240, 242b, 249, 250, 251, 252, 253, 259a and b, 260, 261, 262a-c, 263a and b, 264, 266, 271, 272, 273, 274, 275, 276, 277, 278, 279, 280, 281, 282, 283, 284, 285, 286, 287, 288, 305, 314, 315, 316, 327, 328, 329, 331, 332, 333, 334

Jørgen Meldgaard 198

Jan Nørgård 37, 45, 51, 54a and b, 56a and b, 59, 60, 62a-c, 71, 72, 86, 103, 104, 105, 107, 109, 124, 133, 145, 156, 157, 163, 165a-d, 166, 171, 173a and b, 174a and b, 175, 191, 227, 228, 230, 234, 236, 237, 241, 257a and b, 265, 267a and b, 268, 269, 270, 295, 297b-c, 309, 313, 321, and center picture on back of dust jacket

Dorte Passer 1, 88a and b, 248, 255, 256, 289, 296, 299, 300, 311, 312, 317, 318, 319, 324, and picture on front of dust jacket

Thomas and Poul Pedersen 58, 100, 125a and b, 134, 135, 194a and b, and top picture on back of dust jacket

Eli Ponsaing 330

Emil Rosing 298

Ivars Silis 55, 69, 102, 136, 210, 291, 337, 338, and bottom picture on back of dust jacket

British Museum 11b, 33, 34, 35

Cambridge University Museum of Anthropology and Ethnography 3a and b, 4, 5, 7, 8, 11a, 11c, 15, 19, 38, 39, 87, 153, 225

The Royal Library, Copenhagen 164, 243, 294

Museum of Trade and Shipping, Elsinore 94

National Museum of Finland, Helsinki 41, 42, 44

National Museum, Copenhagen 32, 40, 43, 77, 119, 160, 172, 206, 212, 215, 221, 242a

Musée de l'Homme, Paris 75, 78, 79, 80, 81, 93, 149

Rijksmuseum voor Volkenkunde, Leiden 10, 14, 21, 23-26, 28, 95, 96a-d, 106, 121, 151, 152, 169, 188, 196, 208

Staatliches Museum für Völkerkunde, Munich 83

National Museum of Art, Copenhagen (photographer Hans Petersen) 27, 159, 161, 162, 244, 245, 246a and b, 247, 254a and b, 290, 292, 297a, 301, 302, 303, 304, 307, 308a and b

Figs. 320, 322, 325, and 339 were reproduced directly from the originals

Index of names

66, 161.

Mitsivarniannga. See Andreas.

Moltke, Harald. 1871-1960. Danish painter. 43, 202.

Molle, J. F. Early 1800s. Danish merchant in Holsteinsborg. 91.

Moore, Henry. b. 1898. English sculptor. 118.

Møller, Aqigssiaq. b. 1939. West Greenland painter, author, and school superintendent. 208.

Møller, John. 1867-1935. West Greenland photographer. Son of Lars Møller. 192.

Møller, Lars (Arqaluk). 1842-1926. West Greenland lithographer and editor. 52, 106, 164, 167-68, 169, 170, 171, 172, 187, 190, 192, 207.

Møller, Steffen. 1882-1909. West Greenland painter and lithographer. Son of Lars Møller. 190, 192, 193.

Napoléon I. 1769-1821. French emperor. 170.

Nasmyth, Alexander. 1758-1840. Scottish painter. 158.

Nellemann, George. b. 1930. Danish ethnologist. 28, 64, 65.

Nielsen, Anders. b. 1915. West Greenland doll carver. 120.

Nielsen, Frederik. b. 1905. West Greenland teacher, author, and chief of broadcasting. 52.

Nielsen, Knud. b. 1916. Danish painter. 66.

Nielsen, Malene. b. 1908. West Greenland handicrafter. 120.

Nooter, Gert. b. 1930. Dutch anthropologist. 79.

Nordenskiöld, Adolf Erik. 1832-1901. Swedish polar explorer and geologist. 170, 192.

Nuko, Axel. b. 1949. East Greenland carver. 86.

Nyboe, M. I. 1867-1946. Danish engineer. 45.

Olrik, Christian Søren Marcus. 1815-70. Danish trading-post manager. 96.

Olsen, Gustav. 1878-1950. West Greenland clergyman. Friend and assistant of Knud Rasmussen. 59.

Olsen, Kristian Aaju. b. 1942. West Greenland artist and teacher. 208, 210.

Olsen, Moses. b. 1939. West Greenland poet and legislator. 216.

Osarqaq. b. ca. 1925. West Greenland painter. 207.

Ostermann, Hother. 1876-1950. Danish clergyman. 118.

Panigpak. b. ca. 1850. Polar Eskimo artist and hunter. 199.

Pauli, Johan Georg Leander. 1838-1928. Danish xylographer and editor. 192.

Pavia (= Poul), Around 1900. East Greenland mask carver, father of Nuka and Georg Poulsen. 62, 85.

Peary, Robert Edwin. 1856-1920.

American naval officer and polar explorer. 133.

Pedersen, Carl-Henning. b. 1913. Danish painter. 66.

Petersen, Anders. Active around 1870. West Greenland painter and head catechist. Father of Jonathan Petersen. 193.

Petersen, Johan Christian August. 1867-1960. West Greenland colony manager. 23, 35, 54, 60, 61, 90, 102, 121, 129, 141, 154, 200.

Petersen, Jonathan. 1881-1961. West Greenland drawing teacher, poet, composer, organist, and head catechist. 52, 53, 168, 193, 205.

Petersen, Ole. b. 1894. Former National Council member, Sukkertoppen. 94.

Petersen, Pavia. 1904-43. West Greenland painter, poet, and head catechist. Son of Jonathan Petersen. 53, 193.

Petersen, Takisunguaq. b. 1935. West Greenland carver. 71, 84.

Petrussen, Knud. 1915-74. West Greenland sculptor. 42, 46, 47, 83.

Picasso, Pablo. 1881-1973. Spanish-French painter. 65, 174.

Pisérajik. See Elisa.

Pike, Peter. 1887-1972. East Greenland carver. 118.

Pita. West Greenland hunter, relater of legends to Hinrich Rink in 1858. 173.

Pîvât, Adam. 1904-76. East Greenland carver. 24, 71, 85.

de Poincy, Louis. Mid-1600s. French ethnographer. 143.

Pôk and Qiperok. West Greenlanders who visited Denmark in the early 1700s. 164-65, 170.

Poulsen, Gaba. b. 1910. East Greenland carver. 71.

Poulsen, Georg. 1901-61. East Greenland mask carver and sculptor. Son of Pavia. 62, 66, 67, 85.

Poulsen, Johannes. Greenlandic hunter and relater of legends to Hinrich Rink in 1858, Godthåb District. 173.

Poulsen, Nuka (Utuak). 1912-ca.1970. East Greenland mask carver. Son of Pavia. 62, 85.

Qavigak, Aron. b. 1934. Polar Eskimo carver. 82.

Qarqutsiaq of Etah (Thule), 1900s. Polar Eskimo, carver and hunter. 36, 37.

Qeqe, family. 1900s. East Greenland carvers. 85.

Rasmussen, Aviaja Mørk. 1925-74. Greenlandic painter. Daughter of Peter Rosing, wife of trading post manager Egon M. Rasmussen. 87.

Rasmussen, Christian. 1846-1918. Danish clergyman and linguist. Father of Knud Rasmussen. 195.

Rasmussen, Egon Mørk. 1912-79. Danish trading post manager. 79, 87.

Rasmussen, Knud. 1897-1933. Danish/West Greenlandic polar explorer. 12, 14, 33, 43, 45, 103, 105, 127, 132, 133, 138, 154, 195, 198, 199, 201, 202, 211.

Rembrandt van Rijn. 1606-69. Dutch painter. 191.

Rinatuse, Kristian. West Greenland hunter, relater of legends to Hinrich Rink in 1858. 173.

Rink, Hinrich Johannes. 1819-93. Danish governor, ethnologist, geologist, and explorer of Greenland. 131, 139, 156, 163, 164, 165, 168, 171, 173, 174, 176, 177, 179, 180, 184, 185, 186, 187, 188, 189, 190.

Rink, Signe. d. 1909. Danish author and wife of Hinrich Rink. 16, 164, 173, 184.

Rosen, C. H. 1832-1914. Danish minister in Godthåb. 164, 179.

Rosendahl, Philip. 1893-1974. Danish governor. 156, 203, 205.

Rosing, David. b. 1907. West Greenland carver. 83.

Rosing, Emil. b. 1939. West Greenland artist, teacher, head of the Art School of Greenland in Godthåb. Son of Otto Rosing. 209.

Rosing, Helga. b. ca. 1905. West Greenland handicrafter. 151.

Rosing, Jens B. 1925. West Greenland artist and author. Son of Otto Rosing. 101, 207, 208.

Rosing, Johannes. 1858-1942. West Greenland carver. 115.

Rosing Kâle. 1911-74. West Greenland graphic artist and city treasurer. Son of Kristian Rosing. 207, 209.

Rosing, Karoline Klara (born Kreutzmann). West Greenland painter. Wife of Kristian Rosing. 195.

Rosing, Kristian. 1866-1944. West Greenland teacher, head catechist, clergyman and missionary. 22, 116, 195, 207.

Rosing, Ludvig. b. ca. 1925. West Greenland carver. 83.

Rosing, Otto. 1896-1966. West Greenland painter, author, and minister. Son of Kristian Rosing. 56, 87, 192, 196, 197, 207, 209.

Rosing, Peter. 1892-1965. West Greenland painter and clergyman. Son of Kristian Rosing. 83, 153, 192, 195, 196, 207.

Rosing, Peter Vallentin. 1871-1938. West Greenland carver and hunter. 40, 41, 42, 45.

Ross, John. 1777–1856. British rear admiral and polar explorer. 132-33, 158-59.

Rostock-Jensen, Louis. 1899-1966. Danish naval captain and executive. 197.

Rousseau, Henri. 1844-1910. French painter. 169.

Rudolph, Christian Nicolai. 1811-82. Danish physician and colony man-

ager. 127.

Ruisdael, Jacob van. 1628-82. Dutch painter. 191.

Ruisdael, Salomon van. ca. 1600-70. Dutch painter. 191.

Ryberg, C. J. 1854-1929. Danish governor. 142.

Ryder, C H. 1858-1923. Danish naval officer and expedition leader. 22, 76, 90, 137.

Rüttel, F. C. P. 1859-1915. Danish missionary. 203.

Sackheouse, John. See Zakæus, Hans.

Sameq. See Jonathan.

Schmidt, Hans. 1839-1917. Danish painter. 191.

Seegers, Herkules. 1589-ca. 1640. Dutch painter. 191.

Sehested, family. Danish nobility. 107.

Seligmann, Kurt. German-American artist. 66.

Sikkimsen, Jokum. b. 1906. West Greenland mask carver. 86.

Silis, Ivars. b. 1940. Danish photographer and expedition hand. 131.

Simonÿ, Carl Frederik. b. 1909. danish governor, police chief, and judge. 114.

Simonÿ, Karla (born Bistrup). Danish, mother of C. F. Simonÿ. 112.

Singertât, Efriam. b. 1905. East Greenland mask carver. 62, 85.

Skovgaard, P. C. 1817-1938. Danish painter. 191.

Slania, C. Danish engraver. 208.

Stach, Ado. b. 1917. West Greenland bone carver. 113.

Steenholdt, Vittus. Relater of legends to Pastor Kragh in 1883. East Greenland national pioneer. 164.

Steensby, H. P. 1875-1920. Danish geographer and ethnographer. 121.

Sørensen, P. H. Around 1900. Danish clergyman in Jacobshavn. 96.

Tanguy, Yves. 1900-55. French-American painter. 66.

Tavnâjiik, Thorvald. b. 1930. East Greenland painter and catechist. 207.

Thalbitzer, William. 1873-1958. Danish philologist. 68, 103, 104, 137, 154, 155, 198, 200.

Thalbitzer, Ellen Locher. 1883-1956. Danish sculptor and painter, wife of the above. 200.

Thomassen, Kasper. 1935-74. West Greenland carver. Son of Otto T. 49, 83.

Thomassen, Kornelius. b. 1927. West Greenland carver. Son of Otto T. 49.

Thomassen, Otto. 1895-1971. West Greenland carver. 42, 47, 48-49.

Thomassen, Rasmus. b. 1937. West Greenland carver. Son of Otto T. 49, 72, 84.

Thomsen, Emanuel. b. 1927. West

Greenland carver 85, 120.

Thomsen, T. M. 1870-1941. Danish ethnographer. 90.

Thorsen, Anton. 1927-77. West Greenland carver. 80, 81, 84, 85.

Tinbergen, Nico. b. 1907. Dutch-English animal psychologist and ethnologist. 16, 23, 25, 73, 96, 109, 117, 121, 198.

Toulouse-Lautrec, Henri de. 1864-1901. French painter. 65.

Traustedt, M. P. A. 1853-1905. Danish zoologist. 106.

Tukula, family. 1900s. East Greenland carvers. 85.

Tunes, Nicolai. Mid-1600s. Dutch whaling captain. 143.

Ungaralak, Johannes. 1840-86. East Greenland author and hunter. 170

Utuak. See Poulsen, Nuka.

Walløe, Peter Olsen. 1716-93. Danish explorer. 102.

Vermeer van Delft, Jan. 1632-75. Dutch painter. 191.

Victor, Paul-Émile. French polar explorer. Leader of 1948 and 1954 glaciological expeditions. 75.

Villadsen, Helene. b. ca. 1939. West Greenland carver. 83.

Villadsen, Jens. b. ca. 1939. West Greenland carver. 83.

Vlaminck, Maurice de. 1876-1958. French painter. 65.

Zakæus, Hans. (John Sackheouse). d. 1819. West Greenland painter and interpreter. 132, 158-59.